# Latin America in Caricature

D0647521

The Texas Pan American Series

# Latin America in Caricature

John J. Johnson

University of Texas Press, Austin

BOWLING GREEN STATE
UNIVERSITY LIBRARIES

The Texas Pan American Series is published with the assistance of a revolving publication fund established by the Pan American Sulphur Company.

Copyright © 1980 by the University of Texas Press
All rights reserved
Printed in the United States of America

First paperback printing, 1993

Requests for permission to reproduce material from this work should be sent to Permissions, University of Texas Press, Box 7819, Austin, Texas 78713-7819.

Library of Congress Cataloging in Publication Data

Johnson, John J   1912–
    Latin America in caricature.

    (The Texas Pan American series)
    Includes bibliographical references and index.
    1. Latin America—Relations (general) with the United States—Caricatures and cartoons.   2. United States—Relations (general) with Latin America—Caricatures and cartoons.   3. American wit and humor, Pictoriae.   4. Latin America—Foreign opinion, American.   5. Public opinion—United States.   I. Title.
F1418.J754      301.29'73'08      79-19052
ISBN 0-292-74626-1
ISBN 0-292-74031-X pbk.

∞ The paper used in this publication meets the minimum requirements of American National Standard for Information Sciences—Permanence of Paper for Printed Library Materials, ANSI Z39.48-1984.

For Steven Michael and Sara Christina

POP
CULT
F
1418
. J754
cop. 2

# CONTENTS

# ACKNOWLEDGMENTS

Caroline Ciancutti assisted me immensely during the research stages of this study. Her dedication to the project was unmistakable. Her "reading" of certain of the cartoons established beyond any doubt her remarkable perceptiveness in the field of human relations. I am indeed indebted to her. Had the book developed as it was originally conceived, Margaret Herlin's research on and analysis of stereotypes in elementary and secondary school textbooks would have figured prominently in it. I hope there will be another occasion when her findings can be put to the level of use they so richly deserve. Janet Dubbs was helpful in endless ways when the project was being launched. Michael Gómez, working out of Bolívar House at Stanford, and Avis Poe Trujillo, in Albuquerque, provided invaluable assistance during the wrap-up period.

Two grants from the Institute of American History, Stanford University, helped to finance the research and preparation of the manuscript for submission to the University of Texas Press where, under the watchful eye of Barbara Spielman, it was improved in a number of ways.

Latin America in Caricature

# 1. INTRODUCTION

This study of United States–Latin American[1] relations over the past century is nontraditional in at least three respects. First, it is concerned exclusively with the United States' interpretations of developments. Second, it emphasizes the human dimension of relationships rather than the customary security, economic, and nationalist aspects; more specifically, it explores those racial, ethnic, and institutional images[2] of Latin America held by the interested minority of the dominant White Protestant element in the United States.[3] Third, it largely forsakes conventional sources in favor of editorial or opinion cartoons[4] appearing in leading periodicals and newspapers.[5]

Any merit that the book may have rests heavily upon the validity of the following assumptions: (*a*) Mass communications, to achieve their objective of influencing public opinion, at least to a considerable degree, must reflect the realities, beliefs, and psychological needs of the cultures of which they are a part. (*b*) The "informed public" in the United States is in a position to influence international relations, and its views are therefore important.[6] (*c*) The informed public's responses to hemispheric problems and situations are conditioned by culturally imposed qualities of character which are reflected in its perceptions and evaluations of realities, and, as a consequence, its images of Latin America tell us more about the psychological characteristics of informed United States citizens than about their contemporaries in Latin America.[7] (*d*) Adult citizens of the United States, most particularly those in the more privileged sectors,[8] have considered themselves to be an intrinsically superior species and Latin Americans to be an intrinsically inferior species. At times because of their prejudices[9] and at other times because of an apparent felt need to conform to values of their own group, they have been particularly susceptible to those negative images of Latin America proffered by Washington, the schools, the news media, and other disseminators. (*e*) While overt expressions of racial superiority are tending to disappear in the United States, there are good reasons to believe that underlying prejudices linger emotionally and may be reflected in interactions between Anglo-America and Latin America.[10] (*f*) Although the inappropriateness of judging the peoples of Latin America by United States standards is increasingly appre-

4    ciated, there nonetheless remains a pronounced propensity to measure
Latin American societies in terms of Anglo-American values. (*g*) In most
cases a foreign community's image is not earned but is gratuitously thrust
upon it.[11] (*h*) However optimistic I may be about the long term, I am far
less so about the short term and expect, as a minimum, matrices of conflict to remain at least over the next quarter century.

Historically, the United States has interacted closely with the republics of Latin America, especially those of the Caribbean, Central America
(including Panama), Mexico, Venezuela, and Brazil. Industrial development and trade expansion, a major by-product of which has been a decline
in self-sufficiency at the local level and an increasing interdependence at
the national level, practically guarantee that the future of each part of the
hemisphere will be closely affected by the way its interests mesh with the
interests of its neighbors. Although the nations of Latin America have been
and will remain important to the United States and vice versa, relationships seldom have been salutary. Characteristically, clouds of misunderstanding and suspicion have hung heavily over the hemisphere. Very often
what has been of category-one importance for a given country has been of
category-two or -three importance for another. Time and again one or the
other of the parties involved has perceived, accurately or inaccurately,
that one or more of its goals, purposes, or preferences have been threatened by the intentions or activities of the other.

There are no simple or quick explanations of why the United States
and Latin America have behaved toward one another the way they have.
Scholars, politicians, and the media have historically seen the antagonism
arising from security and economic issues. More recently the intensifi-
cation of nationalism in Latin America and the reluctance of the United
States to accept certain of its consequences have attracted increasing
attention from those who seek to inform opinion about hemispheric
matters.

There is ample reason for the stress that has been placed on security
matters as the linchpin for the explanation of or justification for the failure
of the United States and its southern neighbors to formulate and support
mutually acceptable policies. To say that security, however much the result of irrational fears and frustrations, has been an absorbing concern for
the United States public is practically a truism. Defense was at or near the

core of each of the United States' traditional diplomatic stances: isolation-
ism, freedom of the seas, the Open Door, the peaceful settlement of disputes, the Monroe Doctrine, and Pan Americanism. The Caribbean, Central America, and the Panama Canal have always figured conspicuously in
Washington's security strategies, which with very few exceptions have
been conceived in Washington and also implemented from there. Post–
World War II actions of the United States underscore this point. Although
overall relations between the United States and Latin America were permitted to deteriorate disastrously after the defeat of the Axis powers, cooperation at the security level continued at the urging, one might almost
say the insistence, of Washington. In 1947 the republics agreed (the Rio
Treaty) to the principle that an attack on any American state by any other
power would be considered as an attack upon them all and that collective
means would be taken to repel such aggression. However, formal agreements stipulating cooperation in the field of hemispheric security failed
to restrain Washington when it considered the nation's security threatened. And on three conspicuous occasions since the signing of the Rio
Treaty, Washington has chosen to disregard formal commitments to its
hemispheric allies. The first was when the Central Intelligence Agency
provided Guatemalan refugees with funds, arms, and combat training that
made it possible for them to invade their homeland from neighboring
Honduras and topple the regime of Jacobo Arbenz Guzmán (1954), who
had accepted backing and had received arms from the Soviet bloc countries. The second was the Bay of Pigs incident (1961) when Washington
gave financial and moral support to Cuban refugees intent on ousting Fidel
Castro. The third was during the Dominican crisis (1965). On that occasion President Lyndon B. Johnson ordered troops ashore in the Dominican Republic to avert the possibility of what he described as a "communist
coup." Only after the situation was considered stabilized was the Organization of American States consulted and the participation of its members
in the intervention solicited. The three separate actions tend to confirm
the proposition that, so far as the United States is concerned, the same
principle of national security and assumption of regional hegemony that
were used to justify sending marines into Haiti in 1915 continues in
force.[12] Thus, the late Senator Wayne Morse of Oregon was close to the
mark when in 1961 he fired the accusation that the way the United States
had chosen to achieve its strategic goals had made the country's foreign

6    aid programs of the 1950s and early 1960s one of the most stagnant, unproductive, and misrepresented of all federal activities.[13] Now, over two decades later, it can be added that neither the security-aid mix nor its level of achievement has changed significantly.

Economic issues have contested with security concerns for priority in most analyses of hemisphere relations. But if security and economics have shared major attention, the latter has nearly always generated the greater amount of heat. At times the United States' presence in and influence upon the economies of the republics have been assigned such importance as to make the roles of Latin American nationals and domestic capital appear superfluous to an understanding of the area's industrial growth in this century. Although the facts do not seem to warrant such an extreme position, there is abundant evidence that the United States government and private investors have had a profound impact on the economic evolution of the republics.

With private capital and officials in Washington working in cooperation, United States economic inroads in the area, particularly in the Caribbean, Central America, and Mexico, were quickly consolidated after the War between the States. Before World War I the hemisphere was bound together by flourishing markets, and United States entrepreneurs had launched an all-out economic invasion of the republics.[14] Meanwhile, the United States government had become an apprehensive promoter of economic ties to the south and an active guardian—including the use of customs controls and gunboats—of North American investors. Latin Americans, for their part, had become acutely aware of what they viewed as their disadvantageous position in a system that was developing their immature economies unevenly and leaving them at the mercy of the economic systems of Europe and the United States.

Earlier anxieties of the republics about their subsidiary economic role did not prevent the United States from strengthening its economic penetration after Versailles. It was simply a case of the material desires of the Latin American elites winning out over their trepidations about increasing marketing and financial dependence on the "Colossus of the North." The result was that with the war's end the republics turned to a not reluctant Wall Street, and United States investment soared 70 percent during the decade after 1919.

More than at any previous time hemispheric economic relations between 1930 and 1945 were determined by worldwide phenomena: the
Great Depression and World War II. Shattering as were those developments, in many respects their impact upon inter-American affairs was
limited to abrupt but short-term changes that could be countered by new
strategies and improvisation. And when the world returned to "peace" in
1945 the hemisphere's basic economic relationships and the tactics that
had guaranteed them in the past held steadfast.[15]

The United States emerged from the war against the Axis powers
relatively stronger economically in Latin America than ever before. That
fact alone was perhaps not so important or of as much concern to Latin
America as was the realization that Washington had determined to use
full-scale economic intervention as a means of achieving its objectives
abroad. So far as Latin America was concerned, by the early 1960s several
public financial agencies had been established and funded primarily with
United States capital, and the Alliance for Progress had been initiated.
Washington used its economic control of these agencies to regulate
grants-in-aid and loans, to buy support against international communism,
to stabilize the status quo, and to assist both civil and military regimes that
seemed to give promise of being able to control their constituencies.

In recent times the economic dependency of Latin America, except-
ing Cuba, has continued to give the United States government and private
investors choices denied other nations. Accordingly, "understanding" on
economic issues has remained more a consequence of the republics formulating developmental strategies acceptable to Washington than of the
outgrowth of healthy conflict and balanced compromise. Gunboat diplomacy during the first third of this century was efficacious only against
smaller nations; however, the power of the economic veto exercised
thereafter has meant that the flow of capital could be regulated in such
ways as to influence economic decisions in small and large nations alike.
Furthermore, financial intervention evoked fewer objections at home
than did the "sending of marines."

Nationalism is generally considered to be the dominant variable in
contemporary hemispheric relations. This ideology achieved its current
standing only after several decades of change in its character and objectives. Outcries against foreign economic domination before World War I

8    had nationalist overtones but they were muffled largely by export-import sectors in the republics dedicated to bringing their nations into the mainstream of Western democratic capitalism by means of vastly expanded international trade and large influxes of foreign capital and technology. Two consequences of World War I led to the growth of what might be called cultural nationalism: (a) the seeming decline of France, to whom Latin America traditionally had looked for cultural guidance, and (b) the emergence of the United States, whose culture Latin Americans deeply disdained, as the money capital of the world. The intellectual elites of the republics sought to counter those developments by finding qualities important to national growth within domestic groups who historically had been left to vegetate on the fringes of national life. The Mexican Indianist movement of the 1920s—during which intellectuals from all walks of life, but most particularly anthropologists, artists, and educators, were called upon to rehabilitate native peoples so that they might ultimately justifiably be integrated into society—is one of the better known responses of cultural nationalism to the area's postwar identity concerns.

The intellectuals had not made significant progress when, with the onset of the Great Depression, politicians seized upon the nationalist theme and gave it a strongly populistic coloration and economic orientation. State regulation of wages, hours, and services, tighter restrictions on foreigners in the work force, and protective tariffs were instituted, all designed to appeal to popular elements by providing employment for nationals, retaining within their respective countries a larger portion of the profits of foreign operations, and creating climates in which local industry might supply some of the consumer goods that historically had placed strains on the republics' foreign exchange earnings. The new restrictions soon created heated disputes. In retrospect, one recognizes that foreign investors and managers overreacted to the controls over labor and industry more because of their novelty than their direct impact on production and profits. But, at the time, both sides felt that their futures were at stake.

The antiforeign, anti–North American variants of nationalism were temporarily submerged in the climate of hemispheric unity (seriously strained only by the policies of regimes in Argentina and Bolivia) that prevailed during World War II. By the end of the struggle in Europe, however, more strident nationalism with stronger statist trappings had appeared and was upstaging all other developments in hemispheric relations. The postwar nationalism was and remains distinctly anti–North American. And, while retaining the older cries of exploitation, excessive profits, and foreign domination of local governments, the republics have utilized potent forms of nationalist expression against multinational companies, as well as attempting to circumvent Washington's insistence on the maintenance of an anti-Soviet bloc.

United States responses to the more nationalistic directions taken in the post–World War II era proved markedly negative and unaccompanied by serious or constructive proposals. Instead, each and every program emanating from Washington, including the Alliance for Progress, retained for the United States the privilege of formulating the strategies and tactics under which Latin America was theoretically to develop. Not only is such an approach morally arrogant, but it is also doomed to failure on at least two scores: it overlooks the seriously limited capacity of an external agency to influence and reshape an alien culture and it requires a subservience that Latin American nationalists will no longer abide. As a consequence, the nationalistic distrust of United States motives remains as intense as it is constant and the dialectic of misunderstanding and hostility consequently continues unabated.[16]

The above synthesis suggests the relevance that the United States traditionally has attached to its security and economic interests in the Latin American area as well as the salience of nationalism in contemporary hemispheric relations. What the brief review does not adequately explain is (a) why, historically, the United States government has claimed the right to assume full responsibility for the defense of the hemisphere south of the Rio Grande and unilaterally to determine if and when military forces should be brought into play; (b) why the United States government and private citizens have pursued exploitive tactics in the economic area; or (c) why the United States has so strongly opposed the growth of nationalism in Latin America. I believe, and so contend in this volume, that both our public and our private dealings with Latin American republics have resulted to a significant degree from widely accepted stereotyped negative images of their people, religion, and value systems. I further believe and argue herein that our unfavorable stereotypes of Latin America are largely the product of our cultural assumptions.

United States negative images of Latin America, which have been handed down from one generation to the next, date from the earliest contacts of the two cultures. Most of them were formalized by 1830 and the remainder by 1860. That the images have had a vigorous life for more than a century, as the succeeding chapters of this volume attest, speaks both to their currency over time and to the conviction with which they have been held. Two basic assumptions originally undergirded the images. The first was that the Black Legend,[17] as it developed in England and was exported to Great Britain's New World possessions, realistically represented the Spanish Catholic character at the time of the conquest and early colonization and that the Spanish personality was unmodified by time. In general that assumption served Hispanophobes well throughout the colonials' struggle against Iberian dominance and during the embryonic years of nationhood, when military and political leadership was a near White European monopoly, and yet again before and during the Spanish-American War. The second assumption was that neither of the two other major racial groups—Native Americans and Blacks—nor the large "mixed" elements measured up even to the lowly regarded Iberians. This latter view first found widespread acceptance during the era of Manifest Destiny, roughly between 1830 and 1850. It was reinforced in the 1850s by certain pseudoscientists who more than compensated for their lack of scientific fact with dogmatic assertion. It finally flowered in the 1890s under the guise of social Darwinism and as a rationalization for expansionism.

The Black Legend faulted the Spaniard in a number of areas that would later be reflected in Anglo-American caricatures of him. The legend held him to be decadent, as evidenced by his rejection of progress and, in the highest levels of State, his acceptance of illegitimacy, incest, and gross neglect of responsibility. It identified him as an authoritarian, as manifested in his belief in imposing government from above, by force if necessary, and ruling by decree. The inevitable legacy of such an approach to government, the argument ran, was either strong-man rule or revolution and discontent. This stereotype appeared to be supported by the widespread use of force to attain power and suppress opposition even before independence was everywhere assured. The legend further found the Spaniard corrupt, a by-product that might be anticipated given his view of government office as a route to personal wealth instead of public service.[18] The legend also held that the Spaniard placed a low value on personal toil; his attitude seemed always to be that if work were worthwhile someone else would have grabbed it long ago. The legend labeled the Iberian as cruel, as demonstrated by the atrocities he perpetrated against the Native Americans in his zeal to spread Roman Catholicism and in his merciless exploitation of the defenseless working man throughout the colonial era.[19] The conduct of General Valeriano "Butcher" Weyler and the treatment of inmates in the Spanish concentration camps in Cuba at the end of the nineteenth century, as reported in the United States press, seemed to furnish overwhelming evidence that the Spaniard had not changed.[20]

For more than any other reason, perhaps, initially the Spaniard invited the wrath of Anglo-America because of the Roman Catholic church and the role he assigned it in his society. His Christianity was early and lastingly typified in the Inquisition, associated in the Protestant mind with repression, terror, and torture. His religious views were suspect on the grounds that the life of a monk or a nun was no calling because prayer must be personal, not a way for particular individuals to make a living. He joined Church and State in a manner that made every enemy of the State a heretic. His religion was opposed to both intellectual and political liberty and held itself apart from and above the community, while "American" churches were considered to be on the side of the future and against the "papal past." Even by the early nineteenth century in the United States, the term *pope* had become a by-word for provincial bigotry.[21] The Spaniard's religious institution participated in large-scale lending and landownership, activities that were incompatible with Anglo-American ideas and institutions. His investment of labor and wealth in elaborate church architecture in Mexico, Peru, and elsewhere was compared unfavorably with the modest investment in houses of worship in the United States.

There were bad Spaniards; no right-thinking person would quarrel with that. But what the Black Legend, as propagated in the United States, did was to make badness inherent in the Spaniard and, as it soon developed, also in his direct heirs, the Creoles.[22] As a result, when Spain and Portugal were expelled from the mainland, not only were old stereotypes transferred to the Creoles, but also new ones were created and nurtured. One such stereotype, that of the elites as ideologically immature, appeared even before independence was achieved. Its substance derived from the fact that many of their numbers initially displayed a strong propensity for monarchical government. And that was a position the republican mind saw as if not unfathomable at least backward looking. The Latin

12   American leaders to this day have not shaken the image of their being ideologically unsophisticated, and when certain governments leaned toward fascism in the 1930s and 1940s and others toward international communism and Castroism in the 1950s, 1960s, and 1970s the image was in fact reinforced. At the same time that they were being found lacking in ideological acumen there was being created an image of them as being socially naïve. This stereotype emerged because of their relative lack of prejudice against colored persons and the readiness of their sovereign assemblies to emancipate African slaves during the independence movements.[23] Still another view that became a well-embedded stereotype had them economically improvident because, among other reasons, they were disinclined to defer immediate pleasures of the moment in favor of the greater good of the morrow. Their widely circulated *mañana* spirit added conviction to Anglo doubts about their future prosperity. Finally, the Creoles were portrayed as unnecessarily dependent on standing armies, institutions thoroughly distrusted by Anglo-Americans as dangerous to their civil liberty and freedom. That image has been kept alive and well and has been a popular target of the cartoonists, as Chapter 7 certifies.

At this point a very important qualification is called for, namely, that the Anglo-American indictment of the Spanish Creole males was not extended to their feminine counterparts. Individuals occasionally found the women to be somewhat shallow and priest ridden, but on the whole my evidence rates them well above their men folk. Reports from United States agents, traders, and adventurers generally stressed the women's physical attractiveness and their taste in dress.[24] Chapter 3 provides telling testimony to the cartoonists' strong preference for female symbolism when they have chosen to create a sympathetic image of Latin America.

Returning now to the central theme, what the Anglo-Americans had done within the single decade of the 1820s was to make themselves the near antithesis of the Latin Americans. And the dichotomy between "we" and "they" persists. The speed with which the sharp distinctions were drawn is largely explainable more by what was occurring in the United States than by activities in Latin America. Increasing contacts, both private and public, between Anglo and Latin America came when change in the United States had never been so extensive. Diplomatic and military triumphs had been won. Newly acquired territories and territories yet to be acquired were being peopled. Everywhere there was extraordinary spatial and social mobility. Conditions being so favorable in the United States, closer associations between north and south proved to a majority of Anglo-American thinkers what they had presumed to be true in the first place rather than upsetting old theories in their long-established intellectual foundations. Even those who depicted the Latin Americans in favorable terms[25] equivocated when the destiny of the Latin American nations was measured against that of the United States. Thus, Anglo-American rationality, pragmatism, temperance, honesty, industry, and frugality—basically a list of virtues drawn from the Puritan ethic, stripped of theological trappings[26]—were juxtapositioned against those negative qualities associated with the Latin Americans; it mattered little which Latin American—Mexican, Venezuelan, Brazilian, Chilean, or whomever—all were assumed to possess the same basic qualities. This is the essential point of Chapter 2. The contest, preceded as it was by this kind of early psychological warfare, was unequal and the outcome predictable, if for no other reason than that the rules of the game were decided unilaterally by rule makers suffering from acute cultural myopia.[27] In the knowledge that their own revolution was catching fire, they breathed a confidence understood at the time only by themselves.[28] Little wonder that they gave minimal thought to the possibility that there is no satisfactory criterion as to what constitutes a superior culture.

In terms of hemispheric relations, it is interesting to speculate on what the consequences might have been had Anglo-America "discovered" Latin America at a time when greater value would have been assigned to similarities instead of differences in the two cultures, for the similarities covered a broader range of attitudes and values than is generally appreciated. Both peoples, for example, viewed future European colonialization in the New World in essentially the same terms. They both favored a "limited" state whose primary role over and beyond defense against foreign enemies was the enhancement of individualism through internal order and the protection of private property. And their concepts of private property were less differentiated than the relative size of private holdings in the two areas would suggest. Also, the practice of strictly limiting the electoral franchise was common to both societies, the assumption being that the property holder was an adequate repository for the suffrage because the best interests of the community were represented in him. Each culture saw institutionalized religions as a social stabilizer. In each

14    culture State and Church cooperated in attempts to acculturate native peoples. And both peoples supported an elite educational philosophy that placed great emphasis on cultural continuity.

However, not only were similarities discounted, but also differences were accentuated as the Mestizos (persons of "mixed" European and Indian heritage) almost immediately challenged "White" rule in several of the mainland nations extending from Mexico to Bolivia, and in the United States, Manifest Destiny gripped the imagination of Anglo-America. In its most strident form during the 1830s and 1840s, Manifest Destiny was a psychological mixture of predestination, religion, optimism, and exaggerated nationalism. Its postulates were that (a) Anglo-Saxons are endowed as a race with innate superiority over other races, (b) Protestant Christianity holds the key to heaven, (c) only republican forms of government are free, (d) liberal institutions offer the chance and individualism the motive for success, and (e) the future can be hurried along by human hands.[29] Manifest Destiny thus in affect made White people the model for the human race, and to the degree that other humans differed from the model so much would they be judged to have inherited more of the qualities which ordinarily would preclude their escaping the limits of their civilization. Philosophically, the presumed superiority of the Anglo-Saxon population and republican institutions of the United States quickly ushered in a strong sense of "mission," a civilizing burden. The "American" people were overwhelmed with a Christian obligation to "regenerate" less advantaged peoples. Practically, the ideology initially provided an essentially cultural justification for territorial expansion, domestically against Native Americans, internationally against Mexicans, and ultimately as a patronizing view toward all Latin Americans and Pacific islands peoples as well.

Mexico, whose active population was already primarily Mestizo, felt the impact of Manifest Destiny, first in Texas during the 1830s and there and elsewhere by the late 1840s. Anglo migrants in Texas, after living side by side with the original Mexican settlers for a decade, concluded that they were the degenerate, revolutionary progeny of racially different parents who had inherited not a redeeming feature of the Indian and the worst qualities of the Spaniard. The targeting of the Mestizos as one of the low points of human society amounted to substituting them for the Indians as the negative reference point in the Anglo Protestant's age-old concern about individual morality, family life, and cultural integrity in the New World's wilderness environment.[30] Once the idea of the Mestizo as a negative prototype found acceptance, it quickly gained currency. The attention the Mestizos attracted was due in large part to the fact that the Native Americans could no longer be considered a worthy foe against which to wage cultural warfare. Generally removed from their lands east of the Mississippi, their attacks on White communities subsiding, seen as representing undefined lost values, and, according to the prevailing wisdom, doomed to extinction, the Indians, far from being an object of scorn, were rapidly becoming eligible for the sentimental nostalgia commonly accorded vanquished peoples.[31]

The low regard in which the Mestizo was held following the United States–Mexican War raised what must remain an unanswerable question: To what extent, if any, did the fact that Mexico's population was five-sixths *gente de color*—Indians, Mestizos, Blacks, and Mulattoes—figure in the United States decision not to absorb all of Mexico (and perhaps Central America as well) in the 1840s? Certainly there were individuals in high positions who wondered aloud about such a "mixture." Could it ever be regenerated? If it could be, how long would it take? In the meantime, what should be the status of those people? What effect would admitting them to United States citizenship have on "American" institutions? And how might the "All Mexico" element, who would bestow the blessings of "American" order, peace, and freedom upon their benighted Mexican brethren, have fared had the "New England conscience" been able to subordinate the moral problem of slavery, and its extension, to the getting of land?[32]

The Mestizos never recovered from their early victimization. Wherever they constituted a significant share of the population, and in some places where they did not, they became and for the most part have remained the "sombreroed, lazy, improvident, ungovernable, revolutionary" who, in the dominant North American thinking, has kept the nations of Latin America from becoming "modern" stable societies. Their ubiquitousness to a considerable degree explains why in the succeeding pages Mestizo types appear often and the stereotypical Indian only randomly.

There seems to be no such thing as an "all-duty scapegoat" and the Mestizo has been no exception. As it turned out, they came to share that role with their Black and Mulatto compatriots. Although Anglo-America historically has claimed a profound concern for all of Latin America, the truth is that its interests, whether political, economic, or intellectual, have been concentrated in the Caribbean and its periphery and Brazil. This was especially true until the 1930s when United States hegemony in the hemisphere came under attack, first from fascism, then from communism, and more recently from Latin American varieties of nationalism. And it was in and around the Caribbean and in Brazil that Latin America's Black population was concentrated. More particularly, in several of the countries, for example, Mexico, Colombia, and Venezuela, Blacks centered on the coasts, including the ports frequented by Yankee traders and naval personnel. As a consequence, during the century that the United States showed little other than economic and security interests in Latin America, its population was commonly reported to be comprised of Blacks, with no distinction being made between them and the Mulattoes.[33]

Being identified as Black in the Anglo-American folk wisdom augured badly for the peoples of Latin America. At home Blacks had been stripped of virtually all the rights accorded to White settlers under common law.[34] The few Whites who explicitly denied a belief in White superiority generally betrayed a deeper conviction, namely, that the Black was inferior to the White. Those in the White community opposed to slavery avoided the issue of equality. By the middle of the nineteenth century, anxieties over real and potential slave uprisings were increasingly incorporated into the thinking that had raised genuine, if unfounded, doubts concerning the Blacks' inherent fitness for freedom and the prospects of their incorporation into White society on equal terms.[35]

As the abolitionist debate heated, proslavery forces discovered a "scientific" justification for their beliefs in "craniology," the study of the size of the brain, the shape of the skull, and the nature of suture. Samuel George Morton, the leader of the school in the United States, and his disciples concluded that the skulls of various races ranged considerably in size, the largest belonging to Caucasians. To them that proved conclusively the superiority of the White and the inferiority of the Black races,[36] the substructure on which envenomed racism was built.

Racism[37] gained added momentum in the 1860s when Darwinian biology was popularized and its potentialities as a rationale for racist attitudes became apparent.[38] By subsuming mankind wholly under the grim physical laws of the animal kingdom it confirmed for many that ascent up the ladder of social evolution was closely linked to mental capacity, which was assumed a function of cranial size. Under the dual influences of craniology and Darwinism, White supremacy became the comprehensive philosophy of life that it would remain for the next three decades.[39]

White supremacy, Darwinism, and unsurpassed technological progress gave impulse to two currents of racial nationalism by the 1890s, one defensive and directed against the foreigner within, the other aggressive and calling for expansion overseas. The latter at best led to paternal despotism and at worst to the United States employing extraordinary and sometimes coercive means, especially in Latin America, to reshape the international, political, economic, and social structures of sovereign communities.[40] In the conviction that it had found the key to order and progress, on no less than twenty separate occasions between 1898 and 1920 United States marines or soldiers entered the territories of the states in the Caribbean.[41]

After 1900 racial demagogy declined in intensity, but it would not go away. As distinguished a scholar as Edward Ross, intermittent nativist with fervent populist-progressive views and generally recognized as one of the fathers of sociology in the United States, used the tenets of racism as psychological ammunition in his defense of controls upon immigrant workers and in justification of the traditional social-economic middle groups retaining their cultural hegemony.[42] Many social issues at the local, state, and national levels continued to be stated in Black-White terms through the 1920s when the idea of cultural pluralism provided a new context for conceptions of cultures and cultural relativity.[43] Chapter 5 makes clear that any changes for the better between 1900 and 1930 went unnoticed by the cartoonists who freely employed the physical and verbal stereotypes associated with southern Blacks as a way of communicating their views of the peoples of Latin America.

Gunnar Myrdal, commenting on race relations between Blacks and Whites in the 1940s, noted that, while racism as a comprehensive ideology was still maintained by only a few, prejudice as an attitude remained common.[44] The limited empirical evidence dating from the 1920s indicates that Myrdal's assessment of White prejudices against Blacks could have been applied more or less equally to Latin Americans. There was no

18     longer an encompassing ideology, such as Manifest Destiny or racism, that relegated Latin Americans to inferior status but prejudice against them clearly persisted in the 1940s as it did before and after that date.

As early as 1928, sociologist Emory S. Bogardus found, when he gave a series of 140 questions designed to measure social distance to a sample of 1,725 respondents representing a cross section of the United States public, that only 28 percent would have admitted Mexicans to close kinship by marriage while 15.1 percent favored totally excluding Mexicans from entering the United States.[45] In another investigation of racial prejudices Bogardus asked 110 businessmen and schoolteachers on the Pacific Coast about degrees of social intimacy and found that Mexicans ranked seventeenth in a preferential rating of twenty-three ethnic groups, being favored over Chinese, Japanese, Negroes, Mulattoes, Hindus, and Turks.[46]

More recent and perhaps more sophisticated polls confirmed Bogardus' findings. On December 10, 1940, the Office of Public Opinion Research conducted a nation-wide poll in which respondents were given a card with nineteen words on it and were asked to indicate those words that seemed to describe best the people of Central and South America. The results were as follows:

| Dark-skinned | 80% | Imaginative | 23% |
|---|---|---|---|
| Quick-tempered | 49% | Shrewd | 16% |
| Emotional | 47% | Intelligent | 15% |
| Religious | 45% | Honest | 13% |
| Backward | 44% | Brave | 12% |
| Lazy | 41% | Generous | 12% |
| Ignorant | 34% | Progressive | 11% |
| Suspicious | 32% | Efficient | 5% |
| Friendly | 30% | No answer | 4% |
| Dirty | 28% | No opinion | 0% |
| Proud | 26% | | |

Since respondents were asked to pick as many descriptive terms as they liked, percentages add to considerably more than 100.[47]

If dark-skinned and religious (read Catholic) can be considered negative images, as they unquestionably were in pre–World War II United States, then the respondents showed preference for eight unfavorable terms—dark-skinned, quick-tempered, emotional, religious, backward, lazy, ignorant, suspicious—as descriptive of Latin America before recording a favorable one—friendly—and returning to a negative one—dirty—as their tenth choice. It is no less significant that the lowest score was registered for "efficient," which figures so prominently in the Protestant ethic.

A Gallup poll conducted in 1968 reveals attitudes not unlike those of the prewar years. Respondents were asked to rate twenty-eight nations, five of which were Latin American republics: Brazil, Argentina, Chile, Uruguay, and Cuba. (The method used was the Shapel Scalometer consisting of ten squares or boxes numbered from plus five to minus five.) In the very favorable ratings (plus fives and plus fours combined) Canada, with 64 percent, was ranked the highest. Brazil, rated very favorable by 13 percent of the respondents, tied with Israel for fifteenth in the rank ordering; Argentina, favored by 11 percent, ranked eighteenth; Chile, with 8 percent, tied with India for the twentieth position; Uruguay, with 7 percent, was rated twenty-second; and Cuba, with less than 1 percent, tied with Communist China for the last position. Cuba excepted, all of the Latin America republics were rated above Iran, Egypt, Russia, North Vietnam, and Communist China but not above any "Western" nation.[48]

In summary, at the top of the list of those qualities that have influenced our views of the republics to the south go our racial attitudes and associated sentiments, born of a combination of emotionalism, biological taboos, and hereditarian determinism. Those attitudes and the resultant prejudices have been so much a part of our collective thought processes that it can be argued that the strategies used by individuals and public and private agencies sympathetic to the area and its underprivileged populations may actually reinforce in the United States those images of the republics that historically have worked to their disadvantage. The reasoning is as follows. Missionary welfare groups, such as CARE, make their case for support on the grounds of poverty and/or technological backwardness, the supposed beneficiaries almost always pictured as Indian or Black or "mixed" types. While such a presentation, for whatever reason, apparently is considered effective in seeking philanthropic aid, it tends to lend credence to the popular impression of Latin America as peopled by dark-hued and, it follows, "inferior races," unable or unwilling to help themselves.

The religious views of the historically dominant elements in the United States likewise had the effect of placing Latin America in a disadvantageous position. The republics were Roman Catholic or "papist"; the

United States, at least through the 1920s, was staunchly and combatively Protestant. Protestant literature and standard public school textbooks depicted the Catholic clergy as so grossly ignorant and bigoted as to disqualify it as a standard-bearer of either Christian ethical standards or acceptable cultural values. Those Protestants who questioned the prevailing view were left to search out for themselves evidence of the Church's contribution in the fields of education, science, hospital care, and philanthropy, in each of which it was the central institution throughout Latin America until replaced by the State, a phenomenon of the recent past. If in the last several decades United States Protestants have tempered their views toward Catholicism, it remains a fact that a large share of the classroom literature on Latin America has continued somehow to link Catholicism with the "backwardness" of the republics.[49]

Finally, Latin America's political institutions, which in practice generally have not conformed to the United States model, have served to cast the area in an unfavorable light. Educated to worship democracy founded on faith in the power and courage of free men, the United States public in general has remained firm in the conviction that their style of democracy, despite its failure to provide answers to all the issues born of industrialization and urbanization or to prevent periodic eruptions of class warfare, is superior to political systems in other parts of the world. Given this faith in their perceived experience, it is perhaps not surprising that they have attempted to export democracy to Latin America, which has seemed to enjoy few of the benefits closely associated with responsible government in the United States. Thus, the tendency of the informed public, either out of ignorance or out of conviction, has been to deny credence to alternative traditions and values which may be ill-suited to "democracy" as comprehended in the United States. As a consequence, they gave unquestioning approval to the Good Neighbor Policy in the 1930s and 1940s and the Alliance for Progress in the early 1960s, one of whose major goals was the creation of vital centers in Latin America where a political style fashioned after the United States political pattern would take root and flourish and thereby save Latin America from itself.[50]

There is nothing original about calling attention to the United States' low esteem, when not scorn, for Latin Americans and their institutions. Throughout our history we have been aware that we have been prejudiced unfavorably toward and have discriminated against the people of the various republics. What is perhaps more significant and certainly less often reported is that at no time have we as a society seemed aware that, to the degree our array of ascribed features of Latin America has been actually and philosophically false, it has been unrealistic to expect lasting understanding. Rather we have acted so as to give the impression that immediate gains have been worth the risk of disparaging the peoples and institutions of the republics so long as the consequences did not lead to the immediate collapse of hemispheric relations.

Initially, it was my intent to establish what have been the racial, ethnic, and institutional images of Latin America in the minds of knowledgeable elements in the United States as those images have been revealed in a variety of commonly employed historical sources. In pursuit of that goal I began by examining in some depth diplomatic correspondence of the nineteenth century, especially communications to the State Department from agents in the field and congressional debates. I then turned to memoirs of public officials with experience in Latin America during the early decades of this century. Later, I researched missionary journals and field reports of churchmen covering the period from 1850 to 1920, public school and college textbooks as well as scholarly evaluations of their factual and ideational content,[51] the mass media, and public opinion polls. As the project progressed it became quite apparent to me that cartoonists whose art was appearing in leading publications were capsulizing and marketing to the reading public nearly all the images of Latin America being perpetuated by public officials, missionaries, editors, publishers, and textbook authors and being reflected in the public's responses to social surveyors and professional pollsters. It seemed equally clear to me that cartoonists were recording opinions in a way at least as likely to fix or reinforce impressions in the public mind as were their contemporaries who were depending upon the printed word. I therefore determined to shift my attention almost exclusively to editorial cartoons on the grounds that they would tell the story more concisely and with greater clarity than would the broad range of traditional sources.[52]

Reliance upon editorial cartoons as a prime documentary source raises at least four problems, two of which may be termed substantive and two methodological. The first substantive issue relates to the reliability of cartoons. They are, of course, drawn by artists who make no pretense of presenting the whole truth. On the contrary, cartoonists have a reputation for taking liberties with or oversimplifying the facts in order to make their intent evident. Once at their drawing boards they become first and foremost advocates who invite their viewers to join them in acceptance of policies they favor. The essence of cartooning is attack to the point where heroes are glorified by denouncing their adversaries. As a consequence, a cartoon can be and often is a fundamental distortion of a reality. It tells either more than the truth or less than the truth. Perhaps more seriously, there is no place in a cartoon for reasoned criticism or detailed argument, much less an opportunity to develop a philosophical position. By its very nature, then, a cartoon lends itself to "one side of the story" and has no place for an outline of the converse picture that we have a right to expect in dispassionate scholarly exposition.

The second substantive problem arises from the fact that cartoons are essentially little more than tangible expressions of established myths. By design they exploit the unreflective fusion of the metaphysical and symbolic through the use of reiteration and sensationalism. And on those occasions when cartoons treat issues involving two or more nations, there is added to the above the very present realization that they mythologize the world of international relations by physiognomizing it. They thereby contribute to the all too evident tendency of individuals to think of political sovereignties not as political sovereignties but as persons.[53] I concluded that, since this study would not be concerned, first of all, with the historical accuracy of cartoon reporting on hemisphere matters but rather with the opinions and symbols that cartoonists tapped to elicit an immediate and favorable public response, the ever-present possibility that such cartoons grossly misrepresent the realities of a given situation would not minimize their importance, indeed would accentuate it.

The methodological problems raised in using cartoons as historical documentation are of more consequence. In the first place, valid and reliable data relating to the use of cartoons as a means of communication are sharply limited.[54] Lewis James Davies' sociological study of the form and content analysis of the cartoon as a cultural medium of communication attacks the methodological issue with impressive data, but his work must be considered introductory.[55] LeRoy Maurice Carl presents limited statistical data suggesting that cartoons may generate quite different meanings among members of a single social-economic group.[56] Carl's conclusion does not necessarily invalidate the idea of a substratum of more general beliefs, values, and so on which condition those responses. The remainder of the literature exploring the significance of cartoons as editorial commentary is based largely on intuition or chance observation and is of quite uneven quality. Notably lacking are data of a psychological nature which explore the processes by which a cartoon becomes part of or reinforces an individual's thought pattern, if in fact that actually occurs.

The second methodological problem is that there are extremely few scholarly data on the extent to which cartoons influence public thinking. The "professional students of caricature," as W. A. Coupe calls them,[57] are in general convinced that cartoonists work a fertile field and harvest abundantly. In some cases one need only note the titles of studies to appreciate the conviction with which the case for cartooning is made. William G. Rogers, for example, entitled his book *The Pen Is Mightier Than the Sword*.[58] Scott Long left little doubt of his view when he entitled one of his articles "The Political Cartoon: Journalism's Strongest Weapon" and then went on to contend that "the political cartoon is still beyond doubt the strongest editorial weapon in the whole arsenal of either right or wrong."[59] In a similar vein and with equal confidence in the cartoonists, Bob Eckhardt entitled an article "The 'Art' of Politics: Why the Pen Is Mightier Than the Meathook."[60]

Those who hold that cartoons have significant editorial clout argue their case from essentially three directions. First, they point out that the impact of cartoons is evidenced by the fact that publishers and editors have kept cartoonists on company payrolls, often as the highest paid members of the editorial staff, and have given their art prominent billing for over two centuries.[61] Second, they seek to establish the importance of cartoons by calling attention to cases of public figures who have stated that cartoons have influenced their careers. Few serious students of cartooning miss the opportunity to recall Thomas Nast's role in destroying the public career of Boss Tweed in New York City.[62] Walter Lippmann stated without equivocation in 1931 that the feelings of protest and outrage in the 1920s found their best expression in the cartoons of Rollin Kirby of *New York World*. Historian Allan Nevins declared unequivocally that cartoonists swayed many votes in the Blaine-Cleveland election of 1884.[63]

And Eckhardt, choosing to ignore the fact that politicians are often overly generous with their credits, informed his readers that Presidents Ulysses S. Grant and William McKinley believed that their electoral triumphs were greatly aided by the drawings of Nast and the artists of *Judge*.[64] More recently, former President Gerald Ford, on the occasion of viewing a gallery of United States political cartoons, is reported to have observed, "The pen is mightier than the politician."[65] The fact that a relatively few "credits" are cited over and over suggests, however, that the established number of individuals who have publicly conceded that they were either the beneficiaries or the victims of cartoon opinion may be quite small.

The third category of evidence used to support the position that cartoons do influence the observer breaks down into time and sight elements. According to the time argument, cartoons are instant art, the meaning of which strikes through at a glance, while reading an editorial takes time that many readers are unwilling to sacrifice. Cartoons thus become a substitute for some of the ponderous writing that typifies many editorial pages. The sight argument is apparently as old as Confucius and holds that a picture is worth a thousand or ten thousand words, depending upon whom one chooses to cite. Or, to put it another way, a cartoon creates impressions that are believed to survive those fashioned by the printed word.

Only an occasional author has questioned the view that cartoons are effective communicators. Henry Ladd Smith is one such person. He contended that the first quarter of the twentieth century was the golden age of the political cartoonists because issues were comparatively simple and easily interpreted and there was enough elemental violence in them to satisfy the satirist. Influence of the cartoonists, according to Smith, declined in the second quarter of the century because they lost their monopoly of visual entertainment to other art forms, as for example movies and comic strips.[66] The distinguished cartoonist J. N. "Ding" Darling of the *Des Moines Register*, was even more skeptical of the influence that cartoonists have had. He observed, "I doubt that they [cartoons] ever moved any mountains or changed the course of history."[67] Coupe aligns himself with Smith and Darling when he writes in his reflective article, ". . . fortunately . . . in an age of mass communications and general literacy cartoonists do not have the effect on public opinion that professional students of caricature sometimes impute to them."[68] And Frank Whitford strikes from an-

other angle when he insists that individuals look forward to the daily cartoon only for so long as they are not shocked too thoroughly or their own
beliefs are not held up to too much ridicule.[69]

Those who have been more conservative in their judgments about
the degree to which cartoons may shape or re-enforce public attitudes
stress the economic aspects of publishing. Their position is that only the
very exceptional cartoonists, as for example Thomas Nast at *Harper's
Weekly* and David Low at Lord Beaverbrook's *Evening Standard*, have
been granted an important part in shaping editorial policy because in an
overwhelming number of cases employers have been unwilling to chance
the loss of circulation in the interest of giving their cartoonists freedom of
expression.[70] Also, as cartoonists have become syndicated and appear in
media catering to a variety of views, the tendency to fence-sitting probably has increased.[71] If one accepts that as a group publishers have exercised restraints on editorial opinion, it follows, then, that the vast majority
of cartoonists probably have gravitated to newspapers and journals with
views similar to their own. And if that is true, it would also be true that ( *a* )
most cartoon lecturing is directed to the already converted rather than to
the uncommitted and is designed to arouse the ardor of the reader with
like beliefs and appeals to sentiments well within the context of the viewer's information and knowledge; ( *b* ) political cartoonists draw for a particular kind of reading audience from whom they can expect a certain
amount of support; and ( *c* ) the cartoonist's opportunity to have an impact
is probably less today when newspapers and journals must compete with
other media than it was when they held a virtual monopoly on the public's
attention and quest for news and opinion.[72] This line of argument leads to
a point crucial to this study: namely, that cartoonists have been less opinion shapers and more buttresses of existing opinions.

I believe that the particular nature of this project obviates all of the
more serious problems generally associated with the use of cartoons as
historical evidence. The likelihood that cartoonists follow the editorial
line rather closely and the probability that they draw for individuals who
generally share their views on topical issues appear at worst immaterial
and at best assets in an examination of reader attitudes. That cartoons lack
balance and subtlety and are meant to awaken prejudices or aggressions in
the viewer may disqualify them in certain areas of historical writing; however, in an image study, this merely accentuates their importance. I fur-

26   ther believe that cartoons have very positive qualities that recommend them as evidence for an examination of public attitudes. For example, they often recall incidents that have been all but forgotten by historians but which at a given time could be used to arouse latent dislikes or fears. Also, repetition is the very essence of cartooning. For the cartoonists, no saying is too trite or too banal. Each has a mental storehouse of symbols that have gained credibility through use by successive generations of artists. Cartoonists not only draw upon that armory again and again; they manipulate symbols as though they were puppets which they cannot modify without destroying the meaning built around them. Consequently, cartoonists ordinarily are content to give an innovative twist to such classic symbols as Uncle Sam or John Q. Public and most often settle for something less. Hence, if a cartoon affords surprise it is a familiar surprise founded paradoxically enough on instant recognition. Cartoons thus provide invaluable clues to the mood and mores and underlying attitudes of the society that produced and accepted them. Finally, cartoons contribute highly visual nongovernmental variables to cross-cultural relations.

In a very real sense, the cartoonists themselves have dictated the emphasis of the chapters that follow. Their choice of symbols, their greater or lesser attention to Latin America in various time spans, and their interest or lack of interest in the individual republics and the kinds of domestic and international issues that attracted them were the basic considerations in the decisions I made with respect to which cartoons should be used. Within those broad areas I made judgmental decisions, including attempting to maintain a meaningful balance of topics. The problem of balance led me to underrepresent the cartoonists' representations of Latin America as a whole and their use of non-Black adult males. This resulted in females, children, Black adult males, and military-social issues being overrepresented. But the distortions were not in any sense of a degree to invalidate the overall conclusions that may be drawn about how and why cartoonists used the symbols they did in treating hemispheric affairs.

The distribution of cartoons according to time spans correlates quite closely with the attention that the artists gave to Latin America. Thus, during the decade and a half from 1897 to 1912—encompassing the war with Spain, the subsequent concerns over Cuba, the debates over canal treaties, and the fall of the highly regarded dictatorship of Porfirio Díaz in Mexico

—Latin America appeared regularly on the editorial pages. That is why a
good share of the cartoons are from that era. Then, in the 1920s, Latin
America again became the primary focus of our international relations.
That time it was occasioned by our intervention in the Central American
and Caribbean in efforts to establish political stability as a way of guaran-
teeing our national security interests and private investments, continuing
difficulties with the "revolutionary" administrations in Mexico over subsoil rights and what was seen as President Plutarco Elías Calles' inclina-
tion toward international communism, and, finally, the growing distrust of
the United States by the Latin American republics generally that by 1928
had surfaced at Havana and threatened to totally disrupt hemispheric relations. Latin America did not again capture the attention of the cartoonists
until the early 1960s when initially they lined up nearly unanimously in
support of the goals of the Alliance for Progress and in identifying the military and the economic elite as the obstacles to fulfilling these goals.

The distribution of the cartoons by regions also closely parallels the
relative importance the cartoonists assigned them. An overwhelming majority of the cartoons deal with the Caribbean area, reflecting the United
States' awareness of developments there. When the Caribbean region is
broken down into its component parts, Cuba and Mexico share the lime-
light, with Costa Rica and El Salvador going nearly unnoticed. Until the
1960s and the coming of the Alliance for Progress and a new cycle of military governments, the interests of cartoonists in the republics south of
Venezuela and Colombia were always marginal, except during World War
II and the ideological conflicts related to it. The minimal concerns of cartoonists in the more southern republics speak eloquently to the larger
point, namely that, historically, only under duress has the United States
shown a strong and sustained interest in that part of Latin America not
washed by the Caribbean.

It will be apparent to some readers that certain pervasive issues and
pictorial devices are conspicuous by their paucity in the volume. Again,
this is as the cartoonists would have it. There are few cartoons that even re-
motely reflect the profound antagonism felt before World War II by United States Protestants toward the Latin American varieties of Roman Catholicism. This is because historically the cartoonists have largely avoided
that field, presumably because of respect for reader sensitivities or the
possible economic consequences to publishers taking a pronounced anti-

28 Catholic stance. There are no cartoons that intentionally depict female figures unfavorably, because cartoonists have chosen not to employ feminine symbols for the purpose of communicating derogatory views of the peoples and institutions of the republics. Adult males with pronounced European features and Western dress appear sparingly because with few exceptions the artists have failed to credit Latin American males with playing roles commonly associated with responsible western European or Anglo-Saxon types. Social issues receive only limited attention in the volume because, throughout most of the period covered, cartoonists, much like the public for which they drew, failed to make the association between political instability and social inequities. Only with the appearance of the present generation of artists has this relationship begun to receive a share of the attention it deserves. Finally, the republics seldom appear dehumanized, because only occasionally have cartoonists gone to their animal zoos for symbolic representations of hemispheric issues.

If it seems, as it will to a large percentage of readers, that the cartoons included herein victimize the people of Latin America, it is because the cartoonists ordinarily have portrayed the republics as politically and economically impoverished and culturally deprived. Concomitantly, for the most part, they have been willing participants in a "grand design" to strip Latin Americans of any inherent ability to compete on equal terms in this hemisphere by denying them the very qualities required to compete in Western societies.

# 2. THE HEMISPHERE AS MONOLITH

The republics of Latin America have many features in common but also profound dissimilarities. They share a common experience of adaptation to a New World environment of open spaces and wide horizons. They share the marriage of two profoundly different cultures. They share complex religious beliefs. They share the experience of successfully struggling for independence from their Mother Countries. They share a common political philosophy, a common conception of human rights. Eighteen of the twenty republics share a common official language. Latin American scholars, especially in periods when they have felt their countries threatened, have tended to stress the sentiment of cultural solidarity. The search since World War II for success through myriad international agencies is a recent example of adversity at the national level prompting unity at the continental level.

But the notion of oneness ignores many of the realities of everyday life. Geography and climate have combined to fragment the continent into tropics, cold tablelands, temperate plains, and humid coastal belts, creating problems of communication and nurturing localism. Different indigenous peoples gave rise to distinct regional cultures that have persisted. Political independence did little to solve these differences, while intensifying the chauvinism of the new republics. In the twentieth century pragmatic politicians and concerned intellectuals turned chauvinism into an intense search for "individual" national character, such as *mexicanidad*, *argentinidad*, and *peruanidad*. The reoccurring urge to extend national boundaries led time and again to costly conflict and lasting enmities between Chileans and Bolivians, Peruvians and Ecuadorians, Brazilians and a half dozen of their neighbors, Haitians and Dominicans, Salvadorians and Hondurans—such a list could be extended easily.

Export economies oriented toward western Europe and the United States have tended until quite recently to discourage the development of commercial linkages of the kind that might have assisted the republics in overcoming their profound distrust of one another. Today, for a variety of reasons, the republics are in sharply contrasting stages of economic development, political modernization, social mobilization, and cultural maturity. Argentina and Honduras, for example, have taken radically different paths of development. The racial composition of the populations varies widely not only between but often within the respective republics. In the above context the growth of Pan American agencies and the Organization of American States is explained not by any strong sense of continentalism they hold but precisely because they give support to rather than threaten the concept of national sovereignty.

Historically, cartoonists have chosen to portray Latin America as a single entity or as composed of a number of states without regard for their strong dissimilarities. There are several possible explanations why this has been the case. First, the cartoonists risk the danger of diffusing attention from their argument if they pack their pictures with numerous figures, symbols, or labels. Second, based upon evidence drawn from the cartoons themselves, it seems clear that artists often have been woefully uninformed about the area and its issues, a situation that began to attenuate only after World War II. Third, the area is so complex and the reading public so unmindful of that complexity that there has been little point in artists' attempting to exploit uniqueness, even had they been so inclined. Fourth, the cartoonists have merely reflected the teachings of the standard scholarly literature of the past, which tended to stress commonness rather than differentiation. Fifth, the tendency is for units to converge when viewed from an extraneous angle. Sixth, in graphically presenting Latin America as a single unit, the artists, intentionally or otherwise, have simply opted to pay lip service to what Washington has said and not to what it has practiced in its relations with Latin America. Public officials who would be most unlikely openly to suggest a single policy for a region as diverse as western Europe repeatedly have created the impression that the United States has a single policy for the vast and varied Latin American area, based at different times on the Monroe Doctrine, the Big Stick, the Good Neighbor, or the Alliance for Progress, to mention only four of the better known "cornerstones." Actually, there has not yet been a time when a single United States policy could be applied simultaneously to, say, Mexico, Brazil, and Nicaragua; and Washington has never seriously pretended to be evenhanded in implementing such policies as recognition of new governments, fiscal and military intervention, military aid, hemispheric defense, or economic aid. Quite the contrary, the United States has insisted that its

broad hemispheric objectives be achieved, if achieved at all, through bi-
lateral agreements and / or treaties. Thus, the cartoons appearing in this chapter focus on the practice of artists not to differentiate between the republics. The cartoons and the legends that accompany them are also meant to suggest that the cartoonists' failure to individualize the republics other than by labels has been one of the continuing reflections of the misunderstanding of hemispheric realities by United States Americans.

Following the Civil War, the United States quickly began
to expand its commercial contacts with Europe, the Far
East, and Middle America. Meanwhile, the fleet that had
been assembled during the Civil War was permitted to
rust away to the point where only two ships were considered serviceable. In trading circles, that situation was
viewed as intolerable for a nation in competition with the
imperial powers of Europe, and pressure for more up-to-
date ships mounted. Finally, in 1883, Congress reluctant-
ly appropriated funds for four new warships which became the nucleus of a modern steel navy.

When this cartoon by Thomas Nast, one of the United
States' foremost editorial artists of all time, appeared in
1880, an "unprotected" Miss Columbia, at the time commonly employed to symbolize a righteous United States,
was made to suffer insults from a cross-section of international rivals, including Mexico and Peru. As was the
practice at the time and subsequently of often portraying
the people of the various Latin American republics as indistinguishable one from another, the hair, complexion,
headgear, clothing, cigars, and general demeanor of the
Mexican and Peruvian figures are for all intents and purposes identical.

**1.   The Unprotected Female**
Thomas Nast, *Harper's Weekly*, February 21, 1880.

The Pan-American Exposition held at Buffalo in 1901 was sponsored to promote commercial and social interchange between the republics and the United States. In this cartoon, various Latin American peoples, identifiable only by their labels, lend support to a strident Uncle Sam, determined to defend the Monroe Doctrine against possible German territorial and commercial encroachments. The figure between Brazil and Mexico is labeled Patagonia. This raises the question: was the cartoonist unaware that Patagonia did not exist as a separate nation, was he using poetic license coupled with grand-scale ignorance, or did he possibly confuse Patagonia with Paraguay?

2.  **The Great Balancing Act at Buffalo**
    It takes the Yankee nation
    To make equilibration.
    But every time you turn around
    Pop! goes the Kaiser!
    ( With apologies to the Weasel )
    Albert Levering, *Harper's Weekly*, June 8, 1901.

By the Clayton-Bulwer Treaty concluded with Great Britain in 1850, the United States agreed not to secure exclusive control over the long-talked-about isthmian canal. Thereafter, United States and British interests in the construction of the canal languished until the Spanish-American War when the dash of the battleship *Oregon* from the Pacific coast around South America to Cuban waters impressed upon Washington the advantages of not only a canal but, furthermore, a canal under the sole control of the United States. Great Britain, faced with a hostile Europe and enmeshed in costly war in South Africa, acceded in the Hay-Pauncefote Treaty of 1901 to Washington's suggestion that the Clayton-Bulwer Treaty be superseded by another which would enable the United States to build and control an isthmian canal unilaterally. Thus, Great Britain recognized United States preeminence in the Western Hemisphere and inferentially assigned to Uncle Sam the role of policeman of the hemisphere, charged with protecting foreign interests from the caprices of governments in and around the Caribbean.

In cartoonist Homer Davenport's version of the drama of dividing up the globe, Latin America is stripped even of a geographical identity. This calls attention to a pervasive phenomenon in hemispheric affairs, namely that decisions profoundly affecting the people of Latin America often have been made with little or no input from them or regard for their reactions.

**3. Accepting the Monroe Doctrine**
John Bull gratefully admits that Uncle Sam is the proper custodian of the Western Hemisphere.
Homer Davenport, *Review of Reviews*, January 1902.

At the turn of the century the United States had a negative trade balance with Latin America. The First International Conference of American States (1889) and subsequent efforts to reverse the trend were ineffectual. Latin America continued to sell more to the United States than it bought. This cartoon reflects the importance that the United States attached to that condition. Cartoons of this genre, utilizing similar figures for a number of otherwise differentiated countries, played their part in perpetuating the stereotype of the Latin American republics as ungrateful neighbors.

**4.**   **Only His Neighbors Fail to Patronize Uncle Sam's Big Store**
*North American* (Philadelphia), 1902.

The Latin American republics early built one reputation in the United States for fiscal irresponsibility and another for carefree living. Debt defaults to European nations, especially by Venezuela, that invited intervention in the Caribbean were probably more disturbing to the United States than were the republics' failure to meet their obligations to United States creditors. What was considered the mismanagement of their monetary problems led first to the "Big Stick" policy of Theodore Roosevelt and later to official United States intervention in the fiscal affairs of certain Central American and Caribbean nations.

By portraying all of South America as "our southern brother," Charles L. "Bart" Bartholomew encapsulated the single-entity concept even more neatly than did those artists who relied upon labels to identify their subjects.

5. **Raising the Mortgage**
   If our southern brother would raise more mortgage and less other things, no one
   would object.
   Charles L. "Bart" Bartholomew, *Minneapolis Journal*, ca. 1903.

So far as the United States public was concerned, Germany constituted the greatest single threat to United States hegemony in the hemisphere during the early years of the century. Today scholars generally favor the view that Germany's ambitions and capabilities in the New World were exaggerated by groups in Washington interested in an isthmian canal, expanded trade with Latin America, and the creation of a sphere of influence worthy of a world power. Whatever the reason, any suggestion of German intrusion in the hemisphere was denounced as a potential violation of the Monroe Doctrine and that was more than enough to send the jingoists into action.

This cartoon was occasioned by suspicions that Germany was angling for a toehold in unstable Cuba and/or the Dutch West Indies and that in joining with Great Britain in the blockade of Venezuela—an enterprise which eventuated in the German bombardment of the Venezuelan port of Puerto Cabello on December 2, 1902—the Kaiser's motives went beyond simply collecting debts owed by Venezuela. In pursuing its anti-German policies, the United States did not need or solicit the support of the Latin American republics. This cartoonist chose to establish beyond any possible doubt the United States' ability to go it alone by portraying the republics as equally helpless and equally dependent.

6.   **Five Battleships Ordered,—a Few More Supports for the Nest**
*Philadelphia Inquirer*, 1903.

One alternative to denigrating the republics by denying them individuality was to portray each of them as different from the others but so similar in size, dress, and general appearance as to invite ridicule if not contempt.

7.   **Room for All, If They're Careful**
    William Allan Rogers, *New York Herald*, 1904.

An earlier cartoon (no. 6) depicted the republics as eggs in the "American" eagle's clutch. This caption, taken from the Mother Goose jingle, suggests that by the Third International Conference of American States (held in Rio de Janeiro in mid-1906) the republics at the conference could be lumped together arbitrarily since their appearances and voices were indistinguishable one from another. It is interesting to speculate whether the artist may also have had in mind the next line of the verse, "was not that a dainty dish to set before the king?" who metaphorically could only have been President Theodore Roosevelt. The cook is Elihu Root, secretary of state under Roosevelt and a proponent of strong leadership in Latin America along the lines of Porfirio Díaz in Mexico.

**8.    When the Pie was Open'd the Birds Began to Sing**
Garnett Warren, *Boston Herald*, 1906. Reprinted by permission: Boston Newspaper Division, The Hearst Corporation.

As noted above (see no. 6), Germany—here represented by the Kaiser—was held to offer serious economic competition to the United States in Latin America. In retrospect, it is apparent that the German threat was exaggerated at least in part in order to justify United States responses to it. In this instance, as in many other cartoons, Latin America is assigned a passive role, its fate left to be determined by outside forces.

**9. The Oyster and the Shell**
A condition Secretary Root is said to have faced in South America.
Charles L. "Bart" Bartholomew, *Minneapolis Journal*, 1906. Reprinted with permission of The Minneapolis Star and Tribune Company. All rights reserved.

This 1911 cartoon by Bartholomew appeared as the threat of war in Europe approached. At the time, the United States was stoutly opposed to this hemisphere's becoming entangled in European conflicts. Here Mother Hen Taft's frightened brood of Latin American republics hurries to the protection proffered by the United States. Bartholomew was but one of the many cartoonists who before World War I used the techniques of anonymity and dehumanization, thereby denying the Latin American republics a positive role in hemispheric affairs.

**10. The Real Peace Bird**
Charles L. "Bart" Bartholomew, *Minneapolis Journal*, 1911. Reprinted with permission of The Minneapolis Star and Tribune Company. All rights reserved.

The Pan American Union Building in Washington, D.C., houses the headquarters and many of the agencies of the Organization of American States as well as the Columbus Memorial Library. The original grant for the building came from Andrew Carnegie, industrialist and philanthropist. In May 1911, he contributed an additional one hundred thousand dollars toward completion of the structure.

The above cartoon, with President William Howard Taft in the background, records the recognition accorded to Mr. Carnegie by the American republics in appreciation of the material aid rendered by him "to the cause of peace and friendship between nations." The representations of the various Latin American nations, especially Mexico, still under Porfirio Díaz, whose prestige in the United States remained high, provide some suggestion of their individuality. The overall impression, however, is one of similarity rather than uniqueness.

**11. Benefactor of Humanity**

Mr. Carnegie being presented with a gold medal by the representatives of twenty-one American republics.

*Utica Saturday Globe*, 1911.

54

*The Hemisphere
as Monolith*

When this cartoon appeared in 1912, war clouds hovered over Europe, and the Panama Canal was but a few months away from completion. With those developments in mind, Uncle Sam asserts his claims to hegemony in the hemisphere under the terms of the Monroe Doctrine as unilaterally interpreted in Washington. The artist apparently was in full accord with those in government who would deny the republics a participatory role in policies vitally affecting their well-being and sovereignty.

**12. His Hat (Monroe Doctrine) Is in the Ring**
Charles L. "Bart" Bartholomew [?], *Minneapolis Journal*, 1912. Reprinted with permission of the *St. Paul Dispatch*.

On April 21, 1914, United States marines occupied the port of Veracruz, Mexico, with the stated objective of fulfilling President Woodrow Wilson's announced determination to topple Victoriano Huerta, the military dictator who had seized the presidency of Mexico following the assassination of President Francisco Madero. Huerta refused to buckle under and received support from his political opposition. Wilson, as a consequence, found himself faced with an "unthinkable" Mexican war. The ABC powers (Argentina, Brazil, and Chile) opportunely stepped in with an offer of mediation, which Wilson hastily accepted, as a means of deliverance from a humiliating predicament. ABC delegates and representatives of the United States and Mexico met at Niagara Falls, Canada, in late May and agreed upon a plan which enabled the United States to avoid war. The ABC powers' offer of mediation and their subsequent statesmanship at the Niagara Conference, which took place against a backdrop of war in Europe, provided cartoonists with one of the few occasions in over one hundred years that they have taken to portray the republics in a favorable light. The use, however, of a single figure to represent all of Latin America, except Mexico, implied a cultural unity and agreement on hemispheric policy that has never existed except in the minds of some non–Latin Americans.

**13. United We Stand**

North and South America getting together on the Mexican situation.
Charles L. "Bart" Bartholomew, *St. Paul Daily News*, 1915. Reprinted with the permission of the *St. Paul Dispatch*.

In early 1916, when this cartoon appeared in the *Review of Reviews*, war raged in Europe, and in North America relations with Mexico were tense. Within months the prospects of direct United States involvement in Europe had increased, and nearer home John J. Pershing had been named to lead a punitive expedition into Mexico in pursuit of the revolutionary Pancho Villa. There was good reason for the United States to take advantage of improved relations with the republics resulting from President Wilson's pledge that the United States never again would seek additional territory in Latin America by conquest, his acceptance of the ABC powers' offer of mediation in the controversy arising over United States occupation of Veracruz, and his early withdrawal of troops from the occupied port to make a show of Western Hemisphere unity. The figure labeled "South America" (read Latin America) is shown in an unusual role for a Latin American male personality, that of appearing in Western-style dress and in stature and demeanor the equal of the United States representative, in this case President Wilson.

**14. EUROPE: "If I had only done that!"**
Westerman[?], *Ohio State Journal* (Columbus), 1916. Reprinted by permission of
the *Columbus Citizen-Journal*.

During 1923 the Central American republics agreed to a number of pacts, a key objective of which was that the five republics would not recognize governments that should come to power through a coup d'état or revolution. Before the pacts could be ratified, a defeated presidential candidate in Honduras resorted to revolution. The United States declared its intention to implement the policy of the new pacts. It broke off formal relations, sent warships to both coasts, and landed marines. Washington, in cooperation with Nicaragua, Guatemala, Costa Rica, and El Salvador, selected and recognized a provisional government. At home, continued United States involvement in Honduras raised the question: was Washington primarily concerned with the manner in which Hondurans settled their election disputes or was the main objective of intervention the protection of United States capital already invested in Honduras, especially when rumors of important oil strikes in that country were in circulation? One of the cartoonists' favorite devices has been to portray the Latin American republics as parts of Uncle Sam's anatomy. And when he has felt pain in his neck, chest, shoulders, or lower regions, he has ordinarily prescribed for himself a self-administered "dose of Monroe Doctrine."

**15. Another Little Touch of Sore Throat**

Paul Plaschke, *Louisville Times*, 1924. Reprinted by permission of the *Louisville Times*.

The artist on this occasion apparently was engaging in wishful thinking as a result of the favorable receptions that Charles A. Lindbergh received during his good will tour to several of the republics following his conquest of the Atlantic in the *Spirit of St. Louis*. At no time during the tour did a responsible United States representative publicly propose that Latin America be welcomed even as a partner in respect to the Monroe Doctrine and its interpretation. Furthermore, any expectations for improved relations generated by Lindbergh's barnstorming had dissipated within weeks, and at the Havana Conference hemispheric relations reached what up to then was an all-time low.

**16. The Monroe Doctrine Now Seems to Have a Little Brother**

John T. McCutcheon, *Chicago Tribune*, ca. 1928. Reprinted, courtesy of the *Chicago Tribune*.

Cartoonists and editors offered various interpretations
of the successes and failures of the Sixth International
Conference of American States that met in Havana in
January 1928. But former Secretary of State Charles
Evans Hughes, head of the United States delegation, was
generally acclaimed for having headed off possible dis-
ruption of relations on several occasions. This cartoon
refers to the near breakup of the conference over a resolution that "no state has the right to intervene in the internal affairs of another." The breakup was averted and a
final vote on the resolution headed off when Hughes "in
a supreme effort" defended the right of "interposition of
a temporary character." The United States thus preserved
the right of direct intervention. That right was renounced
within five years and the renunciation was respected in
principle until the United States landed troops in the
Dominican Republic in 1965. In this cartoon, naturally,
only five of the twenty republics constitute the Pan American Union basketball team, and there is no way to identify by nationality any one of them. Collectively, neither
these five nor possible substitutes had any chance against
the United States one-man opposition.

**17.  Guarding the Basket**
J. N. "Ding" Darling, *New York Herald Tribune*, 1928. Copyright, 1928, Des Moines
Register and Tribune Company. Reprinted by permission.

Among the favorite themes of the cartoonists has been one that portrayed the republics as unwilling or incapable of contributing responsibly to their own welfare and development. This drawing appeared when the era of the Good Neighbor Policy had ended and Washington's financial assistance to Latin America was minimal. Aside from stereotypically ascribing to the republics a preference for handouts over hard work and saving, the device of using a single figure to symbolize Latin America served to obscure the fact that the United States hemispheric policies, most especially those in the economic sphere, traditionally have been designed to treat the republics on a bilateral basis.

**18. A Little More Effort, Señor**
Hugh Hutton, *Philadelphia Inquirer*, 1961. Reprinted by permission of *The Philadelphia Inquirer*.

As a century of cartooning certifies, the United States
has held that through pressure from Washington the
Latin American republics would ultimately adopt United
States–style democracy. President John F. Kennedy was
convinced that political freedom could destroy the traditional social barriers. At his insistence the declaration
that political freedom must accompany material progress
was made an integral part of the Alliance for Progress.
There was an abundance of evidence by 1963 that, so
far as democracy was concerned, leaders in many of the
republics were less than apt learners. Here a pedantic
Uncle Sam is thwarted by a uniformly contrary Latin
American class. By portraying the political situation in
the various republics in undifferentiated terms, this artist
reinforced the historically inaccurate view of a "monolith" to the south of the United States.

**19.  The Class Will Please Come to Order—Somebody?**
William H. Crawford, *New York Times,* December 22, 1963. Reprinted by permission of NEA, Inc.

*The Hemisphere
as Monolith*

This 1962 drawing by Bill Mauldin is one of the most ar-
tistically impressive and meaningful cartoons ever to
appear on Latin America. The Alliance for Progress was
only a few months old, but already there was abundant
evidence that it was on its way to failure in a number of
areas, including that of reform. The impact of the cartoon
derives principally from the brilliant exploitation of the
stereotypical image of the "lazing Latin" about to suffer
the consequences of his insincere commitment to meaningful reform.

**20.** Bill Mauldin. © 1962. Reprinted by permission of Bill Mauldin.

# 3. LATIN AMERICA AS FEMALE

At various times in the past, our cartoonists have chosen to portray the Latin American republics as feminine. The occasions of female symbolization and the roles in which female characters have been cast have owed nothing to happenstance. Even allowing for specific differences in interpretation, the general messages that the artists wanted transmitted to their public seem no less clear. It is apparent that certain deep-seated and continuing convictions about role differentiation by sex in the United States have been reflected in such cartoons. A cursory review of the multiple roles that cartoonists have tended to emphasize in their depictions of Latin America supports this claim.

Of the various schools of thought about women in United States society since the Civil War, two dichotomize their status in ways that are particularly relevant to this study. The first emphasizes the changing status of women, changes that are closely linked to new situations arising out of an environment increasingly dominated by industrialization and urbanization. It points to women's ever-heightening intellectual standing; the rights won to hold title to property and to establish businesses; their access to courts, enfranchisement, and new economic opportunities outside the home; and concomitantly their greater capacity to restrain parental and husbandly authority and greater freedom in manners and morals. Those who favor this approach recognize that there are still numerous battles to be fought and victories to be won but nonetheless believe that the lines between male and female spheres, whether intellectual, economic, or social, have blurred.[1] In directing attention to the Western Hemisphere by the use of female symbols, the cartoonists have chosen to disregard those new female roles associated with the late nineteenth and twentieth centuries, preferring instead to depict their Latin American females as dependents, or sex symbols, or simply objects to elicit sympathy, roles associated especially with the early and mid-nineteenth century.

The second school stresses what it sees as the striking continuity of beliefs and attributes about women held by succeeding generations of men. It contends that the dominant influences upon female lifestyles in the United States have been those traditionally associated with the patriarchal society. Nineteenth-century theological assumptions about the weakness and inferiority of women and nativist concerns about the wife and mother in the midst of the rapid industrialization and the wave of immigration around 1900 have been complemented in this century by the pervasiveness of Freudian analysis, which depicts females as passive creatures in contrast to active males. The forces at work, the argument continues, reaffirm woman's alleged dependence upon man for food, shelter, and clothing. She is powerless in her own right. Her destiny becomes marriage, for which she prepares by cultivating seductiveness, gentility, and submissiveness. She is Keats's "milkwhite lamb that bleats for man's protection." In the view of feminist Charlotte Perkins Gilman, sex in effect becomes her economic way of life and hence marriage becomes legalized prostitution. In recognition of her passive virtues, her menfolk have assigned her, as Mother, an official position alongside God and home in the sentimental triad of proclaimed American values. If she be maintained in luxury she plays the added role of status symbol, establishing that her husband competes successfully in a system that places paramount importance on material achievement. In recognition of her purity, the nation, meanwhile, has made her the symbol of peace and justice and the magnanimous goddess of liberty in contrast to the shrewd, grasping, horsetrading Uncle Sam. Cartoonists have depended almost entirely upon this set of traditional images in their representation of Latin America as feminine.

As female, then, Latin America has been White and privileged, as have been women about whom image makers in the United States have been basically concerned. The cartoon characters have played the three basic ascriptive roles assigned to women in the traditional division of labor. Sometimes they are attractive, seductive types seemingly anxious to yield to superior males in return for support. Sometimes they are virtuous but defenseless creatures requiring the protection of chivalrous or indulgent males from the exploitation of undesirable European suitors. Sometimes they have been physically fragile individuals inviting the sympathy and understanding of benevolent neighbors. In sum, Latin America caricatured as female has been weak, dependent, inadequate, in very crucial ways. Nations and peoples so depicted have been denied characteristics which might have qualified them as equal partners in the hemisphere. The feminine representations of Latin America, in fact, seem to lend credence to the dictum that only in the human race has the thought occurred that one sex should be dependent entirely on the other.

The United States, under President Wilson's and Secretary of State William Jennings Bryan's leadership, is shown capitulating to what the cartoonist considered unreasonable demands on the United States by Great Britain over developments in Mexico while failing to protect United States citizens, witnessed by the list in Uncle Sam's back pocket. This behavior is portrayed as womanly and unbecoming. Although Uncle Sam is addressed as "sir," he is in high heels and ruffled pants, his hair in ringlets. The cartoon calls attention to some of the very basic assumptions about males and females that have prevailed in the United States and have been used by cartoonists to establish ordinate and subordinate roles in hemisphere affairs.

**21. Suppose Mexico Should Harm Another Subject of Great Britain?**
Reynolds, *Oregonian* (Portland), 1914.

Prior to 1920, cartoonists commonly portrayed Latin American states as female when seeking to invoke compassion for them. Here defenseless Mexico is cast as a woman—with stereotypical American Indian features—and Catholic (note wall hangings), threatened by Great Britain (*center*), Spain (*left*), and France (*right*), who in late 1861 sent expeditionary forces to Mexico with the stated intention of enforcing the financial claims of their subjects. Public sympathy in the United States was on the side of Mexico, but the Civil War erased for the moment any possibility that Washington, in the name of the Monroe Doctrine, might resist the invaders. Great Britain and Spain withdrew when satisfied that Mexico under Benito Juárez was committed to fulfilling its obligations to the extent that internal conditions permitted. France's ambitious Napoleon III, however, determined to remain and to establish a New World empire. Mexican patriots resisted and the project collapsed in 1867 before the United States became directly involved.

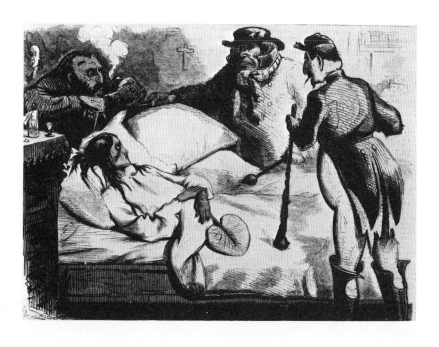

**22. The Sick Woman of Mexico**

JOHN BULL: "Say, Missus! me and these other Gents 'ave come to Nurse you a bit."
Frank Bellew, *Harper's Weekly*, February 8, 1862.

United States agricultural and industrial output spurted following the Civil War, calling forth vigorous efforts to open overseas markets capable of absorbing the mounting surpluses. Latin America, where commercial relations earlier had been left to develop haphazardly, became a prime focus of attention for traders and public officials working in behalf of the private sector.

This cartoon, which called attention to the New Orleans–sponsored "World's International Cotton Centennial Exposition" of 1884–85 and which meant to create a positive image of Latin America as a trading partner, is an early example of what became standard practice among cartoonists of using European-like females to present the republics favorably. The dark-hued figure in non-European attire and labeled La Plata (read Argentina) is interesting because by 1884 the Argentine population, along with that of Uruguay, was the most European in all of Latin America and probably in the entire Western Hemisphere.

23.    Now Peace hath done her perfect work—serene,
Loyal and beautiful, the Southern queen
Bids all the wide world welcome to her door,
Where Industry has spread a varied store,
Where the white splendor of her heaping bales
Answers the snow of crowding foreign sails—
Wise sister, blessed be thy welcoming hand,
Stretched to Republics of the tropic land!
Joseph Keppler, *Puck*, December 10, 1884.

This cartoon, appearing two years before the Spanish-American War erupted, contains all the elements of a melodrama, a highly popular art form of the era. Textbooks, journals, and newspapers had prepared the United States public to view Spain as a villain against humanity in general and against the welfare of Cuba in particular. By the same token, Uncle Sam, backed by a modernizing navy, had become the self-appointed, daring, chivalrous defender of the hemisphere. So long as the cartoonists favored Cuba's cause, it was ordinarily physiognomized as female and Caucasian.

**24. The Cuban Melodrama**

THE NOBLE HERO (*to the* HEAVY VILLAIN): "Stand back, there, gol darn ye!—If you force this thing to a fifth act, remember that's where I git in *my* work!"

C. Jay Taylor, *Puck*, June 3, 1896.

This cartoon appeared soon after the political cartoon became a regular feature of the mass media and at a time when United States interest in Cuba was intensifying. It had been generally agreed that Spain's days in Cuba were numbered and that the United States would not permit events on the island to run their course unattended. There remained, however, considerable difference of opinion on how United States interests might best be advanced. One popular choice was to free Cuba from Spain and annex it as the forty-sixth state in the Union. In his suggestion of a romance in which Cuba plays the subordinate role of a señorita eagerly responding to Uncle Sam's advances, the artist created a scenario that his successors have reproduced with timely variations when seeking to mobilize support for the improvement of relations between the United States and Latin America.

**25. Come Live with Me and Be My Love!**
(Uncle Sam is wooing Cuba, while jealous Spain is plotting revenge in the shadow)
F. T. Richards[?], *Life* (New York), 1896.

This widely reproduced cartoon appeared at a time when demands for Spain's expulsion from the hemisphere had reached fever pitch in the United States. It associates Spanish tyranny with the sixteenth-century conquistadors Cortés and Pizarro as well as General "Butcher" Weyler of "reconcentration" camp fame in Cuba. The emaciated, prostrate female symbolizing Cuban misery was meant to enlist sympathy for the colony where Spain's reported atrocities fed the standard view of its assumed historical inhumanities.

**26. Spain's "Sense of Justice"**
C. G. Bush, *New York World*, 1898.

On April 25, 1898, President William McKinley approved an act of Congress which declared that the United States was at war with Spain as of April 21. Anticipating Cuba's freedom from Spain, this cartoonist drew a slender, bony-armed female with Caucasian features enshrouded in the Cuban flag and arising from the shackles of colonialism. Thus, his public was invited simultaneously to share Cuba's emancipation and to commiserate with the former colony as it faced the uncertainties of the future.

**27. Cuba Libre!**
William Allan Rogers, *Harper's Weekly*, April 30, 1898.

Following the outcome of the Spanish-American War,
influential elements in the United States were sharply
divided as to whether the island should be given its sovereignty or be annexed to the United States. The issue
ultimately was compromised by making Cuba a quasi
protectorate of the United States under the Platt Amendment. Those in favor of annexation had to confront the
view of their opponents that the Cuban people were
basically Black and anarchic and as such unqualified to
practice political democracy. This cartoon reflects the
annexationists' tactical responses to the Black-anarchic
contention: make Cuba "fair" to qualify it for democracy
and female to evoke not only the image of peace and
order but also the need to be protected. A benevolent
United States in turn is symbolized as female.

**28. Miss Cuba Receives an Invitation**

MISS COLUMBIA (*to her fair neighbor*): "Won't you join the stars and be my forty-sixth?"
*Chicago Record-Herald*, 1901.

The annexationists defeated, Uncle Sam prepared to leave the island to a fair maiden, cast in the familiar role of housecleaning, about to apply her broom to Cuban politics. Some United States cartoonists (see chapters 4 and 5) and many informed Cubans, with good reason as it turned out, were dubious both of Cuba's ability to assume the responsibilities of sovereignty and of the United States' intention to allow it a serious attempt to do so.

**29. Packing Up**
*New York Tribune*, 1902.

Many individuals who followed developments in the Caribbean worried that Cuba's chances of survival as a new nation were being jeopardized by excessively severe tariffs levied by the United States on Cuban sugar and tobacco. In this cartoon, the figures representing Congress and the sugar trusts are the villains. If Cuba is revived, it is made to appear that it will have all the necessary ethnic and passive qualities to be acceptable to the United States. In the meantime, right-minded individuals could take pity on Cuba, victimized by greedy monopolists.

**30. Abandoned**
  F. I. Richards, *New York Herald*, 1902.

Independent Cuba soon ran into economic straits. Elements in the United States who felt that Washington had a moral obligation to assist Cuba and those who believed that trade promised the surest way of maintaining effective control of the Cuban people supported proposals to grant Cuban sugar and tobacco special tariff concessions. This position was countered by the beet sugar and tobacco interests, whose lobbyists were influential in preventing the passage of legislation that the lower-tariff advocates considered reasonable and just. This cartoon—one of several that appeared in favor of generous reciprocity agreements—put added weight behind the case by presenting Miss Cuba as unassuming and possessing virtues that were much a part of the United States ethnic: cleanliness, self-reliance, enterprise, and thrift (note handbag).

**31. I Come to Buy, Not to Beg, Sir**
William Allan Rogers, *Harper's Weekly*, November 7, 1903.

Growing international trade and the Spanish-American War in which the United States Navy was called upon to fight in two oceans heightened demands for an isthmian canal. When the second Hay-Pauncefote Treaty of 1901 with Great Britain gave the United States a free hand to build, control, and fortify a canal, it only remained for Washington to choose between the proposed Nicaraguan and Panamanian routes. Each route had had its champions for several years, but by late 1901 congressional and expert opinion had veered sharply toward Nicaragua, largely on the basis of costs. At that point the French-controlled New Panama Canal Company panicked. As heir to the de Lesseps group that had foundered in a sea of debt while attempting to construct a canal across the isthmus, the New Panama Canal Company, fearful of losing out entirely, slashed the asking price for its rights across Panama by 60 percent. The artist saw that gesture as the occasion for a "fickle" Uncle Sam to reject a consenting Miss Nicaragua and direct his attention to Miss Panama, obviously ready and willing to yield to Uncle Sam.

32. MISS NICARAGUA: "O Sam, you fickle thing! They tell awful stories about her!"
*Columbus* (Ohio) *Dispatch*, ca. 1902.

Porfirio Díaz, whose long dictatorial and socially back-ward regime was seen in many quarters as giving Mexico much needed order and fiscal responsibility, had a generally friendly press in the United States. Complimentary reference to him continued to appear in newspapers and periodicals after the defeat of his armies by the rebel forces of Francisco Madero. Here Díaz is depicted as renouncing the presidency to a female Mexico whose physical features and general attractiveness make her a reasonable candidate for the favorable attention of Uncle Sam, whom the cartoonists often portrayed as susceptible to the charms of unthreatening females.

**33. Díaz Making His Greatest Gift to His Country**
(Referring to his renunciation of the presidency)
William Allan Rogers, *New York Herald*, 1911.

Nothing has been more effective in making the United States public receptive to favorable views of Latin America than those conflicts and ideologies born in Europe which have threatened to spill over into the hemisphere and thus to pose security concerns for the United States. This cartoon plays upon that fundamental fact but does not note that strained relations with the newly recognized, strongly nationalist government of Venustiano Carranza in Mexico was an added inducement for the United States to seek better understanding between the remaining republics of the hemisphere. When the cartoon appeared in the February 1916 issue of the *Review of Reviews*, President Wilson had only recently terminated the military occupation of Veracruz, leaving behind an atmosphere of bitterness. During the month following the cartoon's publication, the Mexican rebel leader Pancho Villa and his band raided across the border, taking the lives of seventeen United States citizens. That act prompted the fruitless Pershing expedition which contributed to the further deterioration of trust between the two nations. The artist, then, as a consequence of developments abroad and at home, had good reason to favor hemispheric unity but not, obviously, at the price of recommending a reordering of associations on a man-to-man basis.

**34. Room for All under the New Umbrella**

Charles L. "Bart" Bartholomew, *Minneapolis News*, ca. 1916. Reprinted with permission of The Minneapolis Star and Tribune Company. All rights reserved.

The Fifth International Conference of American States met in Santiago, Chile, during March, April, and May of 1923 in an atmosphere of widespread suspicion over the motives and purposes of the United States. Mexico had refused to attend the conference because Washington had denied recognition to the Alvaro Obregón government. At a more general level, the republics were uniformly resentful over the steadfast determination of the United States to interpret unilaterally the Monroe Doctrine. The artist here suggests a brighter side to a gloomy situation. Presumably as a result of their participation in the war, the peace conference, and the deliberations of the League of Nations, the republics were seen as growing up and already had attained sufficient feminine maturity and charm once again to arouse Uncle Sam's amorous instincts.

**35. My, How You Have Grown!**
Sykes, *Philadelphia Evening Public Ledger*, 1923. Reprinted by permission of *The Philadelphia Inquirer*, 1923.

The sky pilot in this cartoon is Charles A. Lindbergh. Following his solo flight across the Atlantic in May 1927 and his return to a hero's welcome, he was enjoined by the United States government in December to make a good will flight to Mexico. When his reception in Mexico exceeded all expectations, his visit was extended to the Central American states, Colombia, Venezuela, Haiti, and Cuba, in all of which he was warmly received. Many cartoonists, reflecting editorial comment, predicted permanent gains from Colonel Lindbergh's mission. The artist on this occasion went a step beyond the usual love affair theme reserved for such occasions, to unite the United States and Mexico in wedlock.

**36.  The Sky Pilot Performs a Wedding**

Cargill, *South Bend Tribune*, 1928. Reprinted by permission of the *South Bend Tribune*.

In January 1928, less than a month after Lindbergh's triumphal tour, the Sixth International Conference of American States met at Havana, Cuba. At the same time, United States marines were in Nicaragua and United States financial advisers were stationed throughout the Caribbean. Latin American feelings toward the United States had never been more bitter. The republics' deep concern over United States conduct did not prevent this cartoonist from hoping that an engaging and protective Uncle Sam could turn the thoughts of a worried señorita to lighter matters.

**37.** UNCLE SAM: **"It's the wind, rustling the palms."**
Jerry Doyle, *Philadelphia Record*, 1927. Reprinted by permission of Jerry Doyle.

Following the Havana Conference and United States insistence upon the right of "interposition of a temporary character," in December 1928 President-elect Herbert Hoover took a seven-week good will tour to more than half of the nations to the south in an effort to turn the tide of resentment and to present the "real Uncle Sam." The junket temporarily generated good will in some quarters, although numerous knowledgeable individuals failed to share the view of the figure here symbolizing Latin America. Instead, figuratively speaking, recalling the not-unusual consequences of whirlwind affairs for unwary, wide-eyed females, they remained deeply apprehensive of United States intentions, which at best ordinarily placed them in a decidedly subordinate role.

**38. Not as Bad as Painted**
Thiele, *Culver* (Ind.) *Citizen*, 1928. Reprinted by permission of the *Citizen*.

The favorable influences of the Good Neighbor Policy and the hemispheric cooperation prompted by World War II had largely dissipated when Dwight D. Eisenhower assumed the presidency. Throughout his term of office, Europe and Asia commanded Washington's sustained attention to the near-total official neglect of hemisphere issues. Here the artist suggests the Eisenhower-Dulles approach as one detrimental to Latin America and calls attention to a new danger—the Russian bear—in the Western Hemisphere. The artist, as had many of his predecessors, relies upon the traditional strong-male/weak-female roles of the leading characters in order to convey his view of the proper conduct of hemisphere affairs.

**39. Bypassed**
Rogerson, *Newsday*, 1954. Reprinted by permission of *Newsday*.

Soon after his inauguration, President Kennedy launched the Alliance for Progress, designed simultaneously to counter the influence of the USSR and Castro's Cuba and to help Latin America help itself. Congress appropriated initial funds in May 1961, a charter was agreed to in August, and President and Mrs. Kennedy toured Venezuela and Colombia in December to add emphasis to the New Frontier's concern for Latin America's welfare. This cartoon appeared when interest in and hopes for the Alliance were peaking. The euphoria of the time called for the use of a female figure to symbolize Latin America. When disillusionment set in, as it did within months, cartoonists reverted, as they traditionally had, to the use of male figures to represent the republics.

**40. We're Getting Better Gradually—Only Our Parrot Looks Bad**
*New York Times,* December 31, 1961. Copyright © 1961 by The New York Times Company. Reprinted by permission.

The Alliance for Progress had barely been launched when skeptics in Latin America and the United States questioned the validity of its basic tenet: the idea that capital and further incorporation into world trade would solve all problems. For the doubters, large United States public investments in the republics only bought time against expropriation of foreign-owned properties, promoted United States exports, and reinforced direct intervention by Washington in the internal affairs of the republics. It was, furthermore, humiliating for the recipients to comply with conditions attached to "aid funds." In the economic area, those who were unenthusiastic about the Alliance contended that what was needed was price stabilization, improved terms of trade, and, as this cartoon suggests, "trade, not aid." The cartoon appeared about the time that the women's liberation movement began to gather momentum. Whether or not the movement has restrained cartoonists from relying upon the male-female theme, with all that the relationship has traditionally implied, remains to be seen, but the indications are that it has had that effect.

**41. I'd Rather Have Them Drink More Coffee**
Ed Valtman, *Hartford Times*, 1963. Reprinted by permission of Ed Valtman.

# 4. THE REPUBLICS AS CHILDREN

Following the Spanish-American War, cartoonists commonly made use of infant-youth and child-adult symbolism in pictorializing hemispheric issues. Mexico, the Caribbean nations, and the Central American republics were, as a consequence, repeatedly represented as infants or youths to call attention to their immaturity, while the United States was assigned parental and/or guardian roles. The artists scrapped these particular kinds of characterizations about the time of the Great Depression. The phenomenon itself, its discard, and its significance for the better understanding of hemispheric relations are understandable strictly in terms of domestic developments and attitudes.

The generation during which the youth and youth-adult analogies were exploited paralleled those early years of intense public interest in the child and child rearing in the United States. Before, during, and after World War I, parents, nurture writers, educators, religious figures, and public officials, under the influence of the developing sciences, especially psychology, debated endlessly the impact of industrial growth and urbanization, the entrepreneurial system, and immigration upon the child and the child-centered family. Adults were at counterpoint as to whether children should be considered diminutive men and women or innocent individuals who because of their tender years and inexperience must be protected from the worst influences of the environmental changes the United States was undergoing. The God-fearing and those who trusted nature debated the questions. Are children, as the Calvinists had insisted, born depraved and demonic in nature or are they God's little people with the potential for responsible self-fulfillment in adulthood? Would they comprise a better society or were they sons and daughters who would grow up and have thoughts similar to those of their parents? Such questions inevitably led to others. Should discipline be sufficiently painful to break the child's will or should it be limited to deprivation and appeals to the child's rationality? Who should be held responsible and to what degree when a child failed to fulfill achievement norms—child, parent, school, or society?

When the era opened, the individual dominated production and marketing; by its close, bureaucratically controlled industry was fast supplant-

ing family-owned enterprise. The competing systems threatened to produce irreconcilable objectives, and the child often became the victim of
disagreements about how best to serve the needs of a society in transition.
The entrepreneurially oriented elements, who tended toward activity instead of toward an accommodative style of behavior, basically favored
routinized child rearing as a way of inculcating problem solving and self-
control. Youngsters, they thought, should be taught to curb their immediate desires in the interest of satisfying long-range needs. The success ethic,
a cornerstone of their thinking, made idleness and shiftlessness unpardon-.
able sins but Huckleberry Finn's natural boisterousness, self-sufficiency,
and resourcefulness admirable. Achievement was its own reward.

The newly emerging bureaucratic sectors, meanwhile, held a quite
different set of values and attitudes. They tended to reject routinized
training in favor of permissiveness, which they trusted gave children more
freedom for self-determination and would help them to develop a manipu-
lative stance toward their environment. They countered the persisting
view that life is an investment for which the reward would be reaped only
in the future with a consumption-oriented concept that accentuated immediate gratification. It followed that achievement might reasonably be
supplemented by directly rewarding experiences. Permissiveness and
immediate consumption combined to produce a "fun morality" that challenged traditional parental and educational philosophies about work and
play.

The uncertainties about child rearing, great as they were, did not prevent those concerned about youths from reaching consensus in two areas
particularly relevant to our subject. They agreed that female children
started off with virtues lacking in male children and that girls, consequently, were more obedient and cooperative and quicker to develop
those skills, traits, and value attitudes associated with the performance of
present and anticipated social roles. And the disputants realized that,
while there was a genetic relationship of childhood to the future, society
had not evolved any clearly demarcated step or rites by which youth could
advance to adulthood.

Conflicting opinions about children and adult responsibilities to
them provided the cartoonists with a wide range of currently interesting
areas from which to draw when they opted to cast hemisphere issues in
childlike symbols. And they took full advantage of their opportunities.

Sometimes they reflected views held over from an earlier age or from their own childhoods when corporal punishment and humiliations were favored methods of child control. At other times they applied up-to-date attitudes about children and child rearing to international situations, as when they advocated patience and understanding or rewarding of minor achievements. On still other occasions they went beyond the spectrum of commonly debated views, as when they suggested that the lowly regarded Blacks, Indians, and Spanish Catholics might produce offspring capable of evolving responsible political systems within a single generation, thereby seemingly favoring an environmentalist over a hereditary interpretation as a factor in human development. Always they operated on the widely accepted principle that girls have virtues that boys do not possess.

But whether drawing upon the past or the present attitudes toward children and their relationship to adults, the cartoonists' young people were almost invariably abnormal. Their "approved" boys and girls were too neat, too proper, too docile, and at their best when pleasing adults by displaying unrealistic appreciation of what the artist considered responsible behavior. On the other hand, their "disapproved" young people were dishevelled, unruly, quarrelsome, unteachable, impulsive dark-skinned males, determined not to learn the art of self-control. From the "approved—disapproved" dichotomy one must conclude that at the very least the approved had learned how to ingratiate themselves with those adults who took more satisfaction in children being dutiful and having adult interests than in seeing them develop their own unique personalities, and that the disapproved were set on playing undesirable, nuisance roles whatever the costs.

However inappropriate the analogy may have been when applied to sovereign states, portraying nationals as children was a more favorable characterization than representing them as adult females. A child figure at least carried within itself the presumed genetic capacity to grow up without predetermined limitations on the abilities of the eventual adult. On the other hand, as observed in chapter 3, being represented as an adult female strongly suggested that although a nation had reached maturity it could play only a quite limited number of roles and those of a nature that in the United States was considered to require a dominant male partner for successful fulfillment. But if child symbolism was fairer in a relative sense to the recipient, it still helped to perpetuate at Latin America's expense

the tendency in our culture to regard every situation as having a domi-
nance-submission relationship.

Equally to the point, the news media did not permit the public to focus on any hemisphere issue long enough for biological changes to be evidenced, even if some cartoonists at some time might have entertained that possibility. The consequences were that cartoon children never grew up to where they might reasonably be expected to strike out on their own and the reading public was encouraged to think of Latin America as a child-dependent suspended in time.

There is no hard evidence which explains satisfactorily why the cartoonists ceased to portray the Latin American nations as children after 1930. However, four possible factors suggest themselves. First, while child care remained a central concern after 1930, its novelty had worn thin. Second, the newest republics of Latin America—Cuba and Panama— were by the onset of the Great Depression a full generation old. But in that regard it should be appreciated that throughout the period cartoonists had taken the liberty of greatly prolonging Mexico's and the Central American republics' infancy, since Mexico dated its independence from 1810 and the Central American states from the 1820s. Third, there was a growing sensitivity to the implications of social relationships and, hence, of the inequalities explicit in treating some nations as children and others as adults. Fourth, abandoning the use of child symbolism in dealing with inter-American relations coincided with the beginning of the Good Neighbor Policy, a major proposed objective of which was to stress equality among the republics of the hemisphere. Representing Latin America as childlike and the United States as a mature guardian or protector was grossly inconsistent with that goal.

By the close of 1898, Hawaii had been annexed and Spain
had relinquished its sovereignty over Cuba and had
ceded the Philippines, Puerto Rico, and Guam outright
to the United States. The acquisitions launched this country as a full-scale imperial power in competition with
Great Britain and Germany. Cartoonists commonly used
infant and childlike figures to express their views for and
against imperialism and, once debate on that issue subsided, to express their convictions on matters that arose
from United States imperial ventures. Mischievous infants were used in this cartoon to recall two points repeatedly raised by the anti-imperialists: (*a*) empire
would create more problems than it was worth, and (*b*)
the political maturity of the new members of the imperial
family was such that they must in effect be denied full
rights under the constitution.

**42. How Some Apprehensive People Picture Uncle Sam after the War**
*Detroit News*, 1898.

For a decade after the defeat of Spain, trade relations with Cuba and its political and economic instability were high on the United States foreign relations agenda. Controversy in the United States over tariffs on Cuban sugar and tobacco provided the occasion for this cartoon. During this period of intense concern, infants and children symbolizing Cuba were used freely to portray the roles that the artists believed Cuba was playing. In this cartoon, infant Cuba appears incapable of self-help, and the caption indicates that a niggardly Uncle Sam is doing less than his share to improve the state of the island's economic health.

**43.** UNCLE SAM: **I'll give you one teaspoonful, Cuby. More of it might make you sick."**
William "Billy" Ireland[?], *Columbus* (Ohio) *Dispatch*, 1902.

On May 20, 1902, the United States military occupation ended and Cuba was launched as a sovereign state. During the first year the new nation not unexpectedly faced burdensome problems but fared better than had been generally anticipated in the United States. President Tomás Estrada Palma ruled with a relatively even hand and kept congress under control so that there was an acceptable degree of political tranquility. The president's program was especially successful in the economic area, thanks in large part to favorable returns from sugar, despite the failure of the United States Congress to pass a reciprocity treaty favorable to Cuba. As a consequence, the Cuban government had funds to devote to public works, the island established its credit, and the country attracted foreign capital into several industries, notably sugar. If the artist of this cartoon was not sufficiently impressed with the prospects for the future to make his characters "White" he at least made his Black children appear competent and confident in contrast to the Black bunglers that the public had already become accustomed to associate with Cuba.

**44. After the First Mile**
W. L. Evans[?], *Cleveland Leader*, 1903.

Despite disclaimers to the contrary, Cuba's trade with the United States grew spectacularly following its independence from Spain. But the Cuban government's share of the gain was soon being dissipated by a corrupt bureaucracy and appropriations for war veteran pensions. By 1905, the nation's early prospects for success had been seriously blighted, and in July 1906 a revolt forced the first elected regime from power. Meanwhile, Puerto Rico, under United States control, had remained relatively stable. The news media in the United States generally showed little patience when Cuba found itself in political difficulty and did not hesitate to show its hostility. In this cartoon Cuba is triply damned. It is kept a child. It is Black. And the child as a reckless gunslinger is made to play the role of an irresponsible adult.

**45.** UNCLE SAM to PORTO RICO: "And to think that bad boy came near being your brother!"
*Chicago Inter Ocean*, 1905.

Unrest in Cuba over alleged election frauds was so wide-spread by 1906 that President Estrada Palma requested intervention by the United States, which sent commissioners to mediate. Mediation failed. Estrada Palma resigned in July, and on September 29, the United States proclaimed a provisional government until January 28, 1909, when the republic was reinaugurated a second time. The insurrectionists promptly disbanded following the creation of the provisional government and order was restored. In this cartoon Uncle Sam is content with his achievement and with the pacified "White" Cuba that will have to be nursed back to self-government.

**46. The International Nurse**

THE BABY'S UNCLE: "Why, this is not such a bad child, after all."
*Baltimore News,* 1906.

The artist of this cartoon obviously doubted that the United States would relinquish the control it held under the provisional government formed after the downfall of Estrada Palma. For him, "Freedom" turned out to be a marionette presumably to be manipulated by Washington with the United States Navy in a supporting role. Although the cartoonist faults the United States, his rendition of Cuba as childlike and innocent could have done little to convince his viewers that the island was in reality equipped to survive in a world of imperial powers.

**47.  Cuba's Freedom Is Not Far Off**
Thomas May, *Detroit Journal,* 1907. Reprinted by permission of *The Detroit News.*

This cartoon and the preceding one appeared in the same issue of the *Review of Reviews*. Both suggest a friendliness toward the island on the part of the artists. Cuba is here neatly dressed and shows a desire to learn, and neatness and learning were highly valued by the early twentieth-century generation. But that generation also tended to be overly protective of female children. Uncle Sam for the moment is almost out of the picture.

**48. Can She Go It Alone?**
*Toledo Blade*, 1907. Reprinted by permission of *The Blade*, Toledo, Ohio.

Charles E. Magoon was named to head the provisional government of Cuba in October 1906. He sided with the militarists who favored making Cuba a United States protectorate, an alternative opposed by both Secretary of War William Howard Taft and President Theodore Roosevelt. In 1907 the artist responsible for this cartoon had portrayed Cuba as learning to walk on the path to self-government. On this occasion, just months before the provisional government ended in January 1909, an alert Cuba was about to try once again to "go it alone" under the friendly observation of Uncle Sam.

**49.  About Ready to Walk**
UNCLE SAM: "Say, Maggie, let's see if she can go it alone."
*Cleveland Leader*, 1908. Reprinted by permission of *The Plain Dealer*, Cleveland.

Nicaragua, under President José Santos Zelaya, had intervened in Honduras to oust President Policarpo Bonilla;
thereafter, the two nations had signed a treaty and were,
according to the cartoon, at peace. The cartoon blows
out of all proportion the Mexican-Guatemalan controversy which revolved around a Mexican request that a
Guatemalan army officer be extradited to stand trial on
charges of having murdered an ex-president of Guatemala on Mexican soil. The Mexican minister to Guatemala was reassigned to El Salvador and Mexican troops
moved south, but Guatemalan officials had been assured
that Mexico did not intend to push for satisfaction were
its request denied. The cartoon, thus, is a good example
of an all-too-common kind of gross misrepresentation of
developments in Latin America, sometimes out of ignorance, sometimes by intent. The cartoon is also of interest
because Mexico is portrayed as a troublesome infant at a
time when the Mexican president, Porfirio Díaz, was
highly regarded in the United States and his government
was cooperating with Washington in attempts to bring
order out of the instability that Central America was
undergoing.

**50. More Trouble in the Nursery**
Osborn, *Milwaukee Sentinel*, 1907. Reprinted by permission of the *Milwaukee Sentinel*.

This cartoon appeared in the same issue of the *Literary Digest* as the preceding one. Here the same Mexican-Guatemalan incident assumes importance because of its possible effect upon the United States role at the Second Hague Conference where the use of armed forces to collect public debts was debated. Using a minor issue to cast Guatemala and Mexico in such unattractive roles reflected at once a widely held view of Latin America in official and press circles at the time and also, presumably, the public's receptiveness to derogatory images of the republics.

**51.  The Old Man Doesn't Want the Effect Spoiled**

UNCLE SAM: "Now I am going in here to make a peace speech, and I don't want you boys to start any rough house while I'm talkin'."

Carter, *Minneapolis Tribune*, 1907. Copyright © Minneapolis Tribune. Reprinted by permission.

In 1909 Nicaraguan elements supported by United States–owned companies rose against dictator José Santos Zelaya. During the disturbances, two United States citizens were killed. United States marines were landed. Zelaya resigned and José Madriz was named to succeed him. Madriz was not acceptable to either the revolutionaries or Washington, and the United States denied him recognition. United States naval forces occupied the city and port of Bluefields. The United States–favored candidate, Adolfo Díaz, became president in 1911. In sum, the United States became involved in Nicaragua in the interest of United States investors there. In this cartoon, which appeared during the height of the struggle for power, the incorrect inference was that Nicaragua was to be disciplined for violating the Monroe Doctrine when in fact the issue was a strictly domestic one. Given Nicaragua's size and Uncle Sam's determination, not only was the former going to be thrashed, but his dark complexion and sullen expression would also keep him from receiving any sympathy.

**52. Cutting a Switch for a Bad Boy**
McKee Barclay, *Baltimore Sun*, 1910. Reprinted by permission of *The Sun* (Baltimore).

This cartoon appeared during the period when Cuba's prospects of avoiding full-scale United States intervention appeared dim. A "race war" waged in Oriente province led to the landing of a small contingent of United States marines at the town of Daiquirí. And an upcoming presidential election had split the dominant Liberal Party of incumbent chief executive José Miguel Gómez. This division ultimately led President Gómez to throw his support to conservative candidate Mario Menocal, who was victorious at the polls. Up to 1912, cartoonists relied heavily upon infants and inept Black children, using Southern Black colloquialisms or dialects to create the negative images of Cuban politics they sought to convey.

**53. Golly. I've Gone an' Did It Again!**
   (Apropos of Cuba's governmental troubles)
   J. H. Donahey, *Cleveland Plain Dealer*, 1912. Reprinted by permission of *The Plain Dealer*, Cleveland.

The developments in Mexico that led to this cartoon are treated below (see no. 55). Turmoil also reigned in Haiti. Since 1896, nine presidents had "served" and every one of them had been overthrown or killed in office. In July 1915, the government collapsed completely. The president, Vilbrun Guillaume Sam, who was attempting to rule by terror, was seized in the French legation, to which he had fled, and was torn to pieces by a mob. President Wilson, faced with war in Europe and fearful that Germany might take advantage of the chaos in Haiti to seek submarine bases there, consented to United States occupation of the republic. Uncle Sam is trying to devote his attention to Europe and hence is annoyed by the disturbance of the neighborhood "kids," although the artist has them playing "men's" games.

**54. Attending to His Correspondence**
  King, *Chicago Tribune*, 1915. Reprinted, courtesy of the *Chicago Tribune*.

The Mexican dictator Victoriano Huerta went into exile in July 1914. The Carranza, Villa, and Zapata factions that had opposed him could not agree on a common leadership or program. A convention at Aguascalientes in November failed to resolve their differences. Pancho Villa and Emiliano Zapata then formed a loose alliance against Venustiano Carranza, and before the end of the year a civil war broke out and continued throughout the following year. United States lives and property in Mexico were threatened repeatedly. President Wilson's refusal to use force to bring Mexico into line did little to win him friends. Journalists and public officials in Washington loudly urged a tougher policy. In this cartoon President Wilson has a defiant Mexico backed against the wall, and a cleanup appears certain. Readers of *Harper's Weekly* would not have had trouble associating Mexican turmoil and banditry with the approaching need for "the Saturday night bath." However, many of the readers undoubtedly would have related instinctively and sympathetically to the "Mexican" youngster had he been made only a little more appealing.

**55. Isn't It Just About Saturday Night?**
Walter J. Enright, *Harper's Weekly*, August 28, 1915.

In October 1915, the United States extended de facto
recognition to the government of Venustiano Carranza.
Recognition not only failed to moderate Carranza's
nationalistic ardor; it also antagonized Carranza's two
major opponents, Pancho Villa and Emiliano Zapata. In
March, Villa retaliated by raiding across the border into
New Mexico. United States forces sent into Mexico to
pursue him were ordered out by Carranza on the grounds
that their presence violated Mexican sovereignty. In June
a collision with a force of Carranza's troops at Carrizal,
together with the firing on United States ships evacuating
citizens from danger zones, nearly led to war. When this
cartoon appeared, the patience of Congress with Mexico
and with President Wilson's seeming complacence in
regard to the Mexican situation had worn thin. The "civilized" (see wall plaque) appearance and demeanor of the
young people representing Cuba, the Philippines, Nicaragua, and Panama contrast sharply not only with the
dirty, obstreperous, weapon-carrying, booted Mexican
figure, but also with the more usual unfavorable presen-
tations of those four countries by cartoonists. At a more
generalized level the cartoon is notable for the several
pictorial and verbal devices the cartoonist used to indicate his likes and dislikes.

© 1916, by John T. McCutcheon

**56.  It's for His Own Good**

John T. McCutcheon, *Chicago Tribune*, 1916. © 1916 by John T. McCutcheon.
Reprinted, courtesy of the *Chicago Tribune*.

Throughout the 1910s, Cuba was plagued by financial corruption and electoral frauds. Economically the island was dangerously dependent on its sugar industry which was increasingly controlled by large foreign-owned companies. A month before this cartoon appeared in the February issue of the *Review of Reviews*, General Enoch H. Crowder was sent to Havana to advise the Cuban government. Remembering past experiences, the watchbird could have predicted the likely outcome of continued political disturbances on the island. The Cuban republic, represented here by the two young, scruffy, quarrelsome figures, was nearly twenty years old.

**57. A Little Fracas in Cuba**
  Frederick O. Seibel, *Knickerbocker Press*, ca. 1921. Reprinted with permission of
  *The Knickerbocker News*, Albany, N.Y.

President Plutarco Elías Calles (1924–28), shortly after assuming office, alarmed foreign-owned companies in Mexico by making retroactive the expropriation of subsoil properties, originally provided for in the Constitution of 1917. He then proceeded to launch attacks on large landholders and the Catholic church. United States oil companies demanded intervention. Roman Catholic groups in the United States organized protests. Secretary of State Frank B. Kellogg heightened tensions in the United States and anti-Yankee sentiment in Mexico by publicly declaring that "the Government of Mexico is now on trial before the world," and later charged that Soviet agents resident in Mexico were encouraging Nicaraguans to resist United States action in that country. The United States public and most officials adamantly opposed invasion and the prospect of war quickly subsided after President Calvin Coolidge appointed Dwight W. Morrow as ambassador to Mexico. If Secretary Kellogg was guilty of irresponsible diplomatic conduct, as he surely was, the cartoonist in turn can be faulted for helping to prolong the life of the always disrespectful and, by the late 1920s, overworked, practice of representing the Latin American republics in childlike roles. Nearly all artists appearing in establishment journals and newspapers were about to discard that device.

**58.  Lost Something, Didn't You, Frank?**
Howard M. Talburt, *Washington News*, 1926. Reprinted by permission of the
Scripps-Howard Newspaper Alliance.

Political instability provided the occasion for the return of United States troops to Nicaragua from 1926 until 1932. Throughout the occupation President César Augusto Sandino protested the United States presence. His depredations upon North Americans and his repeated embarrassment of United States marines sent in search of him won him acclaim as an anti-*yanquí* man of valor. Meanwhile, the loss of lives among marines made the occupation increasingly unpopular at home. It is noteworthy that this cartoonist assigned Nicaragua to a cradle at a time when portrayal of the republics as children was on the wane and would cease in the 1930s when the Good Neighbor Policy was pronouncing the equality of hemisphere nations. Charles Lindbergh's good will tour is discussed in chapter 3.

**59. Welcome, Lindbergh!**
Cal Alley, *Memphis Commercial Appeal*, 1928. Reprinted by permission of *The Commercial Appeal*, Memphis.

# 5. THE REPUBLICS AS BLACKS

The lynching of 162 Blacks in 1892 marked an all-time high for the United States in that category of crimes against mankind.[1] The lynchings were but one of the more outward manifestations of the full flowering of racism in the United States during the late nineteenth century. Always vulnerable to social and economic discrimination because of color and close association with chattel slavery, the Black in the decades before and during World War I was subjected to both increasingly brutal and more sophisticated forms of repression. Southern mobs by 1890 were torturing and burning their Black victims. Particularly in the South, patterns of violence against Blacks were upheld by the relative lack of fear of legal reprisals from lower courts where the pressures of a deeply prejudiced local opinion were most strongly felt, where judges were often of limited education and provincial backgrounds, and where the few Black lawyers lacked specialization to handle important cases. Outside the South, most notably in industrial areas, ghettoization and segregation were becoming more and more commonplace. Everywhere, racist demagoguery competed with condescension, paternalism, and benevolent sympathy in the imposition of an invidious group identity on all Blacks. Insolence, a lack of the most rudimentary elements of morality, the inability to share "our" democratic opportunities,[2] and an incapacity to behave in their own economic self-interest even under the best of circumstances (a view popularized by labor unions controlled by recent arrivals from Europe) were added to the already widely accepted White stereotypes of Blacks as superstitious, docile, thriftless, emotional, intemperate, unstable, dishonest, promiscuous, happy-go-lucky, and music loving. On those occasions when the race question was permitted to rise to any level of public consciousness, it was treated politically rather than morally.

Formalized racism had reached its peak of power and influence by 1920. Soon therafter it began to be challenged seriously by the emerging liberal environment. By the 1930s, industrialization, technological advances, a high level of mobility, the increasing questioning of the tenets of social Darwinism, and a growing awareness of world animadversion resulted in overt racism losing much of its credibility among the liberal intelligentsia. But if racism as a comprehensive ideology was rejected by many, prejudice as an attitude lingered on, as it still does. And that attitude manifested itself in the continuing inability of Blacks to shed their ancestry; by their failure, ordinarily, to gain access to adequate educational opportunities, good jobs, and union rights; and by their namelessness in occasional pictures appearing in textbooks—to mention just some of the areas in which Blacks were cast as unequal and inferior, thus indirectly providing psychological ammunition for those who would justify the hegemony of established social elements.

The public's determination not to examine rationally the interrelationship between the material facts and their beliefs about Blacks was too apparent and exploitable to go unnoticed by cartoonists in search of ways to direct attention to their views of Latin America. During the three decades (roughly between 1900 and 1930) that racism flourished in the United States, the cartoonists added a profoundly Black image to their repertoire of pejorative and/or patronizing characterizations of the Latin American component of the hemisphere family. Before racism as applied to Blacks fell from intellectual respectability, the cartoonists had cast as Black every Caribbean republic, with the possible exception of Costa Rica. In the process, the artists strongly reaffirmed Thomas Hobbes's conclusion "that, while any person's actual possibility to improve the lot of his fellow creatures amounted to almost nothing, everyone's opportunities to do damage was always immense."

The artists left very little to the imagination as they randomly selected from the long list of physical, oral, and social caricatures with which a prejudiced public could quickly relate. The republics were lampooned variously as cheerful, improvident, carefree Blacks, meant to recall the myth of 'the happy and contented bondsman" or the popular minstrel of an earlier age. They became unintelligent, lazy, dozing people with a consuming appetite for cigars and watermelons or gunslinging, razor-wielding rowdies. And if words were put in their mouths, those words were almost always in southern Black dialect. In brief, a black face and a foreign dialect symbolically transformed Latin America into a stereotype that paralleled the condition of, and evoked from a prejudiced White North American society the same responses as, Blacks in the United States at a time when the prevailing ethic was "keep them in their place."

The cartoonists' use of Black symbolism in portraying Latin America tells us much about their societal role. Their work shows that they waited

nearly a decade after Black racism had luxuriated before commonly ex-
ploiting it in dealing with the republics to the south. And they dropped the
practice only in 1930 when it became evident that the ideology was finally
and definitively on the defensive. This would appear to give strong support to the contention that cartoonists are purveyors rather than makers
of public opinion.

Admiral George Dewey destroyed the Spanish fleet off Manila on May 1, 1898, and Spain's wartime resistance collapsed. Hawaii was annexed two months later. It was apparent that the United States could go the route of imperialism should it choose to do so. The pro-imperialists argued trade, mission, duty, destiny, and defense. The anti-imperialists countered that imperialist involvement would have an unfavorable influence upon the national character and that the "uncivilized" peoples of the potential colonies and protectorates could not be accorded the same rights and privileges guaranteed United States citizens by the Constitution. A major reason that the prospective colonials were held to be unqualified for full citizenship was their presumed racial origin, which Darwinism contended denied them the capability of responsibly participating in and enjoying the benefits of a government designed for "the White race." In this cartoon President McKinley ponders the merits of acquiring territories, including Cuba, considered to be inhabited by inferior peoples of non-Caucasian origins. While the president reflected, public opinion crystallized in favor of annexation of non-White peoples.

**60. The Cares of a Growing Family**

J. Campbell Cory, *New York Bee*, May 25, 1898. Courtesy of the General Research and Humanities Division; the New York Public Library; Astor, Lenox, and Tilden Foundations.

This cartoon is one artist's version of the United States' assumption of an imperial role. The United States stand on imperialism was significantly influenced by the British experience. John Bull, thus, could justly claim some credit for the decision of the United States to join the race for new colonies in areas populated by "lesser breeds without the law," to borrow Rudyard Kipling's words. The British could also take some solace from the prospect of support from a strong United States in the Western penetration of the Orient. But the cartoon is of interest primarily for its depiction of the peoples, including the Cubans, who might compose the empire. The figures are not children, but pygmylike adults with African appearances, including earrings. The implication of inferiority is much stronger here than in the previous cartoon. Children can be educated and do grow up. These figures are already adults, but their size will keep them forever subordinate while their racial features are used to indicate not only race but also lack of civilization.

61. JOHN BULL: "It's really most extraordinary what training will do. Why, only
the other day I thought that man unable to support himself."
Fred Morgan, *Philadelphia Inquirer*, 1898.

Before the United States went to war with Spain, the Cuban patriots had a favorable press in the United States, as their struggle was made to appear as one of civilization against Spanish barbarism. Once troops were landed in Cuba, United States officers quickly concluded that Spanish officers were far more honorable and civilized than the patriots, whose treatment of prisoners and Spanish sympathizers was viewed as savage and brutal. The officers' convictions were soon reflected in the United States news media. As the United States view was modified, the image of the patriot changed from a light-skinned to a dark-skinned person. When civil strife continued after the defeat of Spain, the United States Congress appropriated funds to be paid to ex-patriots who agreed to lay down their arms. In this cartoon all ex-patriots are stereotyped as improvident Blacks, quickly recovered from their wounds (note discarded crutches), content after receiving their share of United States largesse.

**62. This Style of Plaster Will Cure All Their Wounds**
Thomas May, *Detroit Journal*, 1899.

Once Cuba was freed from Spain, there was considerable support in the United States press for Washington to relax its trade restrictions against Cuban sugar and tobacco. While the matter was before Congress the sugar and tobacco trusts lobbied against legislation favorable to Cuba. Though not totally effective, their effort was sufficient to see that Congress granted fewer concessions than the pro-Cuban groups felt necessary if the new nation was to become economically viable. This cartoon speaks to the reciprocity issue and invites sympathy for Cuba. Its most striking feature, however, is the use of attributes associated with the stereotypical Black from the rural South to portray Cuba: shabby gingham shirt, patched overalls, tattered hat, bare feet, oversized bandage on the injured toe, and Southern Black dialect. Compare this with cartoon 53.

63.  CUBA: **"Pahdon me; but would you ge'mmen move aside so's I could get in?"**
James Donahey, *Cleveland Plain Dealer*, 1902.

Despite the great temptation to stay, President Roosevelt stunned the imperialist world by withdrawing from Cuba in 1902. His decision came after the Cubans incorporated the Platt Amendment into their constitution, thus making the island a quasi protectorate of the United States. This cartoon belongs to the same genre as the preceding one and most of the others in this chapter. The exaggerated facial features, the huge cigar, and the language of the caption all invite the viewer to equate Cubans with the caricatured southern Black.

**64.** CUBA: "Yo' watch me, chile, mebbe yo' hab a chance yo'se'f some day."
Westerman[?], *Ohio State Journal* (Columbus), 1902.

President McKinley supported reciprocity with Cuba and President Roosevelt used his influence to keep pressure on Congress in favor of fairer trading arrangements for the island. Yet it took Congress three years to make up its mind. Last-minute differences among the House, the Senate, and the president resulted in postponing the enactment of the measure into law until after this cartoon originally appeared.

**65.** CUBA: "Well, it ought to be a good one, it's been fattening long enough."
Leip, *Detroit News*, 1903.

When Cuba achieved its independence, the status of the Isle of Pines to the south of the main island was left to future adjustment by treaty. In 1925, the United States by treaty recognized it as part of Cuba. In the meantime, United States investors and property owners on the island repeatedly sought to bring it under the United States umbrella, which already afforded protection to other dark-skinned peoples.

**66.  The Isle of Pines Looking for Shelter**
*Binghamton Press*, 1905.

The incongruity of the insistence by the protagonists for imperialism that it was the obligation of the Whites to uplift the benighted, dark-skinned peoples of the Caribbean and the Pacific islands and their insensitivity to the expectancies of Afro-Americans in their midst was seldom called to the public's attention during the era of expansion. This cartoon was unusual for its time in that it spoke to that matter. It is included here to call attention to the possible unfavorable consequences for the Latin American republics of being portrayed as Black by the United States news media.

**67.  Uncle Sam's Burden**

AMERICAN NEGRO: "Lift me up, too; I was here first."
*Ram's Horn* (Chicago), 1903.

On November 3, 1903, the "patriot" Panamanian army
revolted against Colombian authorities. On November 4,
Panama declared its independence. On November 6, the
United States granted the new republic de facto recognition. President Roosevelt had surreptitiously involved
the United States in the movement to separate Panama
from Colombia and then guaranteed Panama's independence by posting United States naval forces off Panama
City to block the advance of troops dispatched to reaffirm
Colombian control. Panama for the moment could justly
be considered a United States protectorate. This cartoon
is one of the many that at once made Panama Black and
infantile, thereby depriving it of independent judgments.

**68.  A Kind Old Gentleman Is Asked to Hold a Baby for "Just a Minute"**
Walker, *Milwaukee Journal*, 1903.

On November 18, exactly two weeks after Panama
claimed its independence from Colombia, the Hay-
Bunau-Varilla Treaty was initiated. On February 23, 1904,
the United States approved the treaty, which provided
for a payment of $10 million down and $250,000 annually and gave this country extraordinary sovereign rights
over a ten-mile strip across the new republic. In this
cartoon the artist, while calling attention to the treaty,
makes doubly sure that it is understood that in his
opinion the United States was dealing with an inferior
people by using a Black child with saliva dripping from
the corner of his mouth in anticipation of a watermelon,
which, according to the wisdom of the day, Blacks found
practically impossible to resist.

**69. They Would Like to Get In**
("The islands of San Andres and Providence want to join the Panama republic."—News item)
W. L. Evans[?], *Cleveland Leader*, ca. 1904.

Colombia resented the United States involvement on the isthmus immediately following the declaration of Panamanian independence. Not surprisingly, there were remarks made in Bogotá and elsewhere suggesting that national pride required Colombia to challenge the United States in Panama. This artist probably exaggerated the seriousness of the Colombian remarks for purposes of effect. Ridicule was a favorite device of early twentieth-century cartoonists, and how better to ridicule than to have a categorically mismatched Black square off against Uncle Sam?

70.  UNCLE SAM: "If you are determined to finish me up, sail in; this suspense is something awful."
G. W. Rehse, *St. Paul Pioneer Press*, ca. 1904.

Ulíses Heureaux became president of the Dominican
Republic (Santo Domingo) in 1882 and retained power
until 1899, when he was killed by political enemies. His
regime gave the nation badly needed peace, but at the
price of corrupt despotism and reckless financial man-
agement. During the half decade after his death, weak
governments rose and fell in quick succession. One of
these regimes ousted the Santo Domingo Improvement
Company, which after 1892, had exercised a measure of
control over Dominican finances and development. Under urging from the State Department the Dominican
government agreed to pay the company $4.5 million (of
a claim of $11 million) in installments, and an arbitral
tribunal ordered that the United States should assume
control over certain customhouses if these installments
were not met. Political unrest and economic irresponsibility caused European debtors to press the claims of
their citizens, and intervention by Germany, France, Bel-
gium, or Italy appeared a serious possibility. Bad as conditions were when this cartoon was published, they
worsened in the months ahead. In a very large majority of
cases, cartoonists portrayed the Dominican Republic as
Black. This caricature not only relied heavily upon standard stereotypical Black images but also exploited the
conviction in the United States that the razor was the
Black man's preferred fighting weapon. The use of "boy"
in the caption gives added emotional impact to the
caricature.

**71.** UNCLE SAM: "Maybe I'll have to bring the boy into the house to keep him quiet."
G. W. Rehse, *St. Paul Pioneer Press*, 1904.

This cartoon appeared at approximately the same time as the preceding one and, like it, called attention to the United States interest in the problems facing the Dominican Republic. President Roosevelt is substituted for Uncle Sam and machetes for the razor as symbols of destructive behavior. The watermelon was, by 1904, a ready-made associational device in the cartooning of developments in the Caribbean republics.

**72. The Strenuous One Will Catch You, If You Don't Watch Out!**
C. G. Bush, *New York World*, 1904.

President Roosevelt concluded that, if the United States would not permit European powers to collect debts by force, it had the "moral mandate" to intervene and compel the reluctant republics to pay their bills. That view was outlined in his annual message to Congress in December 1904, now referred to as the "Roosevelt Corollary" of the Monroe Doctrine. In the same month, Secretary of State John Hay instructed the United States minister in Santo Domingo to determine whether the Dominican president would be favorably inclined to invite the United States government to collect and distribute Dominican customs duties. Soon thereafter a treaty was signed which provided for the United States to take over the collection of customs revenues and to negotiate settlements with the republic's creditors. The United States Senate declined to approve the treaty, but Roosevelt, acting on his own responsibility, established a customs collecting system by executive order. Under United States direction, collections were considerably increased almost immediately. The neat, upright figure symbolizing Santo Domingo—one of a very few dealing with Latin American that portrayed a Black adult in a positive light—calls attention to the change which the artist considered to be for the better. Developments that influenced the cartoonist to portray Venezuela as unkempt and scrubby compared to Santo Domingo are reviewed below (see nos. 77 and 90).

**73. Uncle Sam Invites Venezuela to Occupy a Chair in the International Barber Shop, Just Made Vacant by Santo Domingo**
Clifford Berryman, *Washington Post*, 1905.

Despite generally better economic conditions and relief from creditors after the United States took charge of collecting and redistributing customs duties, turmoil continued to be a featured aspect of Dominican politics. This cartoon and no. 71 were drawn by the same artist. Two years of direct United States influence in the republic's fiscal affairs had not significantly changed his opinion of the Dominican people or their nation.

**74.  Uncle Sam's Periodical Bad Man**
   G. W. Rehse, *St. Paul Pioneer Press*, ca. 1906. Reprinted by permission of the *Dispatch/Pioneer Press*.

On February 7, 1905, President Roosevelt asked the Senate to approve the convention recently agreed to by the Dominican Republic. But enough senators had become disillusioned with expansionism, and resentful of what they considered the president's determination to increase executive power at the expense of the legislative branch, to shun the treaty. Rebuffed, Roosevelt acted on his own and put into operation the machinery to collect and dispense the island's customs duties. A modified treaty, which gave the Senate and the president chances to save face and which paid greater attention to Dominican sensibilities, was negotiated and ratified in 1907. According to this cartoon, the Black, childlike Dominicans, confronted with revolution and political instability, considered the original Roosevelt agreement worth clinging to irrespective of the temper of the Senate.

**75. Still Holding On to It**
"I knows when I's got a good thing."
*Cleveland Leader*, ca. 1906. Reprinted by permission of *The Plain Dealer*, Cleveland.

This cartoon accompanied an article in the *Literary Digest* entitled "Should the United States Intervene in South America?" The thrust of the article was that dictator Cipriano Castro of Venezuela was keeping alive hostilities between his country and Colombia and that constant unrest in the area might compel the United States to intervene to protect its interest in Panama, then a part of Colombia. Castro was satirized unmercifully in the United States press, but in no other instance did the *Literary Digest*, the *Review of Reviews*, *Harper's Weekly*, or *Puck* portray him as a Black. By using the watermelon and the reference to a "southern gentleman," the artist practically guaranteed that his image of Castro as a Black would not escape the reader.

**76. There Seems to Be a Southern Gentleman in the Melon Patch**
G. W. Rehse, *St. Paul Pioneer Press*, 1901.

The tyrant Cipriano Castro had used forces from the Andean region of Venezuela to seize control of the national government in 1899. He openly defied Venezuela's European creditors and, when this led to a blockade of the republic in 1902–03, Castro's countrymen in a display of national fervor gave him their support. President Roosevelt interceded and secured the withdrawal of the blockading fleet and arranged to have the creditors' claims adjudicated by the new international court at The Hague. When the world tribunal scaled down the claims against Venezuela, Castro was hailed as a national hero. During the remainder of his dictatorship he exploited threats from abroad to retain his hold on the country. His cavalier treatment of the Dutch ambassador resulted in the seizure of Venezuelan war vessels by The Netherlands in 1905. The artist used the dictator's lethargic warriors to accentuate his personal need for action in order to retain his domination of the nation.

**77.** CASTRO: **"Carambo, this suspense is killing."**

Reynolds, *Tacoma Daily Ledger*, 1909. Reprinted by permission of the *Tacoma News Tribune*.

In November 1908, President Castro sailed to Europe ostensibly for medical attention, leaving in charge his ablest military officer, Juan Vicente Gómez. Gómez quickly usurped all political power, and Castro was ordered not to return to Venezuela on pain of death. The latter could not accept this turn of events and for several years moved about the Caribbean attempting to organize forces that would return him to power. Foreign nations, with some reason, refused him support, and if there were any champions of the ex-dictator within Venezuela, Gómez kept them suppressed. During the entire Castro era, cartoonists created the unavoidable impression that Venezuela was a Black nation led by a disreputable dictator.

**78.  Sounds Are So Deceiving**
   Thomas May, *Detroit Journal*, 1906. Reprinted by permission of *The Detroit News*.

War between Guatemala and El Salvador broke out when the military and private citizens of El Salvador gave aid to revolutionists in Guatemala bent on deposing that nation's president. Subsequently, a force of Guatemalans allegedly crossed the border into Honduras, whereupon Honduras declared war against Guatemala. Through the good offices of Mexico and the United States, differences among the three republics were settled and, as the cartoon suggests, peace reigned. El Salvador, Guatemala, and Honduras are each pictured as Black children. Given the explicit connotations of casting the republics as Black and childlike, the fact that the cartoonists did not choose faithfully to record the basically Indo-European origins of the republics becomes only secondarily important.

79. **UNCLE SAM: "The kids are in bed and all is well."**
*Seattle Post-Intelligencer*, 1906. Reprinted by permission of the *Seattle Post-Intelligencer*.

The dissolution of the Central American Federation in 1839 left undetermined the boundary between Nicaragua and Honduras. Resolution of conflicting claims dragged on until well into the twentieth century. Border clashes were frequent and might go unreported to the outside world. But when José Santos Zelaya, dictator of Nicaragua (1894–1909), quarreled with his neighbors, all the nations of mid-America and the United States took note. The Central American states went on the alert because the dictator aspired to unite all of Central America, by force if necessary, under his leadership; the United States was worried by his vocal opposition to Washington's intervention in Central America and the threat inherent in such unfriendliness for the United States objective of regulating all transisthmian commercial routes. Thus, when it appeared in early 1907 that clashes between Honduran and Nicaraguan forces might develop into open warfare, concern was expressed in several capitals. The artist, seeing Nicaragua and Honduras from the United States perspective, portrays them as quarrelsome black children, obviously capable of being no more than nuisances in the community of nations. The fact that Honduras had shoes indicated the artist's partiality for that side. The bear presumably referred to "Teddy" Roosevelt.

**80.  A Hint**

Clifford Berryman, *Washington Star*, 1907. Reprinted by permission of the *Washington Star*.

In late 1908, Haiti experienced another of its periodic overturns in government which kept the country in a state of political and fiscal chaos. Eighty-nine–year–old Pierre Nord Alexis, president for the past six years, was the victim. Disorders in the republic prompted speculation that the United States might intervene, as it had in Santo Domingo, to bring order to Haitian politics and finances. As it turned out, the United States avoided intervention at that point, but President Wilson's "missionary diplomacy" led to the landing of marines in July 1915. The alligator as a symbol of revolution in northern Latin America was nearly as commonplace as the Black child was as an indication of political incompetence and irresponsibility.

**81. Alligator Bait**
   The revolutionary alligator may swallow up little Haiti unless Uncle Sam steps in
   and saves the helpless child.
   Thomas May, *Detroit Journal*, 1908. Reprinted by permission of *The Detroit News*.

This cartoon refers to the death of President Vilbrun
Guillaume Sam and the collapse of Haiti's fragile government and financial structure in July 1915 (see no. 54).
The United States promptly landed troops, presumably to
preclude intervention by either France or Germany; and
the Haitians were forced to sign a treaty providing for
United States supervision and financial control. The
worried expression on the child's face may have elicited
some sympathy, but the correlation between United
States intervention in the republics and their portrayal
in the press as inept, simple, naïve Black children was
more than accidental.

**82. I'm In for Something Now**

Hanny, *St. Joseph News-Press*, 1915. Reprinted by permission of the *St. Joseph News-Press*.

United States marines ended thirteen years of guardianship in Nicaragua in August 1925. The following year the marines were returned to that country when General Emiliano Chamorro forced a purged congress to name him president. When a restored congress designated Adolfo Díaz president, the United States hastily extended him recognition. Mexico, meanwhile, recognized Juan Bautista Sacasa, who as vice-president had fled the country at the time of the Chamorro coup. The United States and Mexican positions hardened when Washington accused the Mexican government of sending munitions to Nicaragua in support of anti-Díaz forces and of harboring communists who were giving encouragement to those in Nicaragua opposed to United States–backed parties.

This cartoon appeared at a time when Secretary of State Frank B. Kellogg was leveling a series of charges against the Calles regime in Mexico, including one that it was sheltering and providing arms to Soviet agents seeking to establish a Bolshevist government in Nicaragua. Secretary Kellogg defended the Nicaraguan intervention as necessary to prevent all of Central America from falling into communist hands. Communism was a relatively new element in United States–Latin American relations. In the view of this artist, its appearance did not alter the realities of hemispheric affairs sufficiently to cause this artist to scrap Nicaragua's standard presentation as a Black child in need of Uncle Sam's care and attention. The cartoon is of added interest because it calls attention to the perseverance of a cultural stereotype, regardless of apparent changes in the political-ideological sphere of United States foreign policy.

**83. To the Rescue!**

Craig Fox, *Rochester* (N.Y.) *Democrat and Chronicle*, 1927. Reprinted by permission of the *Democrat and Chronicle*.

By the late 1920s cartoonists, reflecting the emerging climate of opinion that found objectionable the display in print of slurs against certain ethnic groups, began turning away from the use of stereotypical images of Southern Blacks to caricature unfavorably the peoples of Latin America. But as late as 1935 when Good Neighborliness was "in," social sensitivities still had not reached the point where the *Review of Reviews* with its solid middle- and upper-class following could not run approvingly this thirty-four–year–old document with the comment, "This cartoon of 34 years ago finds confirmation in the inauguration of the first Filipino President in 1935." It is telling that with very few exceptions those individuals in the United States who in recent decades have most significantly influenced the making and implementation of policies affecting inter-American relations grew up and received their formal academic training in a social environment that would not find this cartoon an inappropriate portrayal of a Latin American people.

**84.** THE PHILIPPINES: "What yer got?"

CUBA: "Pie."

THE PHILIPPINES: "Where'd yer git it?"

CUBA: "Mah Uncle Sam gin it to me; any maybe ef you was half way decent he' gin you some."

R. C. Bowman, *Minneapolis Tribune*, 1901. Reprinted by permission from the *Minneapolis Tribune*.

# 6. THE LATIN AMERICAN NATIONS AS NON-BLACK MALES

Individuals of Iberian Catholic and Mestizo backgrounds have controlled the political, economic, and religious life of modern Latin America. The racial-religious composition of the leadership of the area has made the republics prime targets for the socially pre-eminent, race-conscious elements in the United States, who traditionally have been quick to make the transition from cultural to political ill-feeling when condemning a particular action or the general "perversity" of the nations to our south. Spaniards and Portuguese historically have been considered the least desirable of all western European peoples. That they have also been categorized as politically authoritarian and economically illiberal has provided added justification for the scorn and disdain directed toward them in the United States. And their association with the Catholic church—which has involved itself in government, engaged in such economic areas as landownership and money lending, insisted on a major role in secular education, and presumably opposed intellectual liberty—was incompatible with the ethos and institutions of North America.

Indians have fared little better. Although, after 1900, eligible for the sentimental treatment the privileged majority has been prepared to accord vanquished people, they traditionally have been denied those attributes which if developed would have qualified them for full-fledged membership in "White" society.

The low status accorded Iberians and Indians nonetheless compares favorably with that assigned the offspring of their biological "commingling." Finding support, at first, in prevailing pseudoscientific theories that held that the children of "mixed" unions inherit the worst traits of the parents and bury their virtues or, later, simply from prejudice, dominant elements in the United States have refused to grant equality to those they have classified as belonging to mixed races. Peoples led by such individuals could be acepted, if at all, for their backwardness, not for any prospects they might have for adjusting to the industrial age.

Although the United States as a whole has found the peoples and institutions of Latin America generally wanting, it has shared with the republics the phenomenon of male dominance. Having, on the one hand, recognized and accepted male "superiority" as a social reality in the republics and realizing, on the other hand, that they have been controlled by individuals of European and European-Indian origins, it is understandable that non-Black males often have been tagged as responsible for those hemispheric developments disapproved by the United States.

The non-Black male adult is the central focus of this chapter. No attempt is made to distinguish between European or "mixed" types. Racial distinctions are essentially meaningless within the Latin American cultural context since in the republics social roles are determined far more by environmental than by biological factors. Most important, cartoonists' intents often are unclear, particularly when they are dealing negatively with Latin America. This is because artists in caricaturing Caucasian and Mestizo peoples ordinarily have disregarded anthropometric and other anthropological criteria in favor of those pictorial symbols that repeated exposure has accustomed the reading public to translate quickly into terms meaningful to them: for example, diminutive and/or emaciated adults; long, stringy, black hair; unkempt dark facial hair, including mustaches; soiled clothing; bare feet; oversized huaraches; sombreros; swords; ancient rifles; bandoleers; and long cigars. On those occasions when the United States has actively sought friends in this hemisphere, for example, in times of war, cartoonists generally have cooperated by transforming the traditionally unattractive Latin American symbolic male figures into standard "Western types," but to date the transformations have not outlived the immediate concern that produced them.

A. K. Cutting, a United States citizen and editor of a newspaper in Paso del Norte, state of Chihuahua, Mexico, was arrested in Mexico in 1886 and charged with libeling a Mexican citizen. Cutting retracted the libelous statement and was released from jail. He thereupon crossed the border, reiterated the charge in print, returned to Mexico, distributed the libelous statement, and was re-arrested. The United States government, acting on incomplete reports, at first demanded Cutting's release on the grounds that he was being held in Mexico for an act committed in the United States, which in the view of the State Department amounted to a claim of extraterritorial power on the part of Mexico. The state of Texas added to the heat of the controversy when its governor declared that his forces would move if Washington failed to insist on satisfaction. United States demands were softened when the State Department accepted Mexico's position, that it was acting on the basis of the original libel committed in Mexico and Cutting's failure to carry out the "reconciliation." This "international incident" finally was settled amicably.

The cartoon perhaps is more noteworthy than the affair itself, since the artist, the incomparable Thomas Nast, as early as 1886 was making use of the numerous artistic devices widely employed over the next half century and still occasionally exploited to fashion unfavorable images of Mexico and Mexicans: superfluity of weapons, menacing attitudes, small stature, dark skin, bristly black facial hair, sombrero, and bell towers dominating the landscape.

**85. It's "Cutting"**

UNCLE SAM: "I must demand his release as an American citizen. I would much rather you would keep him, but law is law."

Thomas Nast, *Harper's Weekly*, August 14, 1886.

Brazilian Emperor Pedro II was forced into exile in 1889, bringing to an end his half century of benign if unprogressive rule; a republic was established under the nation's military leaders. During Dom Pedro's tenure the country experienced an unusual degree of political stability and public order, but the emperor and the statesmen around him failed to grasp the growing importance of civilian elements tied to Brazil's rapidly expanding coffee culture and in turn to the North Atlantic trading community. The military men who succeeded Pedro were as little attuned as the emperor had been to what was transpiring economically. Consequently, quick and widespread discontent followed his departure. By 1893 that discontent was translated into open rebellion when army units revolted in the south and were joined by naval units stationed in Rio de Janeiro. There followed some eight months of civil war before the government could restore order. During the height of the strife the United States, France, Italy, Great Britain, and Portugal kept warships in Brazilian waters and Admiral Andrew E. K. Benham, commander of the United States fleet there, gave protection to the United States merchantmen discharging their cargoes in Rio de Janeiro. Thus, although the only reference to civil disorder, other than this art and poetry to appear in the December 20 number of *Puck*, was a brief comment on British editorializing on bombings by anarchists in France, it is fair to assume that, given the United States government's direct involvement in the Brazilian conflict, the United States informed public had some notion of what was occurring in Brazil.

The cartoon and verse provide interesting evidence in support of the thesis of this work. First, although one must accept that the verse refers to Brazil, since Rio de Janeiro is the only place name mentioned, the tasseled sombrero, sash, and machete make the cartoon figure far less Brazilian than stereotypically Spanish American. Second, the cartoon figure, taken in conjunction with others published in journals directed to the reading public before and after it appeared, leaves no doubt that an abundance of black hair, mustaches, sashes, sombreros, and machetes had become standard devices for signalling attention to political disorder in Latin America generally.

# SUPPRESSED.

E WAS a sturdy patriot,
　And he wore a big sombrero;
And he carried a wicked knife, and lived
　In Rio de Janeiro.

　　He did n't neglect his regular work —
　　　You could n't say that about him;
　　But no revolution could be said
　　　To be complete without him.

　　Whenever his daily toil was o'er
　　　He 'd be plunged in deep dejection,
　　Unless he happened to have a date
　　　To attend an insurrection.

　　But he married a beautiful dark-eyed girl,
　　　A flower of the Equator,
　　And she kicked whenever he did n't get home
　　　Until half-past two, or later.

　Now, when the "*vivas*" rend the skies
　　At midnight, he 's grim and surly,
　For he can't take in any *coup d'état*
　　Unless it finishes early.

So he 's retired from public life,
　And he grieves that his country may be
Lost for the want of his trusty sword
　While he walks the floor with the baby.

　　　　　　　　　　　*W. M.*

**86. Suppressed**
　*Puck*, December 20, 1893.

General Máximo Gómez y Báez was a hero of the Cuban uprising of the 1870s and a leading chieftain of the anti-Spanish forces of the 1890s. A favorite of United States representatives in Cuba before and after the Spanish-American War, General Gómez refused the honor of being the new nation's first president with the words, "Men of war, for war . . . and those of peace, for peace."

The cartoon employs several techniques commonly used by political cartoonists to indicate approbation and disapprobation. The sedate, studious, proper young ladies symbolizing Hawaii and Puerto Rico as diligent students in the art of self-government being taught by Uncle Sam are neatly groomed. General Gómez, also a dedicated learner, is light skinned, his hair trimmed and neatly combed, his clothes clean, his boots polished, and his posture correct—badges of approval. By contrast, the dunce, Emilio Aguinaldo, guerrilla leader who fought first against Spain and later (1898–1901) against the United States for the independence of the Philippines, and the squabbling, perverse Cuban ex-patriot and guerrilla have swarthy skins; stringy, black messy hair; and bare feet—all marks of disparagement.

**87.  Uncle Sam's New Class in the Art of Self-Government**
William Allan Rogers, *Harper's Weekly*, August 27, 1898.

Shortly after his inauguration for a second term, President McKinley made a major tour of the United States. One of his stops was at El Paso, Texas, where it was expected that he and President Porfirio Díaz of Mexico would meet on the international bridge connecting the two countries. The caption of the cartoon, "A Great Day for Old Mexico," referred to the anticipated meeting and what it would mean for Mexico. At the last moment Díaz failed to appear, on the grounds that the Mexican congress was in session and his presence in the capital was required. Díaz' personal envoy, General Juan Hernández, and McKinley exchanged greetings and promises of future cordial relations. The distinguished, manly, almost Anglo-Saxon appearing figure representing Díaz, who, as noted above, was widely admired in the United States, is in sharp contrast to his dwarflike, clownish countrymen, who more nearly fitted the prevailing image of Latin Americans.

**88. A Great Day for Old Mexico**
William Allan Rogers, *Harper's Weekly*, May 11, 1901.

Washington's negotiations first with Colombia and later with Panama for the isthmian canal route, administration of the completed waterway, and auxiliary operations produced one of the most infamous sequences of events in the history of United States–Latin American relations. Theodore Roosevelt was the central figure in the negotiations after May 1902, when the United States decided in favor of Panama over Nicaragua for the proposed route of the canal. Roosevelt's secretary of state, Hay, extracted a treaty (signed January 22, 1903) from Colombia's chargé in Washington, Tomás Herrán. Three days later Herrán received instructions from Bogotá not to sign, but the die had been cast. The United States Senate approved the treaty on March 17. The Colombian senate, objecting to the treaty on the grounds that certain provisions impinged upon the nation's sovereignty and that the financial terms were unsatisfactory, voted unanimously against ratification on August 12, 1903. There were, however, rumors suggesting that, if the United States' initial offer of $10 million was increased to $25 million, ratification would be forthcoming. At that point, if not before, Roosevelt took charge personally, and thereafter the issue moved swiftly to a "solution." On November 3, the US *Nashville* arrived off Colón, and Panamanian insurgents reasoned correctly that it was there to forestall the landing of marine reinforcements from Colombia. On November 4, Panama declared its independence. Two days later the United States granted it de facto recognition. On February 23, 1904, a treaty more favorable to the United States than the one with Colombia was ratified.

During the months of intense bargaining with Colombia, Roosevelt convinced himself that official cupidity was at the bottom of what he considered Bogotá's dalliance. On one occasion he compared Colombian behavior to that of a road agent trying to hold up a man, and this presumably explained the caption of the cartoon which appeared soon after Washington guaranteed Panama's independence. The figure representing Colombia capsulized a long-held view of Latin American politicians generally and provided a commentary on Colombian officials that was readily acceptable to the United States public.

**89. Held Up the Wrong Man**
William Allan Rogers, *Harper's Weekly*, November 21, 1903.

Cipriano Castro, as noted in chapter 5, seized control of war-torn Venezuela in 1899. For nine years he held the nation in the grip of a regime which featured continuous plundering of the treasury and gross internal mismanagement. In foreign affairs he courted disapprobation and earned a well-deserved reputation as an incorrigible international troublemaker.

The United States became actively involved in Venezuela's controversies with its creditors—notably Germany, Great Britain, and Italy—through President Roosevelt's efforts to arbitrate their disputes. Roosevelt held, first, that foreign powers possessed the right to intervene forcibly to collect legitimate debts and, second, that to avoid such possible courses of action in the Caribbean the United States must guarantee the fiscal responsibility of the republics in that area (the Roosevelt Corollary to the Monroe Doctrine).

There is no rational defense of Castro's self-serving behavior, but neither can one find in international law a reasonable justification for the United States' claiming the unilateral right to determine the norms of international conduct in this hemisphere.

The cartoon is of interest because it calls attention to one of the many roles cartoonists assigned Uncle Sam in the Caribbean and also because the artist made such excellent use of further symbols associated with presumed political irresponsibility, notably small stature, evident mental confusion, and witlessness.

**90. Uncle Sam as an Optician**
"Can you read the small print, Mr. Castro?"
Satterfield, *Cleveland Press*, 1905.

224

*The Latin American
Nations as Non-Black
Males*

The power structure upon which the long-lived Porfirio Díaz regime rested was an empty shell by 1910. It cracked under the first attacks of revolutionary groups opposed to the dictator and before those groups were compelled to agree upon a unified set of objectives as a precondition of victory. As a consequence, the moderate Francisco Madero assumed control over a badly divided nation. Elements within the national army, which were permitted to remain intact after Díaz sailed for Europe, took advantage of the discord and of Madero's limited political capabilities and seized the government in February 1913; General Victoriano Huerta assumed the presidency. His usurpation set in motion a power struggle that plunged the nation into a succession of crises over the next several years. In his portrayals of Madero, the army, and the unidentified emerging presidential figure, the artist incorporated techniques that had become accepted through repetition by the profession for caricaturing Latin American adult "White" males. Cartoonists, however, very rarely gave identifiable figures nonhuman features of the kind that this artist used in his depiction of Huerta.

**91.   The Wheel of Fortune**
James Donahey, *Cleveland Plain Dealer*, 1913. Reprinted by permission of *The Plain Dealer*, Cleveland.

As battles raged in northern Mexico between the forces of the debauched dictator Huerta and the capricious *caudillo* Pancho Villa, there was an exodus of women, children, soldiers, and civilians across the Rio Grande into Texas. Total figures for the number that fled north are unknown, but the press reported four thousand refugees in El Paso being cared for by the War Department at government expense. The artist of this cartoon predicted that when United States generosity became known in the south there would be mass desertions, making pointless the continued military struggle for control of the nation. His refugees fit the "Latin type" too neatly not to have raised questions in the minds of some about the merits of the United States government hosting a flood of refugees as opposed to sending forces into Mexico to protect United States lives and property. When the United States army under John J. Pershing crossed the border in early 1916 in pursuit of Pancho Villa, the concept of force triumphed over that of the dole.

**92. Conquering Mexico**

William "Billy" Ireland, *Columbus* (Ohio) *Dispatch*, 1914. Reprinted by permission of the *Columbus Dispatch*.

As viewed from Washington, the United States experienced little but frustration in matters relating to Latin America during 1915. Cuba, where the United States was striving to guarantee a degree of political stability, was once again on the verge of a revolt against an incumbent regime. The Haitian government was in a state of collapse despite Washington's efforts to bring some order into the political arena. Continuing unrest in the Dominican Republic was about to lead to United States occupation of that island republic. Venezuelan dictator Juan Vicente Gómez was finding Germany's predominant political and military philosophies more congenial than those of the United States. Rooseveltian Republicans were resentful that Wilsonian Democrats were prepared to grant major concessions to Colombia in an effort to make amends for the United States role in the Panamanian revolution of 1903. And the opening of the Panama Canal had not brought with it the era of good feeling and trust that Washington had anticipated.

Relations with Mexico proved the most exasperating of all. War had narrowly been averted after the Tampico incident and the subsequent occupation of Veracruz by the offer of mediation from Argentina, Brazil, and Chile. But while diplomats talked, nationalism crested in Mexico and no leader could survive a public acceptance of the terms laid down by the mediators.

This cartoon spoke to the general state of affairs rather than to any specific country or event. The role of "policeman of the Caribbean" was proving to have annoying aspects. The absolute contrasts in size and power of the principals left little doubt of how the artist and, presumably, the public viewed the area's conduct and its place in the total context of the national interest of a United States seriously threatened by a war in Europe.

**93.** Walter Enright, *Harper's Weekly*, October 2, 1915.

Nicaragua was a major trouble spot for the United States throughout the two decades after 1912. Marines were stationed in the capital city, Managua, from that date until August 3, 1925, when they were withdrawn following the election of 1924 and the installation of a United States-approved regime. At the time this country believed that political stability had become reasonably well assured. Nonetheless, even after the withdrawal of troops, Washington kept some citizens in important positions in the Nicaraguan government, as, for example, in the overseeing of expenditures and customs receipts.

Conservative General Emiliano Chamorro seized power three months after the marines departed, but Washington refused recognition, the major factor in his early resignation. The Nicaraguan congress then elected Adolfo Díaz, who was recognized by the State Department despite opposition in the Senate led by William Borah, chairman of the Foreign Relations Committee. At the personal request of Díaz, President Calvin Coolidge landed several thousand marines. The United States forces supervised an election in 1927 and again in 1932 and the last contingents, their safety constantly threatened by the guerrilla leader General César Augusto Sandino, withdrew in 1933.

At the height of Nicaragua's political instability in the mid-1920s, Mexico threw its support to anti–United States elements. Mexico's involvement in Nicaragua came at a time when President Plutarco Elías Calles' policies over land, petroleum, and the Catholic church were contributing to a conspicuous deterioration in United States–Mexican relations. Thus, few were surprised when Secretary of State Frank B. Kellogg insisted that Calles' "socialist" administration had intervened in Nicaragua at the instigation of Moscow. Jingoists in the United States talked of war with Mexico, and President Calles heatedly denied that Moscow was behind Mexico's support of anti–United States groups in Nicaragua; when calmer minds began to prevail in Washington, concern over possible communist "mischief making" quickly subsided.

This cartoon, one of ten dealing with the Nicaraguan question in the February 1927 issue of *Review of Reviews*, is less notable for its casting of Mexicans and Nica-

**94.  The Trouble Is as Close to Him as His Own Coat-tails**
William "Billy" Ireland, *Columbus* (Ohio) *Dispatch*, 1927. Reprinted by permission of the *Columbus Dispatch*.

raguans as well as communist types as undesirable troublemakers—for that was a generally accepted view in the late 1920s—than for its calling attention to an early, if mild, case of hysteria with the realization that the new communist regime in Moscow might possess the capability of agitating against the United States in its presumed sphere of influence.

The issue of *Review of Reviews* in which this cartoon
appeared reported that Chicago had had more bad pub-
licity than any other community in the world. And with
some reason! It was there during the 1920s that professional gangsters and corrupt politicians cooperated to
terrorize the populace while blackmailing the public and
raiding municipal and county treasuries. The lives and
property of those who spoke out against the insiders
were publicly threatened. In the weeks before the April
10, 1928, primary election—to which the cartoon alludes—acts of intimidation ranged from assassinations,
kidnappings, bombings, and machine gunnings to hundreds of small-arms attacks. It was assumed that scores
of fraudulent ballots would return incumbents to office.
As it turned out, when the votes finally were counted,
reformist candidates made important gains, but there
was in no sense a thorough political cleansing.

César Augusto Sandino was a Nicaraguan guerrilla
leader who, depending on one's point of view, had gained
admiration or opprobrium during the several years that
he eluded captivity while harassing and embarrassing
United States marines stationed in his homeland. It was
a striking commentary on conditions in Chicago and
Nicaragua that the artist would imply even in good humor that Sandino and his followers might add a note of
respectability to a Chicago election.

**95. Sandino Comes to Chicago**

Gale, *Los Angeles Times*, 1928. Copyright, *Los Angeles Times*. Reprinted by permission.

The essence of the Good Neighbor Policy was that the United States would abandon intervention in Latin America and make economic concessions to the nations of the area in return for their confidence and good will. It can be argued whether the policy began under Presidents Calvin Coolidge, Herbert Hoover, or Franklin D. Roosevelt. That Roosevelt popularized the concept and that the United States benefited most from it during the Rooseveltian years is certain. There were meaningful economic and political reversals during the Good Neighbor era, but there were only token changes in the vast area of human relationships. United States citizens continued to consider their culture superior and themselves capable of a great beneficence. Latin Americans continued to be viewed as incompetent, troublesome, dependent poor relations or simply as clients. The accompanying cartoon reflects a popular view of Latin America held in the United States. It ignores the declarations of equality made during the early stages of the Good Neighbor Policy. Latin America is stereotypically portrayed as a recipient of United States largesse and seemingly incapable of offering anything in return. There is in fact no more suggestion of equality or of movement in that direction than had appeared in an overwhelming majority of cartoons dating from the late nineteenth century.

**96. Neighborly Call**
Pease; *Newark Evening News*, 1934. Reprinted by permission of the *Newark Evening News*.

Fidel Castro's victory over Fulgencio Batista and his alliance with the USSR brought anticommunism to a fever pitch in the United States. Communists were charged with creating trouble throughout the hemisphere and of promoting antipathy toward the United States. The stepped-up attack on the international communist apparatus served to conceal the reality that anti–United States feeling in Latin America derived largely from Washington's failure since World War II to offer Latin Americans anything more innovative than austerity as a way out of their social and economic dilemmas. This artist seemingly accepted the official Washington view that communism rather than inadequate national development was at the root of the area's unrest and of worsening hemispheric relations. In making a stereotypical Latin American farm laborer—obviously ill equipped intellectually and economically to cope with ideological propaganda—the target of communist influence, the cartoon exploited the United States image of Latin Americans as unlikely to recognize what was good for themselves in any ideological showdown.

**97. Raising Cane?**

Franklin Morse, *Los Angeles Mirror-News*, 1959. Copyright, 1959, Times Mirror Company. Reprinted by permission.

President Eisenhower made a hurried trip to Latin America in early 1960 as a move to counter the possible political consequences of the growing respect in the area for the technological and economic capabilities of the USSR and, especially, its new diplomatic base on the shores of Latin America. The president's repeated emphasis on United States willingness to assist the republics' development and his promise of nonintervention appeared to produce an atmosphere conducive to mutually profitable inter-American cooperation. This cartoon, in one sense, captures the spirit of the time but, in another sense, the sombreroed, seraped, torpid "Latin" figure too closely resembles the stereotypical image of Latin America to give the perceptive viewer much hope that "Brotherhood Week" would last.

**98. Brotherhood Week!**
Jim Dobbins, *Boston Herald American*, 1960. Reprinted with the permission of
*The Boston Herald American*.

This 1962 cartoon hit hard and brilliantly at the phenomenon of Castro's dependence upon the USSR and his administration's difficulties in providing for Cuba's population. But to make his points, the artist relied upon those devices that have served to perpetuate the traditional disparaging image of Latin Americans as ragtag, unaspiring "have nots."

**99. Technically Speaking—We Never Had It So Good**
Ed Valtman, *Hartford Times*, 1962. Reprinted by permission of Ed Valtman.

A central theme of political cartoonists dealing with Latin America has been that the people of the area do not readily grasp the more profound significance of their actions or reactions. Thus, before World War I, President Roosevelt instituted his Big Stick policy because it was held that the fiscal irresponsibility of the Caribbean republics invited intervention by European powers which might remain entrenched after their immediate objectives were satisfied. During World War I, it was believed that President Venustiano Carranza of Mexico flirted with Germany without appreciating the full consequences of his actions. During World War II, Argentina's tolerance of Axis activities within its borders was considered to pose a dire threat to Argentina's sovereignty and to the hemisphere's security. When the Organization of American States was not moved to act against Castro's Cuba as readily as Washington wished, Latin American dilatoriness was seen as endangering the hemisphere, the point of this cartoon. What does not come through in this and other negative cartoons of the Alliance for Progress era is what was expected to be gained by portraying supposedly friendly nations as such sorry characters that they would be incapable of sustained action on their own behalf were they for some reason to make the initial effort.

**100. Why Theese Excitement? Eet's Just a Wooden Horse!**
William Sanders, *Greensboro Daily News*, 1962. Reprinted by permission of *The News*.

The Alliance for Progress was initiated at a time when Congress was closely scrutinizing "foreign aid" budgets. In view of the Congress' attitude toward the public financing of overseas projects, its early appropriations for the Alliance were considered impressive. Still they were not so generous as had been anticipated by firm advocates of the project, and by the third year there was a sharp decline in available public funds. This cartoon calls attention to the drying-up process and also avoids the stereotyping of the recipients of aid. But, intentionally or otherwise, it also gives the erroneous but popular impression that recipients were living off handouts from the United States government, when in fact it was understood from the first that United States contributions to Latin American developmental projects under the Alliance for Progress would be supplemental, constituting a small percentage of the total costs.

**101. From Now On It'll Be Skimmed**
Bill Mauldin. © 1963. Reprinted by permission of Bill Mauldin.

No serious follower of hemispheric affairs doubted that when Lyndon B. Johnson took over from the assassinated President Kennedy the character of the Alliance for Progress and relations with Latin America generally would be modified, as in fact they were. The limited coherence that the Alliance for Progress had given United States Latin American policy was lost as the new president relaxed pressures on diverse interest groups with selfish pressures in Latin America. The Johnson stance could be explained partially in terms of the Vietnam conflict, but there is also a body of evidence which suggests that Johnson held the United States' neighbors to the south in even lower regard than did the United States public generally. The image of Latin America that the public was receiving from the press is well capsulized in this cartoon figure with his outsized sombrero, long black hair, droopy mustache, elbows on the bar, and longing look of anticipation.

**102. New Barman**

Peb, *Philadelphia Inquirer*, 1963. Reprinted by permission of *The Philadelphia Inquirer*, 1963.

The economic situation in Latin America was indeed precarious in 1964, when this cartoon appeared. The republics, already uncertain about Castro's intentions and capabilities, were struggling unsuccessfully to avoid another cycle of military dictatorships. Terms of trade in international markets were running strongly against them. Privileged elements, with their feet firmly implanted in the past, were resisting social change with all the resources at their command. Latin America was low on the Johnson administration's list of priorities, and, as the cartoon correctly suggests, conditions in the republics, figuratively speaking, were being viewed from afar by decision makers in Washington. If one were convinced that it was to the advantage of the peoples of Latin America for the United States to have a deep and abiding concern for their welfare—a conviction not universally shared—there were plenty of reasons for seeing conditions as near catastrophic: inefficient agriculture, large military budgets, poorly qualified civilian bureaucrats, and rapidly expanding populations requiring huge outlays for education and public welfare. This artist directed attention away from his stereotypical representation of Latin America but nonetheless left the impression that, if the Latin Americans were to be saved, the saving would not be by themselves but by Washington.

**103.  We're Taking a New Look at It**
    Herblock, *Washington Post*, 1964. Copyright 1964 by Herblock in the *Washington Post*. Reprinted by permission of Herblock Cartoons.

By the fifth year of the Alliance for Progress there were
good reasons to question where the project had been and
where it was going. President Kennedy had warned
against expecting miracles, and there had been none.
Determination and hope that had initially been shared by
much of the hemisphere had given way to disinterest in
the United States and despair in Latin America. Responsible figures in Washington could no more identify with
any certainty where there had been lasting achievements
or where failures had been repeated than could the non-
contributing sombreroed, mustachioed "Latin type" in
this cartoon.

**104. Where Are We?**
Ed Valtman, *Hartford Times*, 1968. Reprinted by permission of Ed Valtman.

President Richard M. Nixon gave hemisphere problems
scant attention, partly reflecting his personal bias toward
the area and its people but primarily because he believed
that the future welfare of the United States would be determined ultimately by extrahemisphere developments.
Benign neglect caused numerous Latin American officials,
conditioned to periodic injections of United States capital, to suffer withdrawal pains. It can be argued whether
or not it is any longer to Latin America's advantage to
continue to accept at the asking price the kinds of assistance the United States is prepared to offer. But it cannot
be argued that there is in this day and age anything for
the United States public to gain in continuing to deny
Latin Americans—as is done in this cartoon—the physical and mental equipment they will need if they are to
make it on their own.

**105. Mao's Chop Suey**

Jim Yep, *Chicago Daily News*, February 24, 1972. Reprinted by permission of the
*Chicago Daily News*.

In terms of impact upon the quality of national life, Mexico is today for the United States the most important country in the world. It is no less true that no country in the world is more important to Mexico than is the United States, and it is unlikely that the importance of one to the other will change significantly in the foreseeable future.

Within months after President Jimmy Carter and President José López Portillo took office in January 1977 and December 1976, respectively, two long-range issues raised relations between Mexico and the United States to a much higher level. The first was a growing awareness in the United States that annually, for well over a decade, from one to two million Mexican laborers had been illegally crossing the border. The second was the realization that a sizeable part of Mexico is floating on a sea of recently discovered gas and petroleum even as the United States searched frantically for new and reliable energy sources.

Although there were other issues, it was in the context of emigration and oil that the two presidents met in mid-February 1979. The time had come for the two nations to begin to confront those issues. Mexico could no longer expect the United States to absorb its export of labor without limit. The United States could not expect to cut the flow of illegal entries or promote the flow of petroleum and gas from Mexico without a willingness to meet its economically and politically shaky neighbor on equal terms.

President Carter flew to Mexico City prepared to deal with his Mexican counterpart as an equal—the first United States–Mexican meeting of any kind that could be said to have taken place in such an atmosphere. Although there is some evidence to the contrary, it is probable that the meeting of the presidents helped to clear the diplomatic air somewhat. Still the sessions made abundantly evident that the two countries face serious challenges in their future relations. The United States has much to learn before it consistently responds with maturity to changes taking place in Mexico. For its part, Mexico must more fully appreciate that its petroleum reserves at best give it only short-range domestic and international maneuverability. When its oil and gas are depleted, the United States presumably will remain.

This cartoon, supposedly depicting the welcoming

**106.** Ed Valtman, *Hartford Times*, 1979. Reprinted by permission of Ed Valtman.

ceremonies, is remarkable for several reasons. There are no sombreros, serapes, cacti, or unkempt drooping mustaches; the two presidents' left hands suggest the underlying urgencies—assistance and oil—of the meeting. The artist does not have the presidents' eyes meet, as if anticipating that they would talk past one another in forthcoming sessions, as they did a good deal of the time. The presidents' stature and apparel suggest equal status that in fact characterized the meetings and should prevail in the future. Mexico is not a "pipsqueak country" as syndicated columnist Andrew Tully gratuitously labeled it in a March 1979 release.[1] To so portray it is tantamount to performing a disservice to both Mexico and the United States.

# 7. SOCIAL REFORM AND MILITARISM

Of the many hundreds of cartoons on hemispheric topics that appeared in United States newspapers and periodicals during the century ending in 1960 and subscribed to by the "informed public," only a scattering attempted to place on the record the social and military-political environments that were so profoundly influencing the domestic affairs and international conduct of the Latin American republics. Readers, as a consequence, learned of developments characteristically associated with political and economic instability; they were not informed of the cultural, social, and economic chasms that separated the privileged few from the submerged many and thus of the dissidence that echoed throughout the hemisphere. Seldom indeed were readers informed by the artists that the seeming political capriciousness actually reflected the very basic fact that little land was owned by the mass of peasants who constituted the economic backbone of several of the nations or of the burdens of inequitable distribution of income largely carried by urban laborers. Nor did the cartoonists associate social alienation with the quite limited opportunities for education and the scant public funds allocated to social welfare. Armed violence was pictorialized repeatedly but, with remarkably few exceptions, the perpetrators were *bandidos* or *guerrilleros* rather than the national military establishments. The apparent sanctity of the military may be assumed to have resulted at times from a dearth of objective information or interest, but at least it seems equally apparent that the armed forces often escaped the cartoonist's brush because they had associated themselves with either the elite civilian or the personalist regimes approved by Washington.

But if cartoonists for a century largely ignored social issues and the national military establishments, that circumstance changed with the launching of the Alliance for Progress in the early 1960s. Certain cartoonists caught the new spirit and capsulated for their followers the flood of propaganda pouring out of Washington on the political, economic, and social conditions in Latin America considered to be in urgent need of modification. Although they customarily continued to treat Latin America as a monolith rather than a community of individual and unique nations, by alerting the public to the fact that our neighbors to the South suffer chronic institutional illnesses, they undoubtedly made a contribution to inter-American understanding. Their contribution would have been even greater had the artists been less inclined to follow the lead of the instant experts on Alliance for Progress payrolls who cast the republics' social problems in dichotomous rich-or-poor, order-or-chaos, reform-or-revolution terms and had their art focused more on the issues of political economy and less on political leadership per se in Latin America. If the history of Latin America teaches anything, it is that throughout the area the institutional changes take place slowly and grudgingly when at all, the Cuban experience notwithstanding.

As the cartoons in this chapter make clear, since the early 1960s artists have taken a strong stand against the institutionalized armed forces. I hope that the legends accompanying the cartoons make equally clear that, while the artists have helped to keep before the public a disturbing political phenomenon in Latin America, they have left as much unsaid about the armed forces as they have said. The artists are to be faulted in two areas in particular. First, they have failed to note that most Latin American governments are fused coalitions, and, as a consequence, it is unrealistic to make rigid distinctions between the military and civilian spheres. Second, in so forcefully associating the armed forces with the republics' social-economic backwardness, the cartoonists have tended to absolve civilian politicians of their very large share of responsibility for the unsatisfactory social-economic conditions of the popular elements they have so thoroughly dominated.

At least two major conclusions may be drawn from cartoons 107–119. First, contemporary cartoonists are paying closer attention to internal conditions in Latin America than did their predecessors. Second, they still too often resort to the century-long tradition of portraying Latin America at its worst, presumably to satisfy the images and needs of their particular following.

Two considerations recommended that social issues and the centralized armed forces be treated in a single chapter. The first is that in terms of numbers they represent a quite small percentage of the total output of cartoons dealing with Latin America. To have allotted each topic a chapter would have tended to distort their relative importance, given the historical context of the volume. The second consideration is that political problems born of unsatisfactory social environments have been used repeatedly by the armed forces to justify intervention in the civilian area, either on their own account or as spokesmen for the classic corporate structure.

As Figures 120 through 131 suggest, artists have treated the Latin American armed forces on basically three levels. Initially, they were nearly always portrayed as buffoons, although not unusually greedy and irresponsible buffoons, of the variety that "one might expect in banana republics." By the 1940s, the military was more often cast as posing a threat to civilian democratic rule, as was appropriate for an "informed public" which continued to believe that a United States–fashioned democracy offered the surest route to resolving the world's problems. Beginning in the 1960s, the political artists in general shifted their emphasis in order to bring their views more into line with the goals of the Alliance for Progress, and the institutionalized armed forces became *the* institution blocking the way to the reforms that Washington contended would finally launch Latin America on the road to modernity.

The decade after 1900 was a tumultuous one for Mexico. Strikes (and their ferocious suppression), rural disorders, food shortages, the disaffection of leading intellectuals, and the frustrations of Mexican businessmen in the commercial and industrial sectors where foreigners and foreign products were favored by the government were some of the early symptoms of the illness that finally seized the nation during the election of 1910. The aging Porfirio Díaz was the immediate source of the republic's torment. Not only had he again offered himself as the official presidential candidate (which was tantamount to election) but he had also insisted on naming his running mate, thereby precluding for the foreseeable future any reasonable expectation of escape from a political system that had kept the social and economic order suspended in time. Predictably, Díaz and his vice-presidential choice won office, but this time the disparate opposition groups refused to be still. Under mounting pressure from makeshift armies, the regime toppled and the dictator went into exile in May 1911. His departure set in motion the second phase of the civil war, one that would rend the republic for the next half decade.

Contemporary observers in the United States generally viewed the conflict as another in the long series of power struggles in Latin America, meaningful only to the degree that it might affect United States interests in the region. But the conflict outstripped this presumption primarily because industrial workers and agrarian elements, the historical victims of a vicious landholding system and its corollary, peonage, kept the contest alive until it was given a social content to be officially acknowledged in the Constitution of 1917.

But while other cartoonists stuck to traditional themes, centering their attention on the political and international matters created by the revolutionary armies fighting variously under the banners of Venustiano Carranza, Pancho Villa, Emiliano Zapata, and a host of lesser figures, the artist of this cartoon identified the very basic cause of the torment for which tens of thousands were laying down their lives. What inspired him but escaped the others is unknown. It could have been John Kenneth Turner's *Barbarous Mexico* (1911), which exposed in graphic and colorful terms the human misery, avarice,

**107. What Is the Matter with Mexico?**
Barnett, *Los Angeles Tribune*, 1913.

and brutality suffered by the masses, especially the Yaquí and Maya Indians of
Sonora and Yucatán, respectively. Or he may have had access to some of the
thousands who fled to the United States and who knew better than any United
States journalist what conditions were like in Mexico. Whatever the source or
sources of his concern, his sensitivity and perceptiveness in capturing the essence of the struggle that engulfed Mexico make the cartoon perhaps the most
unusual and noteworthy ever to appear on hemispheric matters.

It could be said that in this century the history of Mexico has been largely the history of land and those who possessed it. The ownership of land, whether by the Catholic church, the *hacendado*, the foreigner, the peasant village, the Mexican nation, or the *ejidatario* (a small holder allotted land to which the government retains title), has been an overriding issue. It was a major question of the Revolution of 1910. Land redistribution has been a stated major objective of the monolithic Institutional Revolutionary Party (PRI) since its founding in 1929. Yet today, matters relating to the land repeatedly capture the headlines.

This cartoon, both less artistic and more encompassing, ran a year after the preceding one. The artist employed the same basic concept as did his colleague but moved a step beyond him explicitly to relate social injustice to political irresponsibility, represented here by President-dictator Victoriano Huerta. It is worth recalling that more than half a century later landownership remains at or very near the heart of social unrest in all of rural Latin America, except possibly in Cuba and Panama.

**108. The Real Mexican Government and the Cause of All Revolution**
Kemble, *Leslie's Illustrated Weekly*, 1914.

The Alliance for Progress, the Kennedy administration's response to the rise of Fidel Castro, traveled a near impossible obstacle course before it ground to a halt during the Johnson administration. This artist chose to label the obstacles "feudalism." His choice of a term could be challenged on a number of grounds, but suffice it to say that to apply a term rightly identified with a medieval institution to a modern state is inherently dangerous. But what is considerably more important are the questionable inferences that almost of necessity must be drawn from the cartoon. The first inference is that Latin America was still living in the middle ages, which simply was not true. Since feudalism was, first of all, a rural social-economic institution, albeit with political and juridic overtones, the second inference is that the barriers to progress, as progress was conceived of by the sponsors of the Alliance, were rural in origin. To be sure, some rural institutions were notoriously retrograde, for example the huge, inefficient, largely self-contained haciendas on which archaic agricultural methods and master-servant relationships still prevailed. By the 1960s, however, most of Latin America was urban, not rural. For example, by then over 50 percent of the population of Argentina, Chile, Colombia, Mexico, Uruguay, and Venezuela resided in urban centers. Furthermore, a large part of Latin America, in terms of area and population, was urban dominated. And it was in countries controlled by urban-situated civilians and military politicians—Brazil and Colombia are the best examples—that the Alliance made its strongest bids to prove itself and suffered its most disastrous failures. The third inference is that the obstacles to the success of the Alliance were Latin American in origin. In effect, Washington erected a colossal barrier to success when it demanded that in return for the United States input—estimated at 20 percent of the proposed total expenditure—the Latin American elites discard their traditional, deeply rooted corporatistic tendencies in favor of democratic-liberal capitalism. The leaders of the republics were willing to make that enormous concession only at a much higher price than the United States ever envisaged paying. The fourth inference, and the key one, is that achievement, if there was to be achievement, was

**109. Over the Andes**
   Bill Mauldin, *St. Louis Post-Dispatch*, 1961. © 1961. Reprinted by permission of
   Bill Mauldin.

dependent on the grim determination of the United States. Over time a vast
majority of artists have chosen to relate Latin American inability to achieve at
"acceptable" levels to its racial composition; this one chose institutional grounds
on which to deny the region the chance to elevate itself.

Of the Alliance for Progress cartoons that attempted to identify where responsibility lay in Latin America, this one was remarkably discerning. Jumping Jack Kennedy's finger of guilt is pointed at landowners and industrialists, two of the three principal homegrown culprits, the other being civilian and military bureaucrats. In terms of educating the public, the cartoon is also remarkable in that its "victim" is outfitted in Western-style apparel—usually reserved for statesmen friendly to the United States—rather than the stereotypical sombrero, serape, and buttoned-down pants.

**110. Jumping Jack**
Art Poinier, *Detroit News*, 1961. Reprinted by permission of *The News*.

The Alliance for Progress was justified to the United States taxpayer largely on the grounds that if the Latin American republics did not institute massive social reforms there was no alternative to their experiencing violent revolution which communist agents would exploit. Inherent in that projection was the implication that revolution would see the United States inevitably ending up on the losing side. This cartoon accepts the reform-or-revolution thesis and seemingly gives the advantage to revolution. That position proved wrong, as there were good reasons at the time to believe it would. Aside from the fact that Latin America is far too diverse to be generalized about, there were at least two considerations in favor of a course somewhere between reform and widespread armed rebellion. In the first place, the elites knew better than anyone else the cost to them of losing political control, and throughout the century they had guarded against that possibility by exhibiting just enough flexibility to co-opt emergent urban groups as soon as they entered the political arena. It was reasonable to assume that they would not abandon readily a tactic that had succeeded in every case except Cuba. In the second place, if co-optation somehow failed and it came down to the use of violence, not only did the traditional elites have an overwhelming advantage in weapons and organization, but, furthermore, their military arm, including in many cases the police, alerted by the recent Cuban experience, had begun training in the most up-to-date counterinsurgency strategies to be found anywhere in the Western world. Co-optation and dominance in the exercise of violence may not—should not—be sufficient to keep the privileged groups indefinitely in power, but they have proved remarkably effective to date.

**111. The Race to the Rancho**
Herblock, *Washington Post*, January 7, 1962. Copyright 1962 by Herblock in the
*Washington Post*. Reprinted by permission of Herblock Cartoons.

This is one of the more striking of the cartoons that use the rich-or-poor approach to social dissonance, thereby making revolution strictly a derivative of the economic condition.

Latin America once was polarized into the extremely wealthy and the extremely impoverished, but by 1962 that was no longer so true. The condition persisted in most rural settings, but in the metropolitan centers there were numerous and large intermediate groups whose interests converged at some points and diverged at others, but having in common little to gain from violence. Those intermediate groups were by the early 1960s key factors in the social-political drama. It was in considerable part because large segments of the middle refused to break with the top that those at the bottom were denied through the revolutionary processes, thereby confounding those who predicted that Latin America had no alternative but to accept radical solutions to its social problems.

**112. ─And His Father Lives Up There**
Herblock, *Washington Post*, February 11, 1962. Reprinted from *Straight Herblock* (Simon & Schuster, 1964) by permission of Herblock Cartoons.

This artist seems to have placed responsibility for the success or failure of social-economic programs where it belonged, on the peoples and governments of the republics. The artist thus avoided contributing to the commonly held impression that the United States input under the Alliance for Progress was the critical variable in the process of change. What he did not avoid in making his point was the reform-or-revolution dichotomy and reliance on the sombreroed, dozing figure, one of the more overused stereotypical images of Latin America.

**113. For Some, No Siesta**
Roy B. Justus, *Minneapolis Star*, 1962. Copyright 1962, Minneapolis Star and
Tribune Company. Reprinted by permission.

This cartoon is remarkable for its treatment of the Latin American situation as of 1962. It identified Argentina as the hot spot. There, thirty-five coups against civilian President Arturo Frondizi had just culminated in a successful one engineered by the armed forces. The cartoon holds the elites—rural and urban—collectively responsible for the continuing resistance to reform. It puts the Alliance for Progress in proper perspective. It outfits the central Argentine figure in a stylized, if traditional, costume of his own country. The "hopes for true democracy" were, of course, United States rhetoric.

**114. What Volcanoes? I See No Volcanoes!**
    Richard Q. Yardley, *Baltimore Sun*, 1962. Reprinted by permission of Richard Q.
    Yardley.

Washington was convinced during the early stages of the Alliance for Progress that the containment of Castroism should be the hemisphere's number-one objective. The leadership of the republics in essence argued, for what it was worth in dollars, that the containment of poverty and unrest should receive top attention. The popular elements were not consulted—agreements under the Alliance being between governments—but, had they been, they would have made much the same point that is made in the caption of this cartoon. The cartoon is remarkable for its success in sharply delineating the differences dividing the Alliance's partners. It is also remarkable because the artist thought of having the impoverished speak for themselves and making their representative physically as large as "señor" Uncle Sam. The cartoon is remarkable perhaps most of all because the artist drew Uncle Sam to appear as if he were learning something from a Latin American who knew about the elites from having been stripped of his shoes, socks, shirt, and most of his pants by them.

**115. He's Not the Biggest Threat to This Hemisphere, Señor!**
Richard Q. Yardley, *Baltimore Sun*, 1962. Reprinted by permission of Richard Q. Yardley.

In this cartoon the artist chose a most effective means of transmitting to the public a greatly oversimplified version of the social issue in Latin America. Throughout this century the sombrero has been the one unmistakable, all-purpose cartoonists' symbol for the area. Several considerations contributed to giving the sombrero that status. It has been and remains a readily recognizable item of apparel in Mexico, the area best known to the average United States citizen. As a medium of expression, the sombrero is benign, suggesting neither a determined will nor a military spirit, as did, for example, the German spiked helmet of the World War I era. It thus could be used to capture reader attention while simultaneously assuring that, despite occasional and potentially threatening eruptions in the hemisphere and underlying antipathies on both sides, the United States' security would not be threatened much by aggressive behavior on the part of the southern republics. Also, where official litany held unity and friendship to be the prevailing mood and where unofficially a paternalistic relationship, detested by most informed Latin Americans, was acknowledged to exist, a malleable, fibrous headpiece probably reflected better the United States image of Latin America's role in hemisphere affairs than would any other symbol from the cartoonist's bag.

**116. High Sierra**

Bill Mauldin, *Chicago Sun-Times*, 1963. © 1963. Reprinted by permission of Bill Mauldin.

This cartoon was prompted by the ouster of Brazilian
President João Goulart and the assumption of control by
a military regime which came to power without a social-
economic program and unsure, at least for public purposes, of how long Brazil would "require" military leadership. The cartoon is notable because the artist isolated
several specific burdens of the Brazilian worker and presented them without obvious resort to the stereotypes to
which United States Americans had become accustomed.
Had he added figures portraying privilege, uneven regional development, underemployment, and educational
needs, he would largely have covered the spectrum of
Brazil's social-economic problems.

**117. Presidents Come and Go, but We'll Not Desert You, Señor!**
William Sanders, *Kansas City Star*, 1964. Reprinted by permission of the *Kansas City Star*.

Because wealth and power in Latin America historically have been associated with a triumvirate composed of landholders, the hierarchy of the Catholic church, and the military, it has been assumed that the greatest economic inequalities have occurred in the countryside. That was generally the case throughout the nineteenth century, although in the larger cities the gap separating the very rich from the very poor was already wide and expanding rapidly by 1900. In this century, power in the more developed and populous countries has escaped the landholders and has passed to urban-based bureaucrats and industrialists who at any given time may or may not be aligned with the military. And commerce, industry, and government in the huge and sprawling urban centers have produced greater extremes of wealth and poverty and their attendant consequences than the rural areas ever did. This cartoon with its jumble of worker's shanties vividly records the fact of pervasive urban inequities. "The other . . . summit" referred to in the caption was the meeting of hemisphere chief executives held at Punte del Este, Uruguay, in mid-April 1967, which resulted in the Declaration of the Presidents of America concerning economic issues.

**118.  The Other Latin-American Summit**
Herblock, 1967. Reprinted from *The Herblock Gallery* (Simon & Schuster, 1968) by permission of Herblock Cartoons.

The immediate background for this cartoon can be dated from 1975 when a renewed wave of "land invasions" by peasants put the nation on edge. More immediately, the land problem was given added heat and the peasants increased militancy in August 1976 when President Luis Echeverría declared that he would not leave office without land distribution in the rich west-coast region. As his term drew to a close, he ordered the expropriation of 250,000 acres of prime agricultural land in the Yaquí River valley of the state of Sonora from some 72 wealthy families and its distribution to 10,000 landless peasants. On November 26, thousands of peasants in the state of Sinaloa, south of Sonora and the nation's richest farming region, unwilling to trust the incoming José López Portillo administration, threatened to seize an additional 100,000 acres of private holdings. With the assumption of the presidency by López Portillo on December 1, 1976, his minister of agrarian reform declared that the government would not permit further illegal land invasions. But, in fact, another 107,000 acres were invaded. Negotiations led to compromise that satisfied neither landowners nor peasants. Thus, the artist, as had others before him, called attention to a recurring explosive issue in Mexico and in Latin America generally: namely, the failure to defend the rural masses from exploitation by large landowners, to which group should be added middle men, bankers, and national, state, and local officials.

The aside, "Pancho Villa, where are you?" in the lower left-hand corner, raises a special problem because it is not at all clear what the artist had in mind. Did he conceive of Villa as a reformer, which he was in a thoughtless, erratic way? Did the artist see Villa as a revolutionary, which he was but essentially of the traditional (Latin American) variety? And if the artist viewed Villa as a revolutionary, did he think that Mexico was ripe for a revolution even if led by an unpredictable, military-minded individual such as Villa? Or did the artist resort to Villa as evocative of past struggles or as a symbol that transcends specific historical knowledge yet can be identified by a large, impressionistically informed audience? If the latter were the case, the question posed by the cartoon might be seen as two-edged. First, what basic change, if any, has

**119. Mexican Saddle**
Patrick Oliphant, *Palo Alto Times*, December 23, 1976. © 1976 *Washington Star*.
Reprinted by permission, Los Angeles Times Syndicate.

the Mexican Revolution accomplished? And the answer would be, "a great deal."
Second, does Mexico need, or is the rural situation there dangerously courting,
another social upheaval of the kind that racked Mexico when Pancho Villa, riding
at the head of his makeshift army, was at the peak of his power and influence? And
the answer in both cases is, "no." After fifty years, landownership remains an
issue, but land can no longer pick up the slack or relieve social pressures. Today
the nation's basic problems are water shortages, income distribution, unemploy-
ment, uncontrolled population growth, and urban sprawl.

The twenty republics of Latin America suffered more than one hundred successful revolutions against established national authorities before World War I. The soldier-president was a hallowed tradition by the early twentieth century. The United States public seldom had occasion to take note of the use of force and violence as political instrumentalities by a president in uniform so long as he respected Washington's interest in his region, afforded protection to United States citizens and investments, and conducted his administration in such a way as not to invite intervention by European powers. The United States public was more likely to have called to its attention the posturing and comic-opera blending of military pomp, pageantry, and gaudy uniforms that military presidents used to impress their subjects, as in this instance. F. B. Loomis was assistant secretary of state. He was sent by President Roosevelt to investigate conditions in the Dominican Republic, and in March 1904 he recommended a United States receivership.

**120. Those Little Fellows Want to Look Out When I Toss the Ball**
William Allan Rogers, *New York Herald*, 1903.

Throughout the 1920s, Mexico teetered on the brink of anarchy as the nation struggled to recover from the most devastating civil conflict the hemisphere had ever known. A root cause of its trouble was its armed forces, too often staffed by individuals largely devoid of either military or administrative competence and without concern for their nation or their men. *Current History* of May 1929 claimed that the Mexican army had "more machiavellian morons in high places . . . than any other similar institution in the world." Being awarded a third of the national budget and nearly absolute control over funds budgeted to their divisions was insufficient to satiate their greed for wealth and power. Each presidential election was preceded by a purge, each victory by a military revolt.

The accompanying cartoon called attention to an attempted coup in early March 1929 led by a number of generals in defense of their "prerogatives" and against the recently inaugurated civilian president, Emilio Portes Gil. The coup was suppressed, as had been every other one during the decade, and some of the conspirators faced the firing squad; but the real losers, as the artist makes evident, were the Mexican people. In making his point, the artist employed an unusually wide range of stereotypes associated with Mexico and Mexicans: facial hair, sword, sombrero, serape, cactus, burro, and thatched hut.

**121. Another Popular (?) Uprising in Mexico**
J. N. "Ding" Darling, *Des Moines Register*, 1929. Copyright, 1929, Des Moines
Register and Tribune Company. Reprinted by permission.

On June 4, 1943, the Argentine armed forces overthrew the civilian government and assumed control of the republic. It soon became apparent that decision making within the military regime resided in a highly nationalistic and pro-Axis "colonel's clique" known as the Grupo de Oficiales Unidos (GOU). By mid-1944, Juan Domingo Perón had established himself as undisputed leader of the GOU. When this cartoon appeared, Perón was on the verge of winning a presidential election and beginning what would prove to be a decade-long dictatorship whose chief supporters were the Argentine army, the *descamisados* (shirtless ones), the civilian bureaucracy, and at times the Catholic church.

Being chained to a military dictatorship was no more "The Argentine Way" than it was the way of most of the republics. In fact, over the preceding eighty years, the Argentine record of nonmilitary rule was better than any of the nations except Chile and Brazil and perhaps Uruguay. Furthermore, although in the United States there were sporadic outcries against military dictatorships, neither Washington nor the public had been notably uncomfortable living with a large majority of the presidents-generals. What attracted attention about "The Argentine Way" in 1945 was its fascistic overtones. What is unusual about this wartime cartoon is that it did not specifically associate military dictatorship in Argentina—the traditional variety of which would have been acceptable, as witnessed by the number of Latin American dictators who allied with the United States in the war—with fascism, the "unacceptable" part of such a mix.

**122. The Argentine Way**
    Edmund Duffy, *Baltimore Sun*, 1945. Reprinted by permission of the A. S. Abell
    Company, Publisher.

No single aspect of United States hemispheric policy has generated so much heat and controversy in the United States as the one begun in 1947 (and still in operation on a reduced scale) of making available to the Latin American republics military aid in the form of equipment, maintenance, and technical advice. The policy was an early and direct outgrowth of the Cold War. It was meant to put teeth into the Inter-American Treaty of Reciprocal Assistance (the Rio Treaty) of September 2, 1947, and was approved by the United States Congress in December 1947.

Protagonists of the program justified it on the dual grounds that modernized and standardized weapons and forces throughout the hemisphere were necessary to defend against communism and that, if the United States did not provide military equipment and advice, the republics would obtain them elsewhere. Since the early 1960s, the case for Latin American military establishments as important to the hemisphere defense system has been made secondary to their value as counterinsurgency forces. The most cogent arguments of those who have opposed the military assistance programs have been that they are a form of intervention in the internal affairs of the republics and that they strengthen the power of existing dictatorial regimes, create international rivalries and jealousies, and under no conceivable circumstance can result in the establishment of armed services capable of significantly affecting the outcome of any military threat to the hemisphere from an extra-hemisphere power. Irrespective of the arguments pro and con, the principal result of the programs has been to increase the capability of the armed forces, a capability that has been used, except in Cuba and possibly in Peru, in favor of the traditional privileged elements. When the nationalized forces have remained united, they to date have had their way against armed opposition in every republic, again except Cuba.

This cartoon appeared as the military assistance programs were getting underway. The artist stripped the issue of nonessentials to present simply and compellingly the views of those who believed in the maxim that children should not be permitted to play with matches.

**123. The New Good Neighbor Policy**
Herblock, *Washington Post*, 1947. Copyright 1947 by Herblock in the *Washington Post*. Reprinted by permission of Herblock Cartoons.

Talleyrand is reported to have told Napoleon, "You can do everything with bayonets except sit on them." The civilian leadership in Latin America knows from repeated discomfiture that bayonets were not made to sit on, and the Latin American military establishment knows from prolonged experience that the unsheathed sword is an effective substitute for debate.

This remarkably simple, powerful cartoon leaves very little unsaid about one of the consequences when civilian political institutions clash with naked force. The cartoon is no less remarkable because the artist called attention to a pervasive situation in Latin America at a time when a number of Latin American experts were mistakenly interpreting an apparent lull in the game of military-civilian musical chairs as the beginning of a new era in which civilian politicians would finally triumph over politicians in military uniforms and the republics would somehow inevitably be the beneficiaries.

**124. The Uncomfortable Chair**
Don Hesse, *St. Louis Globe-Democrat*, 1956. Copyright © 1956, *St. Louis Globe-Democrat*. Reprinted with permission, Los Angeles Times Syndicate.

What the preceding cartoon said so very well about the military's ultimate prescription for removing civilian leaders from office, this equally direct one records for the armed forces' bullets-not-ballots strategy for keeping civilians out of office in the first place. The cartoon appeared at a time when democracy (i.e., institutionalized civilian rule) remained an ideal of the Alliance for Progress, but when in reality Latin America was entering upon its current cycle of military-dominant dictatorships. The cycle is now well into its second decade and only Colombia, Costa Rica, Mexico, and Venezuela remain in the civilian camp.

**125. Platform for Democracy?**
    Roy B. Justus, *Minneapolis Star*, 1963. Copyright 1963, Minneapolis Star and
    Tribune Company. Reprinted by permission.

A military junta overthrew Peru's President Manuel Prado y Ugarteche and annulled the June 10, 1962, elections in which Víctor Raúl Haya de la Torre's APRA party, anathema to the armed forces, had won a plurality. It is debatable whether or not "democracy" suffered a major setback as a result of the coup because Peruvian civilian regimes historically had been basically oligarchical regimes more concerned to see the military appeased than democratic processes honored and the masses served. Communism entered the cartoon primarily because of the Cold War climate. But democracy versus communism is not what the cartoon is about, for by giving his stylized Andean Indian center stage, the artist identified the ultimate victim of misgovernment that had characterized Peru's past. Few cartoons have so completely captured the essence of what power struggles have been about in those nations with large Indian populations.

**126. Alliance against Progress**
   Richard Q. Yardley, *Baltimore Sun*, 1962. Reprinted by permission of Richard Q. Yardley.

President João Goulart was overthrown on March 31, 1964, and the Brazilian armed forces seized the reins of power which they have held to the present while brooking a minimum of civilian input. Goulart became a likely target for the armed forces when traditional civilian power elements rejected his programs for stimulating the lagging economy, keeping inflation within reasonable bounds, and maintaining the nation's credit standing abroad. He was doomed when he opted to by-pass established channels and go to the "people" and noncommissioned officers of the armed services, thereby giving the military chieftains a basis for charging him with seeking to set up the country for a Castro-like takeover.

This cartoon, loaded as it is with the symbolism traditionally used to reduce the Latin American "common man" to an object of helplessness and the area's armed forces to scornful unfeeling arrogance, may have aroused emotions in the United States, but it did little better to inform the public of the Brazilian reality shortly after the military usurped power. As rapid-fire reporting from Brazil made clear at the time, the generals and admirals and their anxious middle- and upper-class civilian allies had not "rescued" the nation with any thought of instituting "economic reforms" of the kind that might be of early assistance to the popular elements. On the contrary, their stated objective was to protect the traditional system until it could be made to work. Translated into political terminology, that meant suppressing the dissent and demands of groups newly mobilized by Goulart and his immediate predecessors, not talking to them. And the officers have held to their initial course: the popular elements go unconsulted, basic economic reforms postponed.

**127. Can He See Me Now?**
William H. Crawford, *New York Times,* April 19, 1964. Reprinted by permission of NEA, Inc.

The charter of the Alliance for Progress called for reforms which, if implemented, would have amounted to major structural overhauling in the social-economic-political systems of the Latin American republics. That was asking too much of governments already confronted by nationalist movements from both the left and right, mounting social protests, and enduring civil-military differences. Between August 1961, when the republics subscribed to the Alliance for Progress, and October 1963, when this cartoon was published, seven civilian-led governments —one each in Argentina, Peru, Guatemala, Ecuador, and Honduras and two in the Dominican Republic—succumbed to military juntas. Political discord, to which the armed forces were major contributors then, proved a formidable obstacle to the success of the Alliance. In fact, about the time that this cartoon appeared, the Kennedy administration, out of a growing sense of frustration, issued a policy statement which in effect said, "Enough." The United States would work with entrenched regimes but henceforth no administration coming to power by force would benefit from the Alliance. That policy was aborted less than a year later when Washington, with unseemly haste, rushed to the aid of the Brazilian junta that toppled President Goulart and assumed power. But it bears repeating that to place the burden of responsibility for Alliance failures solely on military juntas, as this cartoon does, was unwarranted. The civilian elite's profound distrust of social-economic change within a framework of constitutional democracy shaped in Washington and the lack of enthusiasm on Capitol Hill once it became apparent that the Alliance was not providing instant answers to Latin America's problems were also factors of equal importance in setting the stage for the Alliance's demise.

**128. The Express Will Be a Trifle Late**
Roy B. Justus, *Minneapolis Star*, 1963. Copyright 1963, Minneapolis Star and Tribune Company. Reprinted by permission.

Nelson Rockefeller, then governor of New York and collector of primitive art, at the request of President Richard Nixon, headed a fact-finding mission to Latin America in 1969. The mission made four separate trips to the area between May 11 and July 6. This cartoon appeared shortly after the delegation returned from the first tour after having visited Mexico, the Central American states, and Panama. Rockefeller is not known to have reported personally to President Nixon prior to the appearance of the cartoon. It thus can be considered a reflection of the artist's view of existing conditions. As it turned out, when the report of the mission was made public in November, it strongly recommended increased assistance to the Latin American military establishments, as bulwarks against communism. It also called attention to the area's pervasive demographic problems, but in deference to the Catholic church and certain nationalist groups, it failed to come out solidly for birth control measures.

Of the seven nations visited on the first trip, four were headed by armed forces officers—El Salvador, Honduras, Nicaragua, and Panama—and the army was the dominant political force in Guatemala. The military establishments in those countries were and remain among the most "primitive" to be found in Latin America, and essentially the same can be said of the actions of civilian elites and foreign investors in those republics. Thus, as the cartoon suggests, the armed forces continue to give a strong flavor to the "art" of the area, and the poor do continue to have children.

**129. It's Part of the Primitive Art That Still Exists!**
Hy Rosen, *Albany Times-Union*, 1969. Reprinted by permission of Hy Rosen.

On September 11, 1973, the Chilean armed forces with the cooperation of the national police overthrew democratically elected Marxist President Salvador Allende Gossens and set up a junta to rule the country. The junta immediately emerged as an authoritarian regime bent on remodeling traditional institutions and remaining in power for a long time. The junta's violations of human rights were brutal beyond anything the more politically sophisticated nations of Latin America had witnessed in at least a half century. Within ten days, arrests had reached into the thousands and summary executions into the hundreds. The working sectors were made to bear the brunt of harsh economic measures designed to slow the rate of inflation and raise production. Political parties were banished and congress disbanded. The faculties of the universities were purged of "leftists" and courses in Marxism. Censorship of the press, including dispatches sent abroad by foreign correspondents, was instituted and rigidly enforced.

The junta's ideological fury reached such heights that individuals burned or in other ways destroyed their private libraries for fear that they might be found to contain materials the military regime would consider subversive. The public burning of posters, pamphlets, and books, to which this cartoon alludes, was yet another aspect of military authoritarianism to run amuck in Chile. The nation had known occasional press censorship even under civilian government, but not since the mid-nineteenth century when the liberal José Lastarría's dissertation and the radical Francisco Bilbao's political discourses were burned had it experienced such irrationality on the part of high government officials.

**130.** Tony Auth, *Philadelphia Inquirer*, 1973. Reprinted by permission of Tony Auth.

Violence has been an accepted feature of the political process in Latin America. Despite their seemingly endless coups and *pronunciamientos*, the national armed forces of Latin America have never enjoyed a true monopoly on the exercise of that violence. For a century after independence was won in the 1820s, private armies characteristically dominated the institutionalized forces at the local and provincial levels. They often successfully competed with them in making and unmaking national presidents and in other ways influencing domestic and international affairs. The great and powerful armies of Emiliano Zapata, Pancho Villa, and Venustiano Carranza which were assembled during the Mexican Revolution of 1910 for all intents marked the end of the personal army as a political instrumentality at the presidential level. Between World War I and World War II, the most spectacular challenge by a noninstitutionalized force came in Brazil. There, in 1930, a combination of private and provincial contingents committed to Getulio Vargas posed a sufficient threat to propel the leaders of the national military services into accepting Vargas as president as against the possible price to themselves and the nation of testing the strength and determination of his supporters on the battlefield. Less than two years later the state of São Paulo, dissatisfied with Vargas' policies and entertaining the thought of secession from Brazil, put fifty thousand troops in the field; but that time the national forces prevailed.

After World War II the challenge to the centralized services began to come from peasant bands and ideological armies, first in Colombia, Bolivia, Guatemala, Peru, and Cuba and later in the Dominican Republic, Argentina, Uruguay, and Chile. To date, except in Cuba, the national forces have prevailed.

The artist of this "nonpolitical" cartoon of 1944 made magnificent use of humor and symbolism to give poignancy to the very real and ever-present possibility for confusion arising from the presence of competing sources of political violence in the republics.

**131. In the Name of the Peasants and Peons National Party—Oh, I Beg Pardon!**
Drawing by Albert Hubbell; © 1944, 1972 The New Yorker Magazine, Inc.

# 8. CONCLUSION

The cartoons reproduced here are believed to constitute a valid visual record of the cluster of United States prejudices against the people and institutions of Latin America. They are at once striking testimony to the cultural underlay of the mainstream of Anglo American society, the concerns of that society about Latin America over the past century, and the gulf that separates the two cultures.[1] Because the cartoons have reflected the culture to which they were directed, they have of necessity been predicated variously upon pseudoscientific theories of evolution, wishful thinking or irrationalities about such amorphous concepts as "national destiny" and national interest, as well as plain and simple misunderstanding of what Latin America is and what it is about. The cartoons, therefore, should be seen as documenting states of mind in different historical eras and as caricaturing instead of inventorying hemispheric realities. Subtlety has not been one of their characteristics; on the contrary, their blows have been that of the club, not the rapier.

The illustrations appear to confirm the view that editorial cartoonists fear the public mind will not grasp anything but the obvious and that simplicity and naïvete preclude more subtle forms of satire. The artists have thus relied upon symbolism, not ideas, and have sought to mobilize support for a cause rather than to enrich debate. It is equally apparent that to the extent to which the cartoonists' symbols have appealed to readers' emotions by calling forth immediate mental and behavioral reactions, they have served to entrench stereotypical attitudes. The relatively narrow range of symbols the artists have depended upon for over a century certifies the public's responses to them and also the fact that concrete historical experiences live on in the present and continue to determine their shape and meaning. Cartoons 107 and 119, in particular, attest to the lasting quality of the symbols.

The cartoonists' lessons have been twofold. First, because of the universal beneficence of its brand of equality and individualism and the superiority of its enterprise and technology, the United States has a civilizing burden in respect to Latin America. Second, Latin Americans are inferior to the point of inspiring little respect or trust and lack the wisdom to know what is best for their own security and economic well-being or to rule themselves effectively. The instruction has taken a quite limited number of forms. Anglo-Americans have been depicted as controlling their destiny while denying Latin Americans, all of whom seem struck from the same mold, the capacity to follow such a path. The republics sometimes have been portrayed as feminine, which in our historically male-dominated society automatically cast them in dependent roles. Not unusually, before the 1930s they were pictured as children requiring the assistance and surveillance of a patient Uncle Sam, compelled to play such roles as doctor, nurse, teacher, truant officer, and doting father. Until about the same date, they often were cast as Blacks, a minority whose values as stereotyped by the dominant White community have represented the antithesis of those associated with the Puritan ethic. When portrayed as "Whites" or Mestizos, the republics have been made to handle their social and political burdens in ways that traverse the spectrum of our social and political negative universe. How Latin Americans have not been portrayed is equally enlightening. They have not been depicted as people who, like the people of the United States, have jobs, raise families, go to school, and grapple with social, economic, and political problems day after day to make their communities and their countries better places in which to live and work. The judgment that the collective symbols, labels, and metaphors scattered throughout this volume and missing from it constitute a form of reductionism appears irrefutable.

Every cartoon in this book was drawn originally for a United States reading public. This was intentional because the purpose of the study was to examine what has gone on in the minds of United States cartoonists to the exclusion of all others in that profession. I took that approach because I consider intrasocial phenomena more important than intersocietal factors for a comprehensive understanding of the sources of cultural misunderstandings. This is simply to say that, to understand others, a society must understand itself. The United States is moving in the direction of better understanding itself but still has a good distance to travel. Large parts of our public sometimes consciously but often unconsciously insist on thinking about other peoples in stereotypical forms. Until they recognize stereotypical traits in themselves, their stereotypes cannot conceivably be expunged. Likewise, until Latin American separatism and its different perspectives are appreciated and accepted, the root causes of those antagonisms that bedevil this hemisphere are out of the question. In the mean- time, parochialism will continue to lead to a want of thought about the requirements of the hemisphere, and while the new may challenge the old, the new will not be victorious.

I have been quicker in pointing out gaps in understanding than I have been in offering suggestions as to how the gaps might best be narrowed. This is perhaps because after being over the ground so many times I am convinced that there are no panaceas, no easy solutions, no dogmas, no formulas, no single prescriptions that will serve all times and all places. On the contrary, acceptable standards of international understanding and behavior require constant review. For example, and speaking figuratively, yesterday the United States thought of Latin America as locked into a hemisphere system engineered by Washington. Tomorrow the United States, to be realistic, will probably have to cope with Latin America's determination to cease being merely a shadow of Washington and to go global. There is the further possibility of such countries as Brazil, Mexico, and, perhaps, oil-rich Venezuela becoming continent-based centers around which their neighbors will orbit. For the United States to handle successfully affairs of that nature will require a respect of cultural differences that has not been exhibited to date. It can be hoped that lessons learned from finally confronting certain of our own racial-cultural problems may provide some very necessary guidelines. But one must hasten to add that to date the consciousness of race as a basis of personal identity seems much more difficult with which to cope than optimists have led us to believe. Finally, to identify a weakness is a far cry from creating the emotional awareness needed to remedy it. I hope that such an acknowledgment does not detract from the message the book conveys.

A case for directly linking the images and stereotypes found herein to the behavior of United States officials and private citizens toward Latin America probably could be made. I have not attempted to make the connection on this occasion for two basic reasons. First, the influence of public opinion and the mass media upon decision-making processes as a field of study is still in its infancy. Many of the issue areas explored by such concerned scholars as Gabriel Almond, Bernard C. Cohen, Robert Dahl, V. O. Key, H. R. Mahood, James N. Rosenau, and Betty H. Zisley, whose works I found most helpful, remain to be tested empirically.[2] For example, to what sectors of the public, if any, have policy makers listened in different historical eras? To what extent do the interests and groups into which the public is divided represent so diverse and conflicting objectives that in peacetime they tend to cancel out one another? To what degree do the Anglo-Americans' values and worries that their generosity may go unrequited make them atomistic rather than corporate individuals of the kind suited to accepting international bargaining? How does the informed citizen's desire to end foreign involvements quickly keep one from maintaining pressures on those in control of public and private agencies engaged in overseas activities? To what degree does the citizen's enmity toward and ignorance of foreign cultures produce a tendency for his or her moods to gyrate between idealism and cynicism rather than to engage in sustained searches for rational responses to international issues? More specifically in reference to Latin America: in what ways, if any, has the fact that historically there has not been in the United States a Latin American pressure group with nationalist attachment to any one of the republics—of the kind that, for example, Irish-Americans, Italian-Americans, Polish-Americans, and Czech-Americans have provided their homelands—given decision makers in the Latin American area a freer hand than they would otherwise have enjoyed? Viewed from another direction, how are voting patterns reflected in the behavior of elected officials and managers of United States companies abroad? And to what extent do informed individuals —through their control of the educational systems that historically have produced the leaders of government, including those in the Departments of State, Treasury, Commerce, Agriculture, and Defense and of the mass media and multinational companies—directly or indirectly influence attitudes toward foreign peoples? My second basic reason for not attempting to relate the stereotypes to policy making, either public or private, is that, despite the importance I suspect the images may at times have had in decision making affecting the entire North and South American continents, I believe no less that major political and economic policies are necessarily multicausal in origin. And since this study relies primarily upon the data of a single input into one of several areas capable of influencing international relations, the overwhelming odds are that any conclusion drawn from it alone would be distorted. If, despite the above disclaimer, the reader wishes to consider the cartoons and the accompanying commentary in policy terms, he or she might begin by taking the two most obvious occasions in this century—the Good Neighbor Policy and the Alliance for Progress—when the United States actively but unsuccessfully sought to promote hemispheric understanding, democracy of the Anglo-American variety, and Latin American "development" and ask the question: what limitations possibly were imposed on the two programs by the kinds of responses to hemispheric affairs that the cartoons appear to invite?

# NOTES

## 1. Introduction

1. "Latin America" is a kind of intellectual shorthand used herein to refer to the Spanish-speaking republics of the Western Hemisphere plus Brazil and Haiti.

2. Although for the sake of variety I occasionally use the term "stereotype[s]," I usually employ "image[s]" because it is not so value loaded.

3. I wish to emphasize at the outset that this book is about racial, ethnic, and institutional stereotypes. I hold only that stereotypes may have been among the more important variables in certain situations and that, while at no time have they been unimportant, they never stand alone. Although I feel that "color" is a greater factor in international relations than "race," I ordinarily use the term "race," in part because it is an accepted social science term and also because, in the field of international relations, "race" is in fact most often associated with "color."

4. As distinguished from social cartoons and humorous drawings of the genre that commonly appear, for example, in the *New Yorker*.

5. The following newspapers and periodicals were consulted: *Harper's Weekly* (1916–1957), *Puck* (1877–1910), *Literary Digest* (1890–1938), *Review of Reviews* (1891–1916), *New York Times* (1940–1972), *Washington Post* (1957–1973). These were journals and periodicals of the quality read by Herbert Blumer's "effective Public"; see his "Public Opinion and Public Opinion Polling," in *Reader in Public Opinion and Communication*, ed. Bernard Berelson and Morris Janowitz, rev. ed. (Glencoe, Ill.: Free Press, 1953), pp. 594–602.

6. I use the terms "informed public," "knowledgeable public," and "attentive public" interchangeably. I conceive of these "publics" as comprised of individuals who, because of cultural background, education, wealth, and interest in public affairs, are more likely than the public-at-large to read about and respond to problems and situations arising from an international climate. Their responses are believed to be conditioned by cultural qualities characteristic of the historically dominant, more socially and economically advantaged, White Protestant elements of the population. They are commonly acknowledged by social scientists to have greater influence on policy than the "ordinary citizen," but that judgment is essentially intuitively based. I know of no empirical study that claims to fix precisely their number or influence on policy. Gabriel Almond, in *The American People and Foreign Policy* (New York: Praeger, 1960), identifies the group by using, among other sources, the recorded observations of informed foreign visitors to the United States, mainly in the late nineteenth and early twentieth centuries. The chapter "Social Groupings and the Foreign Policy Mood," in which he uses such variables as age, sex, income, education, and regional breakdowns, is particularly suggestive. James Rosenau, in *The Attentive Public and Foreign Policy: A Theory of Growth and Some New Evidence* (Princeton: Center of International Studies, Princeton University, 1968), p. 2, reports that "by almost any quantitative standard its [the informed public's] ranks are not large," and on the follow-

ing page he states that "the varying estimates always fall within a range that does not exceed 50 per cent of the adult population." Bernard Cohen is highly skeptical of the public's influence on policy making, but, if I read him correctly, his reservations stem in large part from the fact that to date no one has developed a satisfactory methodology for measuring the how, why, or when of that influence; see Bernard C. Cohen, *The Public's Impact on Foreign Policy* (Boston: Little, Brown and Co., 1973). My conception of the "informed public" conforms in the main to Ernest R. May's in chap. 2 of *American Imperialism: A Speculative Essay* (New York: Atheneum, 1968) and for much the same reasons: namely, that interest in foreign affairs must be fed by a steady flow of information of an international nature available primarily in urban periodicals and magazines of relatively large circulation. Rural dwellers historically have had very limited access to foreign affairs information except through religious journals, clergymen, and an occasional politician. See also Kenneth P. Adler and Davis Bobrow who, in "Interest and Influence in Foreign Affairs," *Public Opinion Quarterly* 20 (Spring 1956): 89–101, identify leadership types in a midwestern suburb as "highly educated, wealthy, Protestant and 'Anglo-Saxon.'"

7. See H. C. J. Duijker and N. H. Fridja, *National Character and National Stereotypes: A Trend Report for the International Union of Social Psychology* (Amsterdam: North Holland Publishing Co., 1960), especially chaps. 7 and 8, which not only discuss national character but also contain extensive bibliographies.

8. I use the terms "policy making" and "decision making" interchangeably. Richard R. Brody, in "Citizen Participa-

tion in Foreign Affairs," *Civis Mundi* 4 (1971): 1–8, makes a distinction between the two that seems valid for his purposes but unnecessary within the context of this study.

9. The term "prejudice" may have positive connotations (as, for example, the United States' prejudice in favor of Great Britain during the two great wars) or negative ones. In this volume, the term will be used solely to refer to the sets of negative attitudes which are assumed to cause, support, or justify discrimination against a socially defined group, i.e., Latin Americans or a person or institution associated with that group. Prejudice appears in varying degrees of extremism. The Preamble of the Constitution of UNESCO, with reference to prejudice in its more devastating form, declares that it, along with ignorance, was a major factor in bringing about World War II.

10. Numerous authors make the point that "race" and/or "color" continue to govern much human behavior and continue to figure in current international affairs. Harold R. Isaacs, "Group Identity and Political Change: The Role of Color and Physical Characteristics," *Daedalus* 104 (Spring 1967): 353–375, provides a well-balanced general discussion of "race" in international affairs. Few studies place as much emphasis on race in international relations as does Robert S. Browne's *Race Relations in International Affairs* (Washington, D.C.: Public Affairs Press, 1961). See also the thoughtful analytical study of Akira Iriye, *Across the Pacific: An Inner History of American-East Asian Relations* (New York: Harcourt, Brace & World, 1967).

11. See William G. Rogers, *Mightier Than the Sword: Cartoons, Caricature, Social Comment* (New York: Harcourt, Brace & World, 1969), p. ix.

12. Hans Schmidt, *The United States Occupation of Haiti, 1915–1934* (New Brunswick, N.J.: Rutgers University Press, 1971), p. 232.

13. *New York Times*, July 14, 1964.

14. Walter LaFeber, *The New Empire: An Interpretation of American Expansion, 1860–1898* (Ithaca: Cornell University Press, 1963), places the stress on the need of agriculture and industry for new materials. Frederick Jackson Turner's warning that the free land frontier no longer existed to siphon off popular discontent was an added factor in the development of Washington's attitudes toward both economic and territorial expansion after 1890.

15. For a detailed development of an essentially similar view of hemispheric economic relations prior to and during World War II, see David Green, *The Containment of a Continent: A History of the Myths and Realities of the Good Neighbor Policy* (Chicago: Quadrangle Books, 1971).

16. For a brief but thoughtful discussion of the influence of nationalism on foreign investment, see Joseph Grunewald, "Foreign Private Investment: The Challenge of Latin American Nationalism," *Virginia Journal of International Law* 11, no. 2 (March 1971): 228–245. See Julio Cotler and Richard R. Fagen, eds., *Latin America and the United States: The Changing Political Realities* (Stanford: Stanford University Press, 1974), for a strongly pro–Latin American and anti–United States presentation of the issues raised by nationalism.

17. For a very ably developed summary of the derivation, pro and con arguments, and historiography of the legend, see the introduction to Charles Gibson, *The Black Legend: Anti-Spanish Attitudes in the Old World and the New* (New York: Knopf, 1971). Although the Black Legend was at times extended to include the Portuguese, the fact is that they for the most part escaped the harshest judgments directed against Spaniards and their culture.

18. Corruption in a variety of forms is a common theme in Glen Caudill Dealy, *The Public Man: An Interpretation of Latin America and Other Catholic Countries* (Amherst: University of Massachusetts Press, 1977).

19. See Gibson, *The Black Legend*.

20. The United States view of Spanish conduct in Cuba during the last years of its rule can be found in numerous studies. David Healy, *U.S. Expansionism: The Imperialist Urge in the 1890s* (Madison: University of Wisconsin Press, 1970), provides a reasoned account of the Cuban situation as seen from the United States. By far the best study of public opinion of conditions in Cuba during the 1890s is Gerald F. Linderman, *The Mirror of War: American Society and the Spanish-American War* (Ann Arbor: University of Michigan Press, 1974).

21. Henry F. May, *The Enlightenment in America* (New York: Oxford University Press, 1976), p. 276.

22. The term Creole refers to individuals born in the New World of Iberian parentage.

23. Arthur P. Whitaker, *The United States and the Independence of Latin America, 1800–1830* (New York: W. W. Norton & Co., 1964), p. 183.

24. See, for example, John M. Forbes, Chargé d'Affaires to John Quincy Adams, Secretary of State, Buenos Aires, July 10, 1822, in William R. Manning, ed., *Diplomatic Correspondence of the Latin American Nations*, 3 vols. (New York: Oxford University Press, 1925), I, 606. The forty-niners who opted for the sea route to California were impressed with the women of Chile's more privi-

320   leged elements; see John J. Johnson, "Talcahuano and Concepcion as Seen by the Forty-Niners," *Hispanic American Historical Review* 26, no. 2 (May 1946): 251–262. Leonard Pitt found that the women of early California were quite respected by Anglo-Americans; see his *The Decline of the Californios: A Social History of the Spanish Speaking Californian, 1846–1890* (Berkeley: University of California Press, 1970). Kevin Starr confirms Pitt's view; see his *Americans and the California Dream, 1850–1915* (New York: Oxford University Press, 1973). To my knowledge, the most competent discussion of Anglo attitudes toward Mexican women in Texas prior to its annexation to the United States is to be found in James E. Crisp, "Anglo-Texan Attitudes toward the Mexican, 1821–1845," Ph.D. dissertation, Yale University, 1976.

25. Harry Bernstein, *Making an Inter-American Mind* (Gainesville: University of Florida Press, 1961), discusses in some detail early intellectual exchanges between North and South America.

26. Stow Persons, *American Minds: A History of Ideas* (New York: Holt, 1958), p. 80.

27. See Bernstein, *Making an Inter-American Mind*, p. 2.

28. May, *The Enlightenment*, p. 308.

29. Frederick Merk, *Manifest Destiny and Mission in American History* (New York: Vintage Books, 1963), p. 265. See also Robert F. Berkhofer, Jr., *The White Man's Indian from Columbus to the Present* (New York: Knopf, 1978), p. 154; idem, *Salvation and the Savage: An Analysis of Protestant Missions and Indian Response, 1787–1862* (Lexington: University of Kentucky Press, 1965), p. 7; and Persons, *American Minds*, p. 158.

30. Gary B. Nash, "Red, White and Black: The Origins of Racism in Colonial America," in *The Great Fear: Race in the Mind of America*, ed. Gary B. Nash and Richard Weiss (New York: Holt, Rhinehart and Winston, 1970), pp. 7–8, 19.

31. See Nancy B. Black and Bette S. Weidman, *White on Red: Images of the American Indian* (Port Washington, N.Y.: Kennikat Press, 1976), p. 135; Ronald N. Satz, *American Indian Policy in the Jacksonian Era* (Lincoln: University of Nebraska Press, 1975), pp. 40–44; and Francis Paul Brucha, ed., *Americanizing the American Indians* (Cambridge: Harvard University Press, 1973).

32. Merk, *Manifest Destiny*, pp. 157, 216.

33. See Carl N. Degler, *Neither Black nor White: Slavery and Race Relations in Brazil and the United States* (New York: Macmillan Co., 1971), and David Brion Davis, *The Problem of Slavery in Western Culture* (Ithaca: Cornell University Press, 1969), for well-argued discussions of the role of the Mulatto in Anglo-American society, including, in this case, Canada.

34. Winthrop D. Jordan, *White over Black: American Attitudes toward the Negro, 1550–1812* (Baltimore: Penguin Books, 1969), pp. 10–12.

35. Winthrop D. Jordan, *The White Man's Burden: Historical Origins of Racism in the United States* (New York: Oxford University Press, 1974), p. 170.

36. The influence of Morton and his disciples on racist thinking in the United States is covered both well and interestingly in William R. Stanton, *The Leopard's Spots: Scientific Attitudes towards Race in America, 1815–1859* (Chicago: University of Chicago Press, 1960).

37. "Racism" is used here to mean a generalized set of stereotypes of a high

degree of consistency, including emotional reactions to race names, a belief in typical characteristics associated with race names, and either conscious or unconscious evaluations of such traits. This definition is from Daniel Katz and Kenneth Braly, "Verbal Stereotypes and Racial Prejudice," in *Readings in Social Psychology*, ed. Eleanor E. Maccoby, 3d ed. (New York: Holt, Rinehart and Winston, 1958), pp. 40–46.

38. George M. Fredrickson, *The Black Image in the White Mind* (New York: Harper and Row, 1971), p. 235.

39. Berkhofer, *The White Man's Indian*, pp. 55–62; Stanton, *The Leopard's Spots*, p. 41 and following.

40. Ernest W. Lefever, "Moralism and U.S. Foreign Policy," *Orbis* 16, no. 2 (Summer 1972): 396–410. For a more general discussion, see Paul Seabury, "Racial Problems and American Foreign Policy," in *Racial Influences on American Foreign Policy*, ed. George W. Shepherd, Jr. (New York: Basic Books, 1970), pp. 60–78.

41. Bryce Wood, *The Making of the Good Neighbor Policy* (New York: Columbia University Press, 1961), p. 5.

42. Edward A. Ross, "The Causes of Race Superiority," *Annals of the American Academy of Political and Social Science* 18 (1901): 65–89; idem, *The Old World in the New: The Significance of Past and Present Immigration to the American People* (New York: Century Co., 1914); idem, *South of Panama* (New York: Century Co., 1915).

43. For an official view of what were considered the less desirable attributes of the Latin American, see U.S. Department of Labor, *The Racial Problems Involved in Immigration from Latin America and the West Indies to the United States*, a report submitted to the Secretary of Labor by Robert F. Foerster (Washington, D.C.: Government Printing Office, 1925), esp. p. 57. Two decades earlier, John R. Commons, director of the American Bureau of Industrial Research, who was highly instrumental in shaping the course of labor history for many years, in his *Race and Immigrants in America* (New York: Macmillan Co., 1907), had expressed a negative view of "tropical peoples" remarkably similar to the one Foerster drew.

44. Gunnar Myrdal makes this point in the introduction to his *An American Dilemma: The Negro Problem and Modern Democracy*, 2 vols. (New York: Harper and Row, 1969), see esp. I, xlii–xliii. For evidence of increasing tolerance of Whites toward Blacks, see "A New Racial Poll," *Newsweek*, February 26, 1979. The report is based on "an updated version of the polls Harris [and Associates] did for Newsweek in 1963 and 1966. This time, Harris polled a nationwide sample of 1,673 whites and 872 blacks in October and November" of 1978.

45. Emory S. Bogardus, "The Measurement of Social Distance," in *Readings in Social Psychology*, Society for the Psychological Study of Social Issues, (New York: Henry Holt & Co., 1947), pp. 503–507.

46. See Katz and Braly, "Verbal Stereotypes." See also the similar findings of Louis L. Thurstone on the prejudices of students in the Midwest in "An Experimental Study of Nationality Preferences," *Journal of General Psychology* 1 (1928): 405–425. Richard T. Morris, in *The Two-Way Mirror: National Status in Foreign Students' Adjustment* (Minneapolis: University of Minnesota Press, 1960), established that Mexicans were still held in low regard in 1960.

47. Hadley Cantril, ed., *Public Opinion, 1935-1946* (Princeton: Princeton

University Press, 1951), p. 502.

48. *Gallup Opinion Index*, Report no. 22 (Princeton: Gallup International, February 1968), pp. 21–24. The problem of extrapolating from such surveys is a serious one. For example, the results of this poll establish that, at the time it was taken, the respondents were being influenced by a specific "anticommunism" as well as the constant of "culture."

49. The Catholic church in Latin America and its implications for hemispheric relations is one area better covered in the printed literature than in cartoons. Because so few cartoons have dealt with the religious issue, they receive only incidental attention in this volume. If the Church were to be treated in any detail, the cartoons prior to World War I would show a very definite anti-Catholic bias. The well-known cartoonist Thomas Nast was particularly anti-Catholic, a view that he expressed on occasion in his art done for *Harper's Weekly*. After World War I, direct cartoon attacks on the Church as an institution are believed to have disappeared. During the interwar years, the few cartoons dealing with religious issues were limited almost entirely to Mexico, and the cartoonists held that the Church there was the victim of godless communist and socialist political regimes, most particularly that of Plutarco Calles. Numerous authors have written on the United States Christian duty; see, for example, Julius W. Pratt, *Expansionists of 1898: The Acquisition of Hawaii and the Spanish Islands* (Baltimore: Johns Hopkins Press, 1936); Merk, *Manifest Destiny*; and such religious periodicals as the Baptist *Standard*, the Presbyterian *Interior* and *Evangelist*, and the Congregationalist *Advance*. Pratt, *Expansionists of 1898*, has noted that many religious journals employed social Darwinist language.

50. For contrasting views of the Good Neighbor Policy, its objectives, and its accomplishments, see Wood, *The Making of the Good Neighbor Policy*, and Green, *The Containment of a Continent*.

51. Linderman, *The Mirror of War*, provides a useful survey of how Spain has been reported in public school textbooks. For more detailed discussion of textbook treatment of Spanish culture and Spanish influence in the New World, see Ruth Miller Elson, *Guardians of Tradition: American Schoolbooks of the Nineteenth Century* (Lincoln: University of Nebraska Press, 1964), and Bessie Louise Pierce, *Civic Attitudes in American School Textbooks* (Chicago: University of Chicago Press, 1930).

52. As noted in note 49 above, the Protestant-Catholic controversy that raged in the United States until well into the twentieth century is a major lacuna in the history of hemispheric relations as recorded in cartoons.

53. Thomas Milton Kemnitz, "The Cartoon as a Historical Source," *Journal of Interdisciplinary History* 4, no. 1 (Summer 1973): 81–93, and W. A. Coupe, "Observations on a Theory of Political Caricature," *Comparative Studies in Society and History* 11, no. 1 (January 1969): 79–95, are probably the best balanced examinations of cartoons as documentary evidence. Kemnitz's article is also rich in bibliographical references. Coupe wrote his article in response to Lawrence H. Streicher's "On a Theory of Political Caricature," *Comparative Studies in Society and History* 9, no. 4 (1967): 427–445, which in turn was written to call attention to what Streicher considered to be theoretical prob-

lems raised by Victor Alba in his "The Mexican Revolution and the Cartoon," *Comparative Studies in Society and History* 9, no. 2 (1967): 121–136, and W. A. Coupe, "The German Cartoon and the Revolution of 1848," *Comparative Studies in Society and History* 9, no. 2 (1967): 137–167. Emory S. Bogardus, "Sociology of the Cartoon," *Sociology and Social Research* 30 (1945): 139–147, was one of the first attempts by a United States scholar to explore the evidential value of cartoons.

Useful monographic studies of cartoons include John Geipel, *The Cartoon: A Short History of Graphic Comedy and Satire* (Newton Abbot, Devon: David & Charles [Publishers], ca. 1972); Rogers, *Mightier Than the Sword*; William Murrell, *A History of American Graphic Humor, 1865–1938* (New York: Macmillan Co., 1938), and *Dick Spencer III, Editorial Cartooning* (Ames: Iowa State College Press, 1949). Ernest H. Gombrich, "The Cartoonist's Armoury," in his *Meditations on a Hobby Horse and Other Essays on the Theory of Art* (London: Phaidon Publishers, 1963), pp. 127–139, provides a brief, thoughtful, and readable discussion of the historical evolution of the cartoon and of the cartoonist's use of metaphors. Books in which cartoons are called upon to carry the burden of the argument include Allan Nevins and Frank Weitenkampf, *A Century of Political Cartoons: Caricature in the United States from 1800 to 1900, with 100 Reproductions of Cartoons* (New York: Charles Scribner's Sons, 1944); Foreign Policy Association, *A Cartoon History of the United States Foreign Policy since World War I* (New York: Vintage Books, 1968); Foreign Policy Association, *A Cartoon History of the United States Foreign Policy,*

*1776–1976* (New York: Morrow, 1975); Mary and Gordon Campbell, *The Pen, not the Sword* (Nashville, Tenn.: Aurora Publishers, 1970); and Lewis Perry Curtis, *Apes and Angels: The Irishman in Victorian Caricature* (Newton Abbot, Devon: David and Charles [Publishers], 1971).

54. Donald V. McGranahan, "Content Analysis of the Mass Media of Communications," in *Research Methods in Social Relations with Especial Reference to Prejudice*, ed. Marie Johoda et al., 2 parts (New York: Dryden Press, 1971), part 2, pp. 530–560, provides a quite useful survey of methodological studies relating to the mass media up to 1950.

55. Lewis James Davies, "Form and Content Analysis of the Cartoon as a Cultural Medium of Communication: A Sociological Study in the Popular Pictorial Arts," Ph.D. dissertation, University of Illinois, Urbana, 1960.

56. LeRoy Maurice Carl, "Meanings Evoked in Population Groups by Editorial Cartoons," Ph.D. dissertation, Syracuse University, 1967.

57. Coupe, "Observations," pp. 77–95.

58. Rogers, *Mightier Than the Sword*.

59. Scott Long, "The Political Cartoon: Journalism's Strongest Weapon," *Quill* 50, no. 11 (November 1962): 56–59.

60. Bob Eckhardt, "The 'Art' of Politics: Why the Pen Is Mightier Than the Meathook," *Lithopinion* 5 (Summer 1970): 64–71. Also, see Bogardus, "Sociology of the Cartoon," pp. 139–147.

61. See, for example, Henry Ladd Smith, "The Rise and Fall of the Political Cartoon," *Saturday Review*, May 29, 1954, p. 7, and Jack H. Bender, "The Outlook for Political Cartooning," *Journalism Quarterly* 40 (Spring 1963): 175–180.

62. Rollin Kirby, *Highlights: A Cartoon History of the Nineteen Twenties,* ed.

Henry B. Hoffman, with an Introduction by Walter Lippmann (New York: W. F. Payson, 1931).

63. Nevins and Weitenkampf, *A Century of Political Cartoons*, p. 15.

64. Eckhardt, "The 'Art' of Politics," pp. 64–71.

65. Stefan Kanfer, "Editorial Cartoons: Capturing the Essence," *Time*, February 3, 1975, pp. 62–63.

66. Smith, "The Rise and Fall of the Political Cartoon," p. 7. On the other hand, Kanfer, "Editorial Cartoons," speculates (his short article is devoid of empirical evidence) that during the 1960s, when public skepticism was abroad in the land, opinion cartoonists gained in popularity because of the pungency of their attacks upon what had been considered the colossal blunders in both domestic and international fields.

67. Bender, "The Outlook," pp. 175–180.

68. Coupe, "Observations," pp. 77–95.

69. Frank Whitford, "The World of the Newspaper Cartoonist," *Twentieth Century* 178, no. 1044, special issue (1970): 3–4.

70. Coupe, "Observations," p. 82, and Long, "The Political Cartoon," p. 59.

71. Whitford, "The World of the Newspaper Cartoonist."

72. Coupe, "Observations," pp. 82–84; Bender, "The Outlook," p. 175; Long, "The Political Cartoon," p. 56.

### 3. Latin America as Female

1. It must be noted that the conclusions reached by those who have dealt in depth with the changing role of women apply overwhelmingly to "White" middle- and upper-class females in urban environments. This is because, to date, the vast bulk of data has been provided by and about that group and also because, until recently, concern for working women and non-Whites attracted little attention.

### 5. The Republics as Blacks

1. George M. Frederickson, *The Black Image in the White Mind: The Debate on Afro-American Character and Destiny, 1817–1914* (New York: Harper, 1971), p. 273.

2. Ibid., p. 164, citing article by the Reverend Joseph Henry Allen of Massachusetts, "Africans in America and Their New Guardians," *Christian Examiner* 232 (July 1862): 114–116.

### 6. The Latin American Nations as Non-Black Males

1. *Albuquerque Journal*, March 19, 1979.

### 8. Conclusion

1. Allen L. Woll, in *The Latin Image in American Films* (Los Angeles: Latin American Center Publications, 1977), reaches conclusions quite similar to mine, including the staying power of stereotypes, such as the childishness of Latin Americans generally and the powerlessness of Latin American males. Woll also notes that in periods of stress (he uses World War II as his principal example) the image of the Latin American improves, but with the return to normalcy producers began to reinstate the traditional filmic stereotypes.

2. Almond, *The American People and Foreign Policy*; Cohen, *The Public's Impact on Foreign Policy*; Robert Alan Dahl, *A Preface to Democratic Theory* (Chicago: University of Chicago Press, 1967); Valdimer O. Key, Jr., *Public Opinion and American Democracy*

(New York: Knopf, 1961); H. R. Mahood, ed., *Pressure Groups in American Politics* (New York: Scribner, 1967); Rosenau, *The Attentive Public and Foreign Policy*; idem, ed., *Domestic Sources of Foreign Policy* (New York: Free Press, 1967); idem, *Race in International Politics; A Dialogue in Five Parts* (Denver: University of Denver Press, 1970); Betty H. Zisk, ed., *American Political Interest Groups: Readings in Theory and Research* (Belmont, Calif.: Wadsworth Publishing Co., 1969). For the best discussion of the backgrounds of foreign service personnel, see Warren Frederick Ilchman, *Professional Diplomacy in the United States, 1779–1939: A Study in Administrative History* (Chicago: University of Chicago Press, 1961).

# INDEX

(Note: A boldface number indicates a reference to a cartoon on that page.)

329

FOR LIBRARY
USE ONLY

F1418.J754
cop.2
Johnson, John J., 1912-
Latin America in caricature

J Ke
Keen
Gett

$5.99
ocm73487706
1st Aladdin Pap 10/26/2010

DISCARD

"That's horrible," I cried. "

"Settle down
I'm going to do
Justine, he added. "I k
ing laws, but right now I have to tell you, it sounds
as if the law is on their side. Justine, if they
come up with t
hold on to the land."

If I was suspicious before, now I was *sure* there
was something fishy going on. "Isn't it a little too
convenient?" I asked. "I mean, that the fire just happened to burn down the building when Rackham
has been trying to buy the land for years?"

"It *is* strange," said my dad. "At the very least, I
would say it's extremely lucky for them."

"Luck, or sabotage," I mumbled to myself.

# NANCY DREW
## girl detective™

**Available from Aladdin Paperbacks**

# NANCY
# DREW
girl detective ™

**#20**

## Getting Burned

CAROLYN KEENE

Aladdin Paperbacks
New York    London    Toronto    Sydney

If you purchased this book without a cover, you should be aware that this book is stolen property. It was reported as "unsold and destroyed" to the publisher, and neither the author nor the publisher has received any payment for this "stripped book."

This book is a work of fiction. Any references to historical events, real people, or real locales are used fictitiously. Other names, characters, places, and incidents are the product of the author's imagination, and any resemblance to actual events or locales or persons, living or dead, is entirely coincidental.

❧ALADDIN PAPERBACKS
An imprint of Simon & Schuster Children's Publishing Division
1230 Avenue of the Americas, New York, NY 10020
Copyright © 2006 by Simon & Schuster, Inc.
All rights reserved, including the right of
reproduction in whole or in part in any form.
NANCY DREW is a registered trademark of Simon & Schuster, Inc.
ALADDIN PAPERBACKS, NANCY DREW: GIRL DETECTIVE, and
colophon are trademarks of Simon & Schuster, Inc.
Manufactured in the United States of America
First Aladdin Paperbacks edition October 2006
10   9
Library of Congress Control Number 2006923519
ISBN-13: 978-0-689-87703-2
ISBN-10: 0-689-87703-X
1209 OFF

# Contents

# Getting Burned

# The Creepy Cloaked Thief

**N**ed and I ran through the streets of downtown River Heights. Our footsteps pounded in my ears like violent drumbeats.

"I think he went this way," I called as I turned left down Sixth Street.

"Right behind you," Ned replied.

As I searched I cursed myself for falling asleep while staking out Olde River Jewelers. If the sound of shattering glass hadn't woken me up a few minutes before, I might have missed the thief completely. Now the slimeball had a lead, but I wasn't about to let him get away. He couldn't have gotten far. I still heard his raspy breathing, after all.

Following the sound, we looped around a large, old warehouse and ended up back on River Street where we'd started—except that now all the buildings were draped in a cool and foggy mist. I glanced at my watch and saw that it was twelve o'clock. This struck me as odd. It didn't seem like noon or midnight. Looking more closely, I realized that the hands were frozen. My watch had stopped, leaving me with no idea of the time. Through the eerie half-light I could tell that the shops on River Street were closed. I figured it was pretty early in the morning.

With the entire world asleep, it was almost peaceful. It would have been romantic, too, if Ned and I weren't chasing a violent criminal.

Let me back up and explain. My name is Nancy Drew, and I'm an amateur detective. I solve mysteries here in my hometown of River Heights, and sometimes beyond. I would call myself a detective, plain and simple, but it's not like I'm licensed or anything. I'm just the type of person who likes helping others out whenever I can. And since I happen to live in a town where corruption grows faster than the weeds, my help usually involves solving mysteries. I'm very good at it too—maybe because I'm a natural, or maybe because I get so much practice. It's probably a combination of those two factors. The how and why doesn't really matter, I suppose. Solving mysteries is just what I do.

This particular slimeball had been on a crime spree

for months, breaking into places all over town. He'd already robbed four homes on Bluff Street, the First Bank of River Heights, and two antique stores, making off with lots of cash and some valuable old silver. He'd even broken into my friend Harold Safer's cheese shop and taken an entire shipment of award-winning French Brie. (I know. I was thinking the same thing: awards for cheese? Apparently they do exist, though.)

I had a hunch that he'd be striking the jewelry store next, so I was on a stakeout. My boyfriend insisted on tagging along, not that I minded. Ned Nickerson is the greatest—smart, sweet, and supportive. We've been together since practically forever, and he's always there for me when I need him. Plus, he's got beautiful, twinkling brown eyes, soft, floppy dark hair, and a smile that makes my knees go weak—figuratively speaking, of course. I mean, who could catch criminals with weak knees?

Just then I spotted the creep. It wasn't easy. He was wearing a heavy, black, hooded robe that blended into the dark shadows cast by the surrounding buildings. We followed him down a narrow alley, and I soon found myself in a part of town that I wasn't so familiar with.

It smelled like rotten food, and everything was damp. I was heading downhill, and moments later I was splashing through murky puddles. Before long, my sneakers and socks were soaked through. Turning another corner, I heard some squealing and whipped around in time to see a small, furry thing dart behind a pile of bricks.

A rat—yuck!

What was this place? I turned around, thinking I'd ask Ned if he'd been here before. But there was no Ned, and no sign of him. It was like he'd vanished into thin air.

The tall buildings towered overhead. They seemed to be closing in on me. I felt the skin on the back of my neck prickle. My hands started shaking a little too. This was getting eerie. River Heights doesn't have buildings this tall.

When I heard the clatter of trash cans—too loud to have been another rat—I spun around. Then, swallowing my fear, I hurried toward the sound. A ripple of black cloak disappeared around the corner.

That's when I realized it was time to call in the big guns. (Actually, the only guns, since I don't carry one myself and never would.)

Reaching into my pocket, I carefully pulled out my cell phone. I called the River Heights Police Department, which was on my speed dial.

"Chief McGinnis, please," I whispered to Tonya Ward, the police department receptionist.

"Nancy, is that you?" Tonya asked.

"Yup," I replied. "This is an emergency, so can you please put me through?"

"Right away," she said before transferring me over to her boss.

"Hello?" said a very gruff chief of police.

I guess he'd been tipped off that it was me calling. See, I'm not exactly his favorite person. Chief McGinnis thinks that mystery solving should be left to the professionals. It's not that I don't trust the police department. It's just that there's plenty of crime to go around for everyone—unfortunately. So I try to pick up the slack. "I found your jewel thief," I told him.

After grunting impatiently he asked, "What jewel thief?"

"You'll see. Know the back alleys behind River Street?"

"Yes," said Chief McGinnis.

"Meet me there as soon as you can, and bring backup."

"Well you've sure got a lot of—," Chief McGinnis began. He was probably going to say *nerve*, but I'll never know for sure since I hung up on him. There wasn't any time to waste. I had to keep my eyes on the thief.

Creeping around one of the brick buildings, I saw his black hood poking out from behind a tall stack of tires. He thought he was hiding, I guess. If I stayed quiet and close, he probably wouldn't move.

But what about when he heard police sirens? Surely he'd run. I had to come up with a way to keep him in one place. Glancing around the alley for something to use, I saw nothing but a bunch of garbage and some old car parts. There was a stack of bricks against the wall, and also, just an arm's length away, a second pile of tires—tires that could be useful.

I carefully lifted one from the top of the pile, thinking I'd drop it over his head so he'd be easier to catch. I moved slowly, easing the tire up on one shoulder and creeping over to where the crook was crouched. I lifted the tire over my head, and then, holding my breath, I began to lower it. In just another second I'd . . .

"AHH!" I screamed, feeling a cold hand on my shoulder.

The tire fell to the ground, landing on my foot. "Ouch!" Spinning around, I found myself face-to-face with a very stunned Ned.

"Sorry, Nancy!" he said.

I was sorry too, because now the thief was on the run again. I tore after him through the alley.

"I didn't mean to startle you," Ned said as he followed.

"No problem," I replied, pumping my arms harder. Picking up the pace, I leaped over a dented trash can, only to land ankle deep in another puddle.

"The cops are on their way," I called, still running. My feet slid around in my soaking wet shoes and socks. "We've just got to keep him close."

"I'm right behind you," said Ned.

"Where did you go before?" I asked.

"What do you mean?" he asked. "I've been here all along."

It wasn't true, but this was no time to argue. I had a thief to catch.

Moments later, we all ended up at a dead end. The thief was cornered. I heard sirens in the distance—finally. As I kept my eye on him, Ned whipped out his cell phone, called the police, and told them exactly where we were. I just hoped they found us soon.

"So who are you, anyway?" I asked. Sure, I was curious, but I was also trying to distract him. Too much silence could leave him time to think up an escape plan, and I wasn't about to let the guy get away.

The slimeball pulled off his hood, revealing a pale face, a mess of stringy white hair, and black eyes that were as lifeless as two marbles. His cold gaze was unwavering, and his mouth was set in a severe, straight line. He clutched a brown paper sack, tightly—the jewels, I figured.

Chills ran up and down my spine. Suddenly it felt like the temperature had dropped by about twenty degrees. Something about this guy wasn't normal. And I know this sounds crazy, but it's true: He didn't seem human.

When the first cop car screeched around the corner and sped toward us, I was so relieved. Another case wrapped up—or so I thought. Suddenly the thief threw the bag of jewels at me and flew away.

Huh? I blinked and gazed toward the sky. The guy was flying high, his dark cape rippling as he soared through the air. Seconds later, he disappeared into the early morning light. I've seen weird things in my life, but this was on a whole different level. This was in a whole different realm.

"What happened? How did he do that?" I asked Ned, who just shook his head, speechless.

Another cop car pulled up next to me, and Chief McGinnis, all six feet of him, stepped out. "Nancy Drew," he said, and not kindly.

"You're a few seconds too late," I said, handing over the bag of jewels. "The thief was just here."

"Sure he was," said the police chief.

"He—you're not going to believe this, but the guy flew away." I felt ridiculous for saying so, but I was only being honest.

Chief McGinnis scrunched up his bushy eyebrows. "You're right," he said as he tossed the jewels to another officer. "I don't believe it."

"Well, fine," I said. "But—"

Chief McGinnis didn't let me finish my thought. Instead, he grabbed my arm, twisted it behind my back, and slapped a pair of handcuffs on my wrist. "You have the right to remain silent," he began as he secured my other wrist.

As if! "What are you doing?" I asked, struggling in vain. "This isn't funny. The real criminal is getting away."

"The real criminal has been getting away for a long time now," said the chief. "But I've finally caught you."

"That's crazy," I cried. "You're making a huge mistake."

The chief shook his head. "You had a great cover with this amateur detective business, Nancy. You really had us going there for a while."

"What are you talking about?" I asked.

"Think about it," said the chief. "Whenever there's a crime, you're always involved somehow. And it's not just here in River Heights, either. You go to Costa Rica, and some endangered birds are almost smuggled out of the country. You visit a friend in Key Largo, and suddenly someone's sunken treasure is at risk. Music students get kidnapped, and keys turn up hidden in old clocks, all under your watch."

"But everything always works out," I said. "I solved those mysteries."

Chief McGinnis snorted. "That doesn't change the fact that wherever you go, Nancy Drew, bad stuff happens."

I struggled to break free and quickly learned something about handcuffs: They hurt—a lot, especially when you're trying to get out of them. The more I pushed against them, the tighter they squeezed.

Turning to Ned, who seemed almost as stunned as I did, I said, "Tell him. Tell him there was a thief—and that he flew away. . . ." I stopped talking because by that point, even I realized how crazy it sounded. I didn't want the entire police force to think I was a raving lunatic, even though I was telling the truth.

Ned had this strange expression on his face. His mouth kept opening and closing, like he was struggling to speak, but he kept choking on his words. It was as if he had no voice. Our eyes met. Mine widened, and his did too.

The sirens were getting louder. More cop cars were speeding toward me. Officers in navy blue were surrounding me, staring me down. There were so many of them that their faces blurred, and they were treating me like a dangerous criminal.

What was happening?

The sirens grew louder and louder still. It was like they were blaring right in my ear.

I squeezed my eyes shut, tightly. This couldn't

actually be happening. No way could it be real.

Opening my eyes, I found myself in darkness. Where had the time gone? Had they thrown me in solitary confinement? Did I black out? I blinked a few times so my eyes could adjust.

I found myself in my bedroom, which is when I realized I'd been dreaming. There was no creepy-cloaked, flying jewel thief. There was no line of police officers staring me down, and there were no handcuffs.

I sighed in relief, but then realized that there *were* still sirens going off. They were coming from somewhere nearby, and they seemed to be getting louder.

I glanced at my bedside clock and saw that it was five a.m.

Leaping out of bed, I ran to the window just in time to see three fire trucks racing by. They were heading toward the south side of town, where I saw billows and billows of heavy gray smoke.

Grabbing my jacket and car keys, I ran downstairs and outside. Once in my blue hybrid, I turned on the car and raced toward the smoke. Speeding through town, I had the worst feeling about where it was coming from. Still, I hoped that my premonition was wrong.

Ten minutes later, I was at the River Heights Animal Shelter, where I volunteer once a month. What *used* to be the animal shelter, I should say. Now the building was engulfed in flames.

A ring of firemen surrounded the mess. All were working hard to hose down the structure. The flames were high and fierce, seemingly relentless.

Thinking about the poor, defenseless animals inside, I cried out and ran toward the burning building. I didn't give a thought to my own safety. All I could think about were those animals. I had to save them.

# 2

# Up in Smoke

N ancy, wait!"

I was just a few yards away from the entrance when someone grabbed my arm and stopped me from entering the burning building.

Turning around, I was surprised to see that it was Justine Tamworth, the executive director of the River Heights Animal Shelter. Justine was so crazy about cats and dogs, I'd have expected her to be leading the rescue effort. Yet here she was holding me back. I didn't get it.

"But what about the animals?" I asked.

"It's okay, they're all gone," Justine said.

I looked around and, sure enough, there wasn't a dog or a cat in sight. The fire had already eaten its way through half the building. The firefighters were still trying to hose it down, but the water seemed to make the flames grow larger.

My heart sank. "Gone?" I cried. Straining my ears, I listened for barking dogs and screeching cats, but all I heard was the crackling fire. "How can you be sure? Maybe it's not too late."

"I mean they're not here," Justine explained as she pulled me away from the fire. "All of the animals were moved to the shelter in West River two days ago. There are none in that building."

We'd been standing so close, my entire body felt overheated. Beads of sweat were forming above my eyebrows. But now, at a safe distance, we both watched as the flames danced wickedly in the early morning breeze. "That's such a relief," I said.

"Tell me about it," Justine replied, her dark brown eyes crinkling in sadness as she watched the burning building.

"But why were the animals moved?" I asked.

"We were in the middle of having the building painted, and I was worried the fumes would be bad for them. Imagine if they were still in there."

"It would have been the worst thing I'd ever seen," I said.

We both shuddered at the thought.

Standing on the sidelines, I noticed that the scene was growing. When I'd first pulled up, I'd seen only the firefighters and then Justine. While we were talk-ing, a few police cars had arrived. Some of my friends from River Heights had trickled in too. I recognized a few animal shelter employees and also some vol-unteers, but that wasn't all. Joshua Andrews, a baker who's famous for his banana bread, was there. So was Mrs. Diver, the music teacher, with wild, curly red hair—and Harold Safer. People kept coming. Ten minutes later, it seemed as if half the town were there.

As soon as Chief McGinnis strolled onto the scene, a pale guy dressed in running shorts and a T-shirt approached him. They shook hands and spoke for a while. The guy was short, with dark brown hair. I didn't recognize him, and my curiosity was piqued. They spoke for a while, gesturing toward the burn-ing building. Unfortunately I was too far away to hear what they were saying.

Minutes later, the firefighters put out the blaze for good. With the flames gone and the smoke clearing, all that was left at the scene was the building's charred frame.

"Years of hard work down the drain," Justine said with a sigh as she kicked at the dirt with her sneakers.

I could only imagine how heartbreaking this was for her. Justine is passionate about animals. She'd given up a successful career in investment banking in Paris to move to River Heights to attend veterinary school. Before she came along, the River Heights Animal Shelter was tiny and run-down, but Justine quickly changed that. Almost single-handedly she'd raised the money and supervised the construction of a brand-new, state-of-the-art facility. Thanks to Justine, our town's strays have an excellent place to go—at least, they did until this morning.

"We'll build a new one," I said, resting my hand on her shoulder. "It's horrible, yes, but at least none of the animals were harmed."

"This is true, but I still can't believe this is happening. That so many years of hard work are now gone, up in smoke." Justine glanced at the cluster of firemen huddled nearby. "I'm going to talk to the firefighters. Maybe they'll know what caused this."

"Mind if I tag along?" I asked.

"Not at all," she replied.

By the time we'd walked over to the group, which included Cody Cloud, the chief of the fire department, Chief McGinnis was there.

I hung back, behind Justine, figuring things would go more smoothly if I stayed out of Chief McGinnis's line of vision.

"Excuse me," she said, tapping Chief Cloud on the shoulder. "I'm Justine Tamworth, executive director of the River Heights Animal Shelter. What can you tell me about the fire?"

"Cody Cloud," said the chief, wiping the sweat from his brow with the back of his hand. "Nice to meet you, and I'm very sorry about your building. I only wish we'd gotten here sooner. Then we'd have been able to save more of the structure."

"I'm just glad you got here before anyone was hurt," said Justine. "No one was hurt, right?"

Chief Cloud shook his head. "Not a soul. It's amazing luck that the animals had all been moved."

"So what caused the fire? Do you have any idea?" Justine wondered.

"It's hard to tell just yet. There are no obvious signs, but we're thinking it's a case of faulty wiring," the fire chief replied.

Justine's forehead wrinkled. "But that's impossible," she said. "I just had the entire place inspected, from top to bottom, by an excellent electrician. She certainly would have told me if there was a problem."

"Sorry, Ms. Tamworth," Chief McGinnis said. "I know this is a huge loss for you and the entire community, but accidents happen." He was writing in his notebook and didn't even look up at Justine when he spoke. "You know how these old buildings are."

"Actually," said Justine, "the building was kind of new. It was only built three years ago."

The police chief smiled and said, "Then that must be the reason. You know they just don't make things like they used to."

"We'll do a more thorough search, but I can't promise you we'll find anything," Chief Cloud added.

"Ah, don't bother," said Chief McGinnis, closing his notebook and putting it in his back pocket. "This building was new, so obviously there was a design flaw of some sort. If you think the fire was caused by faulty wiring, then I'm sure that's what it was."

That's exactly the kind of thing that drives me crazy about Chief McGinnis. Too often he takes the easiest explanation as fact, without really doing a thorough investigation. "But you've hardly done an inspection!" I cried.

Suddenly noticing me, Chief McGinnis smirked and crossed his arms over his chest. "Well, if it isn't Nancy Drew," he said.

I'd meant to let Justine handle this by herself, but it was too late now. I stepped around from behind her and said, "Surely an electrician would have found an electrical problem, especially since that's what she was looking for in her inspection. Aren't you at all suspicious?"

"No," said Chief McGinnis. "Accidents happen. It's a sad fact of life." Yawning, he looked at his watch. "And I need to get going."

"We'll conduct a thorough investigation, Nancy," said Chief Cloud. "Don't you worry."

I thanked the fire chief but turned back to Chief McGinnis and asked, "I was wondering, who was that guy you were talking to before? The one in the running shorts."

Chief McGinnis said, "That was David Wells, the guy who called 911."

"Why was he out here so early?" I wondered.

"He was out jogging and saw smoke. Good thing, too. See that office park over there?" asked Chief McGinnis, pointing to a group of buildings in the distance. "That's part of Rackham Industries. Imagine if the fire had spread to there—to the biggest employer in all of River Heights. Now *that* would have been truly horrible."

"It's truly horrible now," I said. "And I still think there's more to the story."

Chief McGinnis rolled his eyes. Pointing at me, he said to Justine, "Don't let this one fill your head with ideas of scandal. You'll only waste your time."

I couldn't believe this. "Come on," I said. "Don't tell me you're not looking into this."

Chief McGinnis stared down at me. "Look, Nancy. In all my years on the force, never have I had to answer to a young woman wearing pajamas with pink bunnies all over them, and I don't intend to begin now."

I felt my face burn red. I didn't need to look at my outfit to realize what Chief McGinnis was talking about. I just wish I'd noticed it sooner. I was in such a hurry to get to the fire this morning that I hadn't bothered to change. I was plenty mad at the chief of police, but I was also embarrassed. It figures that while all of my other, regular pajamas are perfectly respectable, I just happened to be wearing the pink bunny ones on the day that the entire town saw me. Dad got them for me for Christmas last year, and I hardly ever wear them. Seriously, I don't.

As Chief McGinnis walked away, Chief Cloud told me and Justine that we could check in with him later in the afternoon.

"Do you have any other theories?" I asked.

Chief Cloud tipped his hat back and scratched his forehead. "Too soon to say. We'll keep investigating, but it's not likely that we'll find anything definitive," he said.

"Thank you for trying," said Justine, handing him her card. "This is my number. Please call day or night if you have news."

"Will do," said Chief Cloud. "Nice to meet you, Justine. Nancy, good to see you."

As he strolled to his truck, I turned to Justine and said, "Sorry about that. It was wrong to question the police chief so blatantly. I just couldn't help myself.

It's too soon to jump to conclusions, you know?"

Justine put her arm around my shoulders. "I'm not surprised by the police chief's attitude, Nancy. That's why it's good that we have you around."

"Well, I don't care what Chief McGinnis says. I'm not going to let a pair of pink bunny rabbit pajamas stop me from investigating things further."

Justine laughed. "Now *that's* the Nancy Drew we all know and love. I'm going to meet with the shelter employees, but let's talk later on today."

"Sounds good," I replied.

As Justine walked away, Harold Safer rushed over to me. "Isn't it horrible, Nancy?" he said.

"Yes," I said. "But at least the animals weren't harmed."

"But where will they go?" asked Harold. "The West River Shelter is tiny. They don't have room to keep them all. And you know what happens at *that* shelter when it gets too crowded. . . ."

Even though my body was still sweating from the heat of the fire, I suddenly felt my blood run cold. Harold raised an issue that hadn't even occurred to me.

There are two types of animal shelters in the world: kill and no-kill. A no-kill shelter will keep animals for as long as it takes to place them. A kill shelter is one that will put animals to sleep after a certain amount of time. The length of time varies, depending on the shelter's policy. It could be three months or three days. The River Heights Animal Shelter was very humane and strictly no-kill, of course. But as far as West River went, well, I didn't know, and I was afraid to find out.

I shivered, then changed the subject. Remembering my dream from the night before, I asked, "Hey, Harold, is there such a thing as award-winning French cheese?"

"Of course," he said, looking at me strangely.

"And do you ever worry about it getting stolen?"

Harold raised his hand to my forehead. "Are you feeling okay, Nancy? Are you sure you didn't get too close to that fire?"

"I'm fine," I said. "And don't worry about the animals. We'll come up with a solution."

"Good," said Harold. "I like your outfit, by the way. It's good to see young people taking fashion risks."

"Thanks," I said, not realizing until it was too late that he was teasing me.

We both laughed. "See you later, Harold," I said, waving.

"Always a pleasure, Nancy."

I scanned the crowd for some sort of clue and noticed the pale guy in running shorts—the one Chief McGinnis told me had called 911.

I walked over to him, asking casually, "Crazy fire, huh?"

"Yup," he said.

"I don't think we've met. I'm Nancy Drew."

The guy offered his hand. "David Wells."

"Do you live in River Heights?" I asked.

"Yes, I just moved here from New York City. I'm the vice president of new business development at Rackham Industries."

"Chief McGinnis told me you discovered the fire," I said.

"It's true. I'm the one who called 911," he explained.

"What were you doing out here?" I asked.

"Jogging," he said, meeting my eyes with his cool, brown-eyed gaze. "I always jog early in the morning.

Suddenly I felt a strange sensation—chills running up and down my spine. Something wasn't right. The problem was, I didn't believe David. Sure, he was wearing jogging shorts and a T-shirt, but he was also wearing shiny brown loafers, which is a strange choice. Who goes jogging in loafers?

I didn't question his footwear, but he answered me like he knew what I was thinking.

"I just moved here. Meaning, my stuff is still on the way. I had to get out and run, but my sneakers haven't yet arrived."

"Do you live nearby?" I asked. There were lots of beautiful places in River Heights to go running—the park, the country roads, the dirt path along the river—and this was not one of them.

Apparently, this was the wrong thing to ask. David Wells got really hostile. He narrowed his eyes and took a few steps back. "Look here, I don't need to defend myself to you. I've done nothing wrong. I saved the day, in fact. Who are *you*, anyway?" he asked.

"I never said you did anything wrong," I said, completely surprised by his quick change in attitude.

Suddenly I felt someone tap my shoulder. "Ms. Drew," said a familiar voice.

Uh-oh. Gulping, I turned around and said, "Hi, Chief McGinnis."

"Didn't I ask you not to go poking your nose into other people's business?" he asked.

"No," I said. "But even if you had, I wouldn't have listened. I've been volunteering at the shelter for ages, so technically, this is my business."

"Last time I checked, harassing the innocent citizens of River Heights is illegal," said Chief McGinnis. "If you don't believe me, I can take you downtown and we can discuss it at the station."

I couldn't believe that Chief McGinnis was almost threatening to arrest me, like he had in my dream. What was going on?

"I wasn't harassing David," I said. "I was just asking him a few questions."

"Actually," David said, "it kind of felt like harassment."

"I'm very sorry," I insisted, holding my hands in the air as if to surrender. "Honestly, I didn't mean it. I'm just trying to get as much information as I possibly can because I'm worried about the shelter. Um, welcome to River Heights." I turned to leave, realizing I'd have to figure out some other time why David was so defensive. There had to be a reason, and I wasn't going to get anywhere with Chief McGinnis watching my every move.

I went to find Justine, who was still talking to some of the shelter's employees. After pulling her aside, I told her what happened.

Justine sighed. "I appreciate your help, Nancy, but I don't want you to get in trouble with the police."

"I'm not worried about that," I said. "I just want to figure out how this fire started. You said you were having the building painted, right? Who was doing the painting?"

"Peter Sandover, of Peter Paints," said Justine. "It's a new business."

"And he was painting the inside of the building?"
Justine nodded. "Yes."

"Does that mean he had keys to the shelter?"

"Yes, he did," said Justine. A worried look crossed over her face. "I hope I didn't make a mistake. He seemed like a nice guy."

"I'm sure it's nothing, but I'm going to check it out, just to be safe. Do you have his phone number?" I asked.

"He gave me a flyer, which I left in my office in the shelter," said Justine, frowning at the remains of the building. "I probably wrote it in my organizer, but that's at home."

"No big deal," I said. "I can look it up. I'll call you later."

Justine said, "Thank you, Nancy. I really appreciate this."

"Don't thank me, yet. I haven't done anything."

"Well, you're willing to look into the matter. That's more than I can say for the police department in this town."

Not wanting to bad-mouth the chief, which would have been too easy, I said good-bye and headed on home.

After showering, getting dressed, and shoving my bunny pajamas into the back corner of my pajama drawer, I turned on my computer so I could research David Wells. I checked the online archives of the *River Heights Bugle* first. Sure enough, there was an article about him in last week's business section. He'd been hired to head the new business development team.

It was a pretty big job. Rackham Industries is one of the largest companies in the entire Midwest. Like David had mentioned, the article said he came from New York, where he was working at a big bank. Before that, he worked for an energy company in Houston, and before that, he was at Harvard Business School, where he graduated at the top of his class. There was a photo accompanying the article. In it, a slightly younger version of the David Wells I'd met that morning smiled brightly. All in all, there was nothing out of the ordinary about what I read, so I don't know why the nagging feeling that something was awry persisted.

While I was online, I decided to look up Peter Paints, the company Justine had told me about. But there was no business by that name in River Heights, or in any of the surrounding towns. This was surprising, but not shocking. Sure, we're in the twenty-first century, but not everyone is technologically adept.

I turned off my computer and checked the phone book. Strangely, I couldn't find the name of Peter's painting company *or* Peter Sandover anywhere. I called information and they didn't have a listing either.

It got me thinking—sure, Justine said the company Peter Paints was brand new, but what if it didn't actually exist at all?

# 3

# Added Threats

**S**omething didn't add up—but it was too soon to tell what, exactly, it was. Later that day I was still thinking about the fire at the River Heights Animal Shelter, when I heard a knock at the front door.

I wasn't at all surprised to find that Justine had come to visit. "I was just about to call you," I told her. "Please come in."

"Thank you, Nancy." Justine walked inside. She looked tired and stressed, not that I could blame her. I was feeling the same way myself.

"Hannah just made some delicious iced tea. Can I get you a glass?" I asked.

"Did someone call my name?" Hannah asked as she bustled into the entryway, carrying a duster in one hand. Hannah Gruen works as our housekeeper, but she's more like family. I've known her forever, and love her dearly. She takes excellent care of me and my dad.

When she saw Justine, her face clouded over with concern. "Oh hello, dear. I'm so sorry to hear about the fire. Such horrible news."

"Thanks for the concern," Justine replied with a sigh. "It's a horrible thing, but I keep trying to get myself to look on the bright side. No one was hurt—human or animal."

"That's true," said Hannah. "You know, my cousin's nephew's restaurant burned down years ago, and it turned out to be the best thing. He rebuilt it and tripled his business."

Justine seemed too puzzled to respond, and I felt the need to step in and explain. "That's one of the amazing things about Hannah. She never fails to have an anecdote at the ready for every single occasion."

"It's true," said Hannah, smiling bashfully.

"And they're always related to her distant family members too," I added.

"Okeydokey," said Hannah as she headed back toward the kitchen. "I'll get that iced tea."

"Thank you," Justine and I said.

Once we were seated in the living room with our drinks, I told Justine that I couldn't find any information about her painter.

"Oh, I'm not surprised," said Justine. "The company is brand new. In fact, the owner, Peter Sandover, offered to paint the shelter for half price in order to help drum up business."

"That's a nice offer," I said. "What was he doing before he started painting?"

"Oh, he told me that he's been a painter for years, and that he used to work for a large company in Florida. He wanted to branch out on his own and figured River Heights would be a good spot, so he moved here a few weeks ago."

"I'd love to speak to him," I said. "Perhaps he saw something suspicious. Did you ever find his number?"

"I'm afraid not. I looked in my organizer, but for some reason, I don't have it. Things have been so crazy. I guess I forgot to copy it down. It's a shame that I only had one copy of the flyer, and now it's gone—incinerated," said Justine.

I frowned. "I searched online and called information, but he's not listed."

"Oh, right," said Justine. "His landline wasn't working yet, so he gave me his cell phone number."

"That's too bad," I said.

"I know," Justine replied. "I wish I could tell you more, but my life has been so hectic lately, I guess I haven't been paying close attention. I'm in my last year of vet school and I have some really big exams coming up. It's all I can do to get dressed in the morning, I'm so busy studying."

"Well, don't worry about this. I still might be able to track him down. Can you tell me what Peter Sandover looks like?"

"Sure," said Justine. "He's tall and pale, with scruffy, bleached-blond hair and green eyes. I'd guess he's in his thirties."

"How much had he painted?"

"Not much." Justine took another sip of her iced tea and then set the glass on the coffee table. "He'd just started working two days ago."

"And what was the rest of his crew like?"

"His crew?" Justine asked. "Actually, every time I went to check up on him, he was working alone. I thought that was a little strange, so I asked him about it. He told me he'd have more help next week." Glancing at her watch, she added, "Oh, but I don't want to keep your father waiting."

"My father?" I said.

"Yes, there are some legal issues surrounding the shelter, and I need his help," Justine explained.

My dad is one of the busiest lawyers in River Heights. Besides representing his regular corporate and individual clients, he does a lot of pro bono work, mainly for nonprofit organizations that wouldn't ordinarily be able to afford legal assistance. Dad has been representing the animal shelter, free of charge, ever since Justine built it.

"The shelter's having some sort of legal problems?" I asked.

"Now, Nancy," I heard my dad say.

I turned around to find him standing in the doorway with his arms crossed over his chest and his eyebrows raised.

"I'm just asking out of concern, Dad," I said.

"I know, honey, but you have to respect my clients' privacy, even when that client is a friend."

Justine stood up and smoothed out her skirt. "It's okay, Carson. I don't mind letting Nancy know what's going on. She's been volunteering at the shelter for some time now, so this concerns her, too. In fact," she said, turning to me, "do you want to join us?"

She didn't need to ask twice. I stood up and followed them into Dad's wood-paneled study.

"What seems to be the trouble?" Dad asked, once Justine and I had each settled into one of the two leather club chairs opposite his desk.

Justine sighed. "It's Rackham Industries. As you know, they own all of the buildings and most of the land surrounding the River Heights Animal Shelter, but apparently that's not enough for them. They want the shelter's land, as well. They've made me many offers over the last few years, even though I've been quite clear that I have no intention of ever selling."

Dad nodded as if he knew all about this. It was news to me, though.

"What's the problem?" I asked.

"Well," said Justine, "they just made me another offer this afternoon. And it's one that I may not be able to refuse."

"That's crazy," I said. "The fire was a huge setback, but you're going to rebuild the shelter. No *way* would you ever sell that land."

"Believe me," said Justine, "I have no interest in selling. They know that better than anyone. This is the third offer they've made this month. The problem is, I don't have the money to rebuild. And according to the zoning laws, as their team of lawyers just informed me, if I can't rebuild the shelter, I must accept any reasonable offer of purchase for development."

I looked to my dad, confused. He cleared his throat and explained. "In other words, if she doesn't have immediate plans to develop the land, she'll have no choice but to sell it."

"That's horrible," I cried. "Dad, you can't let this happen."

"Settle down, Nancy," said my dad. "You know I'm going to do everything that I can." Turning to

Justine, he added, "I'll take another look at the zoning laws, but right now I have to tell you, it sounds as if the law is on their side. Justine, if you can't come up with the money to rebuild, then you can't hold on to the land."

If I was suspicious before, now I was *sure* there was something fishy going on. "Isn't it a little too convenient?" I asked. "I mean, that the fire just happened to burn down the building when Rackham has been trying to buy the land for years?"

"It *is* strange," said my dad. "At the very least, I would say it's extremely lucky for them."

"Luck, or sabotage," I mumbled to myself.

For some reason, Dad didn't like this. "Nancy," he said, "please don't jump to conclusions. Not everyone in River Heights is corrupt, and without ample evidence, you can't be so quick to accuse."

"I'm not accusing anyone," I said. "I'm just saying that it all seems a little suspicious. At the very least, it merits an investigation."

"True," said Dad. "But you must allow for the fact that sometimes there is no mystery, just bad luck."

Okay, something was definitely up. Dad is usually proud of the fact that I solve mysteries. Of course he doesn't like it when I do things that he thinks are dangerous, but he's never so blatantly discouraged me from trying to help out. What's more, he was a big supporter of the animal shelter, and he was thrilled that I volunteered there. He's also a good friend of Justine's. So, what was going on here?

"Don't you want me to do everything I can to help?" I asked.

Rather than look at me, Dad started fiddling with the stapler on his desk. "To be honest, Nancy, I got a call from police headquarters a little while ago."

"And?" I said.

He shifted in his seat before answering me. "Chief McGinnis asked me to have a talk with you."

"You've got to be kidding. All I was doing was trying to help."

"I believe that," my dad replied. "Now, I'd never try to stop you from doing what's right, and I know that you and the police chief don't always see eye to eye, but I'd prefer you not to get in his way. He *is* the chief of police in this town, and he deserves respect."

I leaned back in my chair, completely stunned. "I can't believe he called you," I said.

"I was surprised too," my dad admitted. "And I defended you, of course. But please, do me a favor and try not to step on any toes."

"I won't," I said. This was irritating and crazy, but I didn't want to argue in front of Justine.

Dad turned to her and said, "Don't worry. Rackham Industries is not going to get that land without a fight. I promise you that I'll do everything in my power to keep it from happening."

"Thank you, Carson," said Justine as she stood up to leave. "How long do you think all of this will take?"

"Months, perhaps," said my dad.

Justine sat back down again. "Oh, dear," she said. "I was afraid of that. You see, West River only agreed to hold the animals for a week. They're overcrowded as it is."

"I'm sure you can work something out with them," my dad said.

"Actually," said Justine, "I've already spoken to them. They'll give me an extra two weeks if they have to, but that's it. And here's the biggest problem: While the River Heights Animal Shelter is strictly no-kill, West River Shelter can't make that promise."

I felt chills travel up and down my spine. "What are you saying?" I asked.

Justine paused and took a deep breath. When she answered, her voice trembled. "The animals are safe for now. And if I can scrape together enough money quickly, we can at least come up with a temporary structure to house them before breaking ground on the actual building. . . ."

"How much do you need?" I asked.

"Twenty thousand dollars, minimum," Justine replied.

"That's a lot of money. What happens if you don't get it?" I asked.

Justine shook her head and wiped the dampness from her eyes.

No one said anything. No one needed to. We all knew how gruesome this could turn out to be.

# 4

# When Monkeys Fly

**T**his is heart wrenching," said Justine as we left my dad's office. Shoulders slumped, she shook her head. "I can't believe that so many years of hard work have suddenly become meaningless, overnight. And all because of one fire and one little law."

"It's not fair. We can't let Rackham take that property," I said.

"It would be a disaster if they did, but I don't know how we can stop them," Justine replied sadly. "I'm going to run home and go over the shelter budget again, but I'm pretty sure that the money just isn't there."

As I walked Justine to her car, I realized what we could do. "If a lump sum of money is the only thing holding us back right now," I said, "we should have a benefit concert."

Justine turned to me and grinned. It was the first time I'd seen her smile all day. "I'm intrigued," she said. "Tell me more."

Biting my bottom lip, I looked over my shoulder. I didn't want Dad getting upset with me. And, okay, he'd asked me not to meddle in the investigation of the fire—but he didn't say anything about not helping the animal shelter. The reality was that I *had* to do something. There was no way I could just sit back and let the animals suffer some horrible fate. Dad would understand that.

"Well, there are tons of animal lovers in River Heights," I explained. "Some of them have to be musicians. We can get a bunch of them together for a benefit concert. Mrs. Diver will help out, I'm almost sure of it. She was at the fire, so she knows how devastating it was. I'll give her a call."

"That's a wonderful idea. Mrs. Diver adopted a cat from us a few months ago," said Justine. "There's only one problem. I'm behind on my studying. I don't think I can organize a concert *and* pass my exams."

"Don't worry about that," I said. "I'll organize the entire thing. I love doing stuff like this."

"Are you sure?" asked Justine. "It sounds like a lot of work."

"I'm positive. I can't think of anything I'd rather do. Well, besides finding out if that fire really *was* an accident—but there's time for that, too."

Justine laughed as she got into her car. "Thank you, Nancy, but be careful. I don't want you getting into trouble—with your dad or with the police."

"I'll be fine," I said, waving good-bye as she pulled away from the curb.

Hurrying back into the house, I called my partners in anticrime: Bess Marvin and George Fayne, and, of course, Ned. They'd all heard about the fire. Everyone in town must know by now. But the news that Rackham Industries was trying to take the animal shelter's land was a shock to all three. All of them wanted to help, and luckily they were all free to meet me for lunch that afternoon to hear my plan.

By the time I got to Susie's Read & Feed, Bess and George were already sitting in a booth at the front of the café. Each had a tall glass of lemonade in front of them. By the way, Bess and George are first cousins who grew up together—and they're my best friends. "I'm so glad you're here," I said, sliding into the booth next to them.

"It's my pleasure," said Bess. "I just finished changing the oil in my car and fixing the engine in my dad's, so I'm totally free for the rest of the day."

George grinned and said, "I'll bet she's the only person in town to go from working under a car to

40

changing into a pink sundress with a matching cardigan."

I had to agree.

"You should learn a thing about style," Bess argued jokingly as she surveyed George's khaki pants and solid green T-shirt.

"I know everything I need to know," George countered, "like that I should never go out in public in pajamas with bunny rabbits printed all over them."

Leaning my elbows on the table, I covered my face with both hands and groaned. "You heard about that?"

"*Everyone's* heard about that," said Bess. "But no one is surprised."

This town is small, and people know me well. I get so focused on mysteries that I often forget about stuff like matching my clothes and brushing my hair. Luckily no one holds that sort of thing against me.

"So, how's Justine doing?" asked George.

"She's depressed, but hanging in there," I said.

"I don't blame her," said George. "I biked to the shelter site this morning. There's nothing left but ash and rubble."

"Yeah, it's grim," I said.

Just then, Ned strolled into the café. Checking his watch, he asked, "Am I late?"

"You're right on time," I said.

"Good." Smiling, he bent down to give me a kiss and then slid into the booth opposite me. "So, what's the plan?"

"Well, as I mentioned on the phone, we need to raise a lot of money, fast, or the animal shelter—and perhaps the animals that were in it—will be history," I began. "I was thinking of throwing a benefit concert. I already spoke with Mrs. Diver, and she loves the idea. She's going to call a few of her more promising students to see if they'll be willing to perform. We'll make money off ticket sales, and we can set up a bake sale at intermission too. I'll bet Joshua will donate a batch of banana bread for the cause."

Joshua Andrews was a shelter volunteer, and he also owns the best bakery in River Heights. Usually he only bakes banana bread on Thursdays—but I had a hunch he'd make an exception for the cause.

"Ooh," said Bess. "Last week I waited in line for an hour for a loaf. And it was totally worth it. Just thinking about that banana bread makes my mouth water."

"Glad to hear your mouth is watering," said Susie Lin, the café owner. She stood over us with her order pad in one hand and a pen poised in the other. "So, what will it be?"

After we all ordered lunch, Ned said, "I have a friend

in the River Heights University Orchestra. I'll bet he could convince the other musicians to perform."

"Excellent," I said. "Then we can—"

I was cut off rudely by none other than Deirdre Shannon, who'd just come into the café and was lingering by our table. "Ned Nickerson!" she exclaimed, taking off her sunglasses before giving Ned a hug.

Typical. While Deirdre can't stand me or my friends, she's always had a thing for Ned. She seems completely baffled by the fact that he'd rather date me, and she makes no pretense of hiding her feelings.

I had to give her credit, though. She is skilled in some ways. She somehow figured out how to flirt with Ned while turning her nose up at me, Bess, and George at the very same time.

Deirdre is my age and her dad is also a lawyer here in River Heights, but that's about all we have in common. Most people would agree that Deirdre is a snob, and I wouldn't argue with them. Her family has a lot of money, and she thinks that makes her better than everyone else.

Flinging her dark, curly hair over one shoulder and adjusting the strap of her designer purse, she said to Ned, "You should join me and my friend at the back. I'm having lunch with Langston Murphy. You know Langston—he lives in that huge house in Mission Hill."

"Sure, I know him," said Ned, not exactly impressed and more than a little uncomfortable.

"We have a better table," she said, putting her hand on his shoulder and batting her eyelashes. "And it would be much more fun if you were there."

George rolled her eyes. Bess shook her head. I just sat there smiling up at Deirdre and acting like she didn't bother me. Of course, that always seemed to annoy her even more.

"I'm okay here, thanks," Ned replied, winking at me.

"Are you sure?" she asked.

"Positive." He nodded. "We're just discussing how to help out at the animal shelter. Did you hear that it burned down?"

Deirdre wrinkled her nose and said, "Yes, and good riddance."

"That's a horrible thing to say," said George.

"Well, I'm sorry, but the entire place smelled like animals," Deirdre replied.

"Is she serious?" George asked in a whisper.

I shrugged.

"Anyway," said Deirdre, "I heard that none of the animals were hurt, and we don't need a shelter here anyway. Anyone who wants a dog can get a pure breed from a breeder."

"Why pay for a fancy, name-brand dog when there

are so many adorable, unique stray mutts?" asked Bess.

"Because mutts are gross," Deirdre said as she scrunched up her nose. "And they're so common."

Bess almost choked on her drink. George narrowed her eyes at Deirdre. "Do you mind letting us eat?" she asked.

"Sorry," said Deirdre. "I should have just stayed at the country club for lunch. I don't know what I was thinking."

As she walked to her table, Susie came back with our food.

"Great," said George. "I'm starving." She took a huge bite of her turkey club sandwich.

I turned to my friends. "Now, where were we?" I asked.

George chewed and swallowed. "The concert is a good idea, but I was thinking . . . you know Nikki Kolista?"

"Of the Flying Monkeys?" I asked. "Of course. She's the lead singer of the biggest band around."

"Didn't the last Flying Monkeys albums go platinum?" asked Bess.

"Yes," said George. "Actually, all of their albums have. Nikki does solo stuff, too. And did you know that she's from River Heights? And that she's a big animal rights activist?"

Realizing where George was going with this, I grinned. "You don't think she'd come here, do you?"

"Why not?" asked George, with a shrug of her shoulders. "There's no way of knowing until we ask."

Bess's eyes widened. "People would come from all over the place to see a Nikki Kolista concert. Can you imagine how much money that would rake in?"

"With hope, it'll be enough to save the shelter," I said.

"But how are we going to get in touch with her?" asked Bess. "She's a huge rock star."

"I'll bet I can find her agent's information online," said George. "Let's go to my place after lunch."

"Great," I said, already feeling better.

As we were finishing up, Deirdre walked over to our table and said, "Ned, can you give me a ride home?"

Although he was halfway out the door, Deirdre's friend Langston overheard and turned around. "I'll take you home, Deirdre."

"That's okay," said Deirdre. "My place is on the way to Ned's."

"It's on the way to mine, too," said Langston.

"I said I didn't want a ride from you, Langston," said Deirdre. "Good-bye."

"Sorry," said Langston, throwing up his hands and backing out of the café. "I'll see you later."

Bess and George both raised their eyebrows at me.

"Um, Deirdre," said George, "didn't you drive here?"

"Yes, but my car is making funny noises," said Deirdre. "A lot of these new fancy models just aren't that reliable. It's crazy, since they look so good and they cost so much money, but—oh, well. I'm afraid that if I drive it anymore, it'll break down."

"I can take a look at it," said Bess, dabbing at the corners of her mouth with a napkin. "What kinds of noises is it making?"

"Um, it's hard to describe," said Deirdre. "I'd much rather have a professional work on it. In fact, I already called the garage to come tow it. So what do you think, Ned?" She put her hand on his shoulder again. "It's on your way, isn't it?"

"He's not going home," said Bess. "We're all going to George's house."

"Actually," said Ned, "I promised my dad I'd help him cut down some trees after lunch. So I guess I will be heading home."

"Perfect," said Deirdre. "I'll be waiting outside."

Once she was gone, Ned pulled out his wallet and left some money on the table. Standing up, he shook his head. "Sorry about this, everyone."

"It's okay," I said. It was, too. I wasn't going to blame Ned for being too polite to refuse to help

Deirdre, even if she didn't really need help. It wasn't his fault she was such a flirt. A few minutes later, we loaded George's bike into the back of my car and then drove to her house, with Bess following in her car, close behind.

Once in her room, George pulled out one of her laptops and searched for Nikki's information. In a matter of minutes she'd managed to track down a phone number for Nikki's talent agent.

Bess called him up and explained the situation. The agent was nice, but he couldn't give us Nikki's phone number. He didn't want to violate her privacy, which was understandable. Bess turned on the charm, though, and managed to get him to agree to give us her e-mail address.

We wrote to her right way, explaining about the fire and the animals over in West River and the Rackham Industries threat.

Then we played a couple of card games, just to kill time. We also listened to the latest Flying Monkeys CD for good luck. Nikki was incredible. Her voice was so powerful, and she was amazing on guitar.

I was getting ready to leave when George got a new message in her in-box.

Hey Nancy, Bess, and George,
Thank you for writing. Wow—I haven't been

back to River Heights in ages, and I can't
think of any better reason to come now than
to help our town's animals. You've caught me
at a great time. My band is on break, and I
have some new material I've been wanting to
try out. Definitely count me in. You said you
needed this done quickly, so how is Saturday
night?
Talk to ya soon,
Nikki

Bess, George, and I looked from the screen to one
another, too stunned at first to actually speak.

"The famous Nikki Kolista is actually coming
to River Heights," George said, still blinking at her
computer screen.

"I can't believe it," I marveled.

Bess clapped her hands and jumped up and down.
"This is the best news!" she exclaimed.

"The animals of River Heights will be saved," I said.

All at once, we started to cheer and give one
another hugs.

Rejoicing with my friends at that moment, I was
filled with such hope. Everything seemed so bright. I
had no idea that things were about to take a turn for
the worse.

# 5

# Deirdre Shannon Strikes,
# Again

**W**ord that Nikki Kolista was coming to perform in River Heights spread faster than the poison ivy I got last summer. Everyone was talking about it, and it sounded like everyone planned to come to the concert. Luckily our friend Mayor Simmons helped us secure the town's largest concert venue for free. The concert hall was downtown, and it was large enough to hold two thousand people. The show was going to be huge, and I was thrilled. Of course, between selling tickets and dealing with the staging, sound, lighting, and concessions, it was going to be a ton of work—too much for Bess, George, Ned, and me to handle on our own, which is why we put out a city-wide call for volunteers.

We were all gathering at one of the conference

rooms in the town hall at seven p.m. When I walked into the meeting five minutes early, I was shocked to find the room so packed. It seemed as if half of River Heights were crammed inside. The chairs must have filled up a while ago, because lots of people were sitting on the floor, and some were even lined up at the wall in the back.

Mrs. Diver rushed over to me right away and gave me a hug. "Nancy Drew, I don't know how you did it, but I'm thrilled that you did."

"I've been trying to call you," I said. "I feel bad that you already asked your students to perform. I don't want you to think there isn't room for them. Maybe they can be the opening act."

"Don't be silly," said Mrs. Diver, waving her hand in the air as if to dismiss the thought. "My students are just as excited as I am. And, by the way, one of my students is the star act. I taught Nikki Kolista how to play the guitar."

"Really?" I said.

Mrs. Diver nodded. "Yes, I'm really aging myself by admitting this, but she started coming to me when she was eight years old. I always knew she had tons of talent, but I'd never imagined she'd become a world-renowned musician. It's so thrilling to see a former student—especially one who was so sweet—become so successful."

"Well, I am so happy to have you," I told her.

"Any help you need, just ask," said Mrs. Diver. "But we can talk about that later. I'd better get back to my seat before I lose it."

"Thanks, Mrs. Diver."

My heart warmed as I looked at all the friendly faces. Joshua Adams was there. He not only had agreed to donate a batch of banana bread to sell at the concert, he'd also offered to make the bread every single day for the next week, donating all proceeds to the River Heights Animal Shelter.

George's little brother, Scott, was a huge Flying Monkeys fan, so he was volunteering in hopes of getting to meet Nikki in person. He'd even brought his friend Nelson Fadley. Nelson is a cute kid—skinny, with large brown eyes that you hardly ever see because his floppy dark bangs are always falling in his face. He rides his skateboard everywhere and is hardly ever seen without his pet iguana, Iggy. Iggy was even at the meeting now, snoozing on Nelson's shoulder.

But before I made it across the room to say hello, I saw my dentist. "Hi, Dr. Wolfson," I said. "I didn't know you were a fan of Nikki Kolista."

For some reason, Dr. Wolfson's face got bright red. "Oh, Nancy. I should have known you were behind this. I'm not a fan, exactly," he said, coughing. "I

52

mean, I don't know her music very well."

I tilted my head to one side and smiled at him. "So you must be here because you love animals."

"Actually, I'm allergic to all things furry," said Dr. Wolfson. He eyed Iggy the iguana cautiously. "And amphibians just make my skin crawl. You don't think that thing will get loose in here, do you?"

"Nelson keeps him on a leash. I'm sure we're safe," I said, trying to suppress a grin. (I didn't want Dr. Wolfson to think I was laughing at him, even though I was—but in a strictly good-natured way.) "So if you don't like Nikki's music and you don't like animals, why are you here? I mean, if you don't mind my asking."

Dr. Wolfson shrugged. "I just, well—I had some time, and I thought it would be good to do something for the community."

"Fair enough," I said. What else could I say? Dr. Wolfson is always kind of awkward when he isn't in his lab coat, peering into a patient's mouth. Whenever I see him in town, like at the grocery store or on River Street, I always say hello, and he always seems quiet and withdrawn. Right now, though, he seemed even more uncomfortable than usual.

I decided to start the meeting. Clapping my hands, I called everyone to attention. "Welcome, everyone. Thanks so much for coming! Justine Tamworth couldn't be here tonight—she is busy studying—but she wanted me to express her gratitude. She'll be thrilled to hear that so many people want to help raise money so we can rebuild the shelter. I thought we'd start by introducing ourselves." I turned to my right. "Bess, do you want to go first?"

"Sure." Bess stood up and smoothed down her yellow corduroy skirt. "My name is Bess Marvin."

As everyone stated their name, I looked around the room. It was a familiar crowd. I saw a bunch of volunteers from the shelter, and also some neighborhood friends. In fact, we were halfway through with the introductions before I saw someone I didn't know. He was a tall, bald man with green eyes. His name was Stefan Kinsley, and he said he worked at Rackham Industries.

I thought it was a bit strange that someone from Rackham would volunteer for this cause. If we were successful, they wouldn't get to build. I wondered if Stefan worked with David Wells. Had David sent him to the meeting to spy? Maybe this was somewhat far-fetched, but my other leads were drying up. I'd spent a little time that evening looking for contact information for Peter Sandover and I hadn't found anything. I needed something to go on, so I made a mental note to talk to Stefan later on.

After George, Scott, and Nelson introduced themselves, it was my turn.

"Hi, everyone. My name is Nancy Drew. I've lived in River Heights all my life and I've been volunteering at the River Heights Animal Shelter for years. Now I suppose we can—"

"Excuse me," said Deirdre, interrupting me as she strolled into the room, twenty minutes late.

"Oh, don't worry about it," I said, completely unfazed by her rudeness. But what was she doing at this meeting? "Um, Deirdre, this is a meeting about the benefit concert for the animal shelter. You know that, right?" I figured she was in the wrong place, since she'd made her opinion of the shelter and its strays very clear before.

Deirdre glanced at her manicured nails and asked, "This is the committee that's organizing Nikki Kolista's concert, right?"

"Yes," I said.

"Then I'm in the right place," Deirdre said. "I'd like to be involved in this. After all, Nikki is my cousin."

"Really?" I said, unable to hide my surprise.

"Yes," said Deirdre, "which is why I think I should be in charge of this committee."

"That's ridiculous," George called as she stood up. "This whole thing was Nancy's idea, and she's already worked so hard. You've never even been near the River Heights Animal Shelter."

"True," said Deirdre, "but Nikki's mom and my mom are sisters. Plus," she added, turning to me, "Nancy is always in charge of everything. Why not give someone else a chance? I mean, why is it that she always has to be in the spotlight?"

I groaned. Deirdre was *so* missing the point, and it was time someone told her. "I'm not in the spotlight," I said. "And that's not why I'm doing this. This isn't about a rock concert. It's about raising money for the animal shelter."

"*And* it's about hosting the most famous rock musician in the world." Deirdre crossed her arms over her chest and narrowed her eyes at me. "Don't pretend like you're not thrilled with the idea of meeting my cousin."

"I'm interested in meeting anyone who's willing to help us rebuild the shelter," I answered honestly.

"Are we going to get started?" asked Harold Safer. "Because the movie version of *South Pacific* is coming on at eight o'clock, and I really want to be home for it."

"Sorry," I said. People were starting to talk among themselves, and we really needed to move on before all focus was lost. "Deirdre, why don't you have a seat and we can discuss this after the meeting."

"No," said Deirdre, staring me down. "I want you to explain why you get to be in charge, yet again."

This was getting embarrassing. I didn't want to debate with Deirdre. All I wanted to do was start the meeting so we could be that much closer to rebuilding the shelter.

"Nancy does have lots of volunteer and fundraising experience," Bess pointed out. "Deirdre, what have you done for the community lately?"

"Lately," George mumbled. "How about, ever?"

"Shh." Bess elbowed her lightly in the side and whispered, "I'm trying to be diplomatic here."

"I was on the committee that organized the charity ball at the country club last year," Deirdre said proudly. "It was a fabulous event. Everyone who's anyone in River Heights was there."

"You mean, all of River Heights's *richest* people," said George, rolling her eyes.

If Deirdre heard George, she didn't let on. "I have lots of connections to the philanthropic community and, as I said, Nikki is my cousin—so it only makes sense. I want to be in charge of this, and I *deserve* to be in charge," she finished.

I honestly didn't know what to do next, so I was really happy when Ned stood up and said, "Why don't we take a vote."

It was a great idea. Deirdre thought so too. "Thank

you, Ned. You're so brilliant," she said. "You're like my knight in shining armor."

She really was too much. Her last comment confused everyone.

"All those in favor of having Deirdre run the fundraising committee, raise your hands," said Ned.

A few people raised their hands, including Nelson, who asked, "Does Iggy get a vote too?"

"Who?" asked Deirdre.

"My iguana," said Nelson, standing up so everyone could get a better look at the green and brown amphibian sitting on his shoulder.

Deirdre shuddered and said, "Yuck."

Nelson grinned as if Deirdre had complimented him. "Iggy wants you to be in charge, Deirdre," he said, before sitting down.

"And all those in favor of Nancy?" Ned asked.

Almost everyone in the entire room voted for me. It felt good to know that I had the support, but I felt bad for Deirdre. It had to be embarrassing for her—not that she seemed to mind making a stink in the first place.

"Okay," I said, relieved that this silly feud was over. "Let's get started."

"Wait a minute," Deirdre called, standing back up. I'd expected her to quit, but instead she said, "At the very least, let me organize a party for Nikki after the concert."

I had no problem with this. And actually, throwing a party for Nikki would be a great way of thanking her for coming out to perform. "That sounds great to me, Deirdre."

Deirdre smiled and said, "Perfect."

Once we were through with that nonsense, I started assigning people to various committees. Joshua and Harold were in charge of food and beverages. Mrs. Diver would take care of sound. Dr. Wolfson would handle the lighting. Stefan was interested in working on security, which I didn't think we needed, but he was pretty convincing. George, Bess, Scott, Ned, and I were in charge of ticket sales and general coordination on the day of the event. Nelson wanted to help Deirdre, but she was too grossed out by his iguana, so she sent him over to work with my group.

Once we had a plan in place, I excused myself so I could talk to Stefan. I caught up to him just as he was leaving. "Hey Stefan, I just met a guy you work with," I said. "David Wells."

Seemingly surprised, Stefan turned around and said, "I don't know anyone by that name."

"Really? I thought everyone over at Rackham knew David. There was a big article about him in the paper last week."

"Oh, *that* David Wells," said Stefan, glancing at his watch and then out toward the parking lot. "The new guy—yeah, I know who he is, but we don't work together."

"You know that Rackham is trying to buy River Heights Animal Shelter's land out from under them, and that this whole concert is happening so we can stop them, right?" I asked.

Stefan cringed. "I do know that, Nancy. Can you please do me a huge favor and keep quiet about my involvement. I love my job, but I love animals more."

"No problem." I grinned, realizing I was probably jumping to conclusions. It was possible to be an animal lover *and* a businessperson. And just because Stefan worked for Rackham didn't mean he had to agree with all of their decisions.

"Do you have any pets?" I asked.

"Sure," said Stefan. "I have a golden retriever named Ollie. In fact, I'd better get home to walk him."

"Okay," I said. "And don't worry. Your secret is safe with me. It's not like I hang out with anyone who works at Rackham, but even if I did, I wouldn't say a thing."

"I appreciate that," said Stefan, before getting into his silver sports car and driving off.

I turned around and walked back inside, thrilled that everything was falling into place. Nikki Kolista's concert was going to be huge. I was sure we'd raise enough cash to save the shelter.

I was about to head back to my group when Ned pulled me aside. With a sheepish look on his face, he said, "Uh, Nancy, you're not going to like this, but Deirdre convinced me that I had to help her with her party. It seems that she's already fired the rest of her committee."

I had to laugh. "I'll bet she did. That's just so typical."

Ned looked confused. "So, you're not mad?" he asked.

"I have no time to be," I told him. "Between organizing the concert and trying to figure out who set the fire, I've got too much to juggle. Deirdre is always going to be pulling stuff like this, and I can't waste time stressing over it. Plus, I trust you."

"Ned!" called Deirdre in a shrill voice. "Can you get back here, please? I need your help with something."

"Nancy, you're the best," said Ned, leaning over and kissing me on the cheek. "I'll still help out with your committee too. Don't worry."

"I'm not worried," I called, grinning as he walked back to Deirdre.

When she put her hand on his shoulder, my smile faded. I tried telling myself not to be upset. Ned is an amazing boyfriend, and I trust him completely. He was only helping Deirdre because he was too nice to say no. I knew that—yet, for some reason, I still had this icky feeling in the pit of my stomach.

# 6

# Following Leads

**T**he next day, **I** spent the entire morning trying to track down some sort of information about Peter Sandover. My first stop was with Layton Bourdevarx, a local painter who lives at the other end of town. I figured that if there was new competition, Layton would know all about it.

Layton was helpful. He hadn't heard of any business called Peter Paints, but he was able to give me some good leads: three hardware stores that had the best prices on paints. Anyone in the business would go to one of those three, he was sure.

After calling Justine to find out what color the shelter was going to be painted, I went to each of the three hardware stores—but not one could recall selling any paint to Peter.

"Are you absolutely positive?" I asked the salesman at the third shop, just to make sure. "He's a tall guy with bleached-blond hair, and he would have been buying eggshell white. He may have been using a different name."

The salesman shook his head. "Sorry, Nancy. I've checked my sales records. No one has bought eggshell white in weeks. Other versions of off-white, sure—but not eggshell."

"Okay, well, thanks for your help," I said as I made my way out of the store.

Once in my car, I pulled out my cell phone and called all of the other nonprofits in town to see if Peter had offered to paint their buildings. He hadn't.

Next, I called some apartment buildings and the local real estate agencies to see if there were any new people in town who matched Peter's description. A couple of brokers mentioned David Wells, but it seemed like he was the only new guy in town. No one had heard of any Peter Sandover. Even going by just his description got me nowhere. Apparently, no tall, blond, pale, green-eyed guy in his thirties had recently moved to town—or if he had, he hadn't gone through normal channels to find a place to live.

I was starting to get suspicious. Worse than that, I was out of leads. How do you track down a guy who isn't who he says he is? A guy who may not even exist?

The only thing I could think to do was try a new angle. No one can develop land in River Heights without a permit, and the whole Rackham Industries connection to the River Heights Animal Shelter was curious. It definitely merited further investigation, so I headed to city hall.

Ms. Talby, the secretary of the Land Use Department, knows me very well, and was happy to give me access to the archives in the basement of the building.

Digging through the recent permit applications, it didn't take me long to find the file that I needed. Turns out, Rackham Industries had filed their request to expand their property weeks before the fire. All the plans had been worked out and submitted by an architect. That meant someone who wanted to build had assumed that the animal shelter wouldn't be a problem. Yet Justine assured me she'd told Rackham in no uncertain terms that she had no intention of selling. I dug through the file until I found the person at Rackham who had applied for the permit: David Wells.

I had to wonder, did David grow tired of hearing Justine say no, and decide to take matters into his own hands? Did he wake up in the early morning hours to set the fire, and then wait until the building was almost destroyed to call the fire department? Did he have some connection to Peter Sandover, or to whoever was pretending to be a painter named Peter Sandover? Or was that just a strange coincidence?

I wanted to look into things further, but then I noticed the time.

Justine and I had plans to meet at Mugged near the university. Of all the Muggeds in town—and there are a bunch—that one's my favorite, and I was going to be late.

As I was driving over, George called me on my cell. She was all excited because she'd created a website for the show, so it was now possible to buy tickets online. They'd sold two hundred tickets in the first few hours that the website was up.

I was eager to share the great news with Justine. Once I got to Mugged, I ordered a cappuccino and then went to find her.

She already had a table at the back of the coffee shop. From the looks of the area—she had books all over the place, three open notebooks, an empty coffee mug, and a plate with a half-eaten croissant—she'd been there for a while.

"Hey, Justine," I said, sitting down across from her. "How's the studying going?"

"Hi, Nancy," she said. "It's been better. You wouldn't believe how many bones there are in the body of an anteater. Here's something I have to re-create from memory on Thursday morning."

She showed me an intricate-looking diagram of an anteater with at least one hundred arrows pointing to various bones and body parts. At the bottom of the page was a list of names printed in tiny letters. Just looking at it gave me a headache.

"Anyway," said Justine, closing her textbook and rubbing her temples with her fingertips, "Harold told me about the meeting last night. I am so thrilled that you're doing such a great job."

"It's my pleasure," I said. "I just hope we raise enough money to rebuild."

"You're not the only one," said Justine. "But when we spoke, it sounded kind of urgent. What's up?"

"Well, for one thing, I've been trying to track down Peter Sandover everywhere, and I can't find him." As I explained the steps I'd taken to find Peter, the worry lines around Justine's eyes deepened.

"So you think he may have something to do with the fire?" she asked. "I don't know why I trusted him. This is all my fault. I feel horrible."

"It's not your fault," I said. "And this is just a theory. But you won't believe what I found out about David Wells."

Justine leaned in closer and whispered, "What?"

I lowered my voice too. "He filed the paperwork to get a permit for his expansion into the animal shelter's property weeks before the fire. It's almost as if he knew what would happen—that the River Heights Animal Shelter wasn't a real obstacle. I'm wondering if he hired someone to pose as a painter to get the key to building."

Justine shook her head. "Well, that would certainly explain the news I just got from Chief Cloud."

My ears perked up. "What's that?"

"He said the fire was definitely set from the inside. That means whoever started it probably had a key."

"How many keys were there?" I asked.

"Four," said Justine. "I had one, and two employees had keys. And there was one spare key, which I gave to Peter Sandover."

"Does Chief McGinnis know about this?" I asked.

"He does," said Justine with a sigh. "But Chief McGinnis seems to think that a fire starting from the inside supports Chief Cloud's original theory about electrical problems."

"Even though he knows you just had the building inspected?" I asked.

"Even so," Justine replied gravely.

"That's crazy," I said. "It could be so many things. Chief Cloud didn't rule out arson, did he?"

"Nope." Justine shook her head. "I tried to tell him, Nancy. And please, do me a favor—don't talk to Chief McGinnis. I don't want your dad getting upset with me. He's doing so much to help out. How will it look if I get his only daughter into trouble?"

I took a sip of my cappuccino to hide my disappointment. "I can promise you I won't talk to the police chief yet, but I'm not going to stop investigating the fire. There are too many loose ends. I can't just walk away from this."

"And I wouldn't ask you to. Please, just be careful," said Justine.

"I will," I said. "Don't worry."

After quizzing Justine on anteater anatomy, I went home for a quick dinner before the evening concert committee meeting.

Before I even walked into the conference room, Deirdre pulled me aside. "Nancy, we need to talk," she said, in an urgent-sounding whisper. She had a piece of paper in her hand. Thinking it was connected to the fire investigation, since that's all I had on my mind, I followed her down the hall.

"What is it?" I asked.

Deirdre smiled. "Nancy, I hate that I have to show you this. Believe me, it's not easy. I feel horrible, I truly do. But you can't control people's feelings, can you?"

"What are you talking about, DeeDee?" DeeDee is Deirdre's nickname from back when we were kids. She can't stand it when I call her that, and I actually wasn't trying to annoy her. The nickname just popped right out of my mouth.

"It's Deirdre," she answered curtly. "And I think you'd better take a look at this."

She handed me the paper. It was a note, scrawled in pencil.

Deirdre,
I love the way your green eyes shine.
I only wish that you were mine.
Sincerely, N

"What is this supposed to be?" I asked, completely confused.

"A love letter," Deirdre replied, unable to restrain the huge smile on her face, "from your boyfriend."

I looked back down at the note. It was signed by N, which I guess she thought stood for Ned. As if.

"First of all," I said, "this isn't even Ned's handwriting."

Deirdre grabbed the note out of my hands. "Maybe he wanted to disguise his normal writing so you wouldn't find out."

I shook my head. "There's no way. Ned is not a sneaky guy, and we've always had a very honest relationship. If he was interested in someone else, he'd tell me and we'd stop dating."

Deirdre carefully folded the note and placed it in her purse. "Keep believing that, Nancy Drew," she said. "But when all is said and done, you can't say I never warned you."

# 7

# Ollie or Riley?

**I was really stuck.** Somehow I knew that David Wells was connected to the fire. I just didn't know how. Nor did I have enough evidence to prove that he was guilty. And I couldn't even approach him. Something told me that even if I asked David the most innocent question, he'd run straight to Chief McGinnis. The two had become very chummy all of a sudden. I saw them eating lunch at the local steak house yesterday. And over breakfast this morning, my dad happened to mention that David had joined the police chief's weekly poker game.

My best link to David was through Stefan. I waited for him after the next meeting. He was on the security team, which got out just a few minutes after my team. As I walked him out to the parking lot, I asked,

"So, I was wondering. Do the Rackham executives know about the concert and how big it's going to be? I'll bet they're worried about not getting that land."

"I don't know," said Stefan. "That's not the kind of thing I'm involved in."

"Oh," I said. This wasn't going so well, but I wasn't about to give up. "What department did you say you worked in again?"

Stefan's eyes darted to the left and then right as he ran his hands through his short hair. That was funny. When we met, he was bald. I'd assumed he'd lost all his hair naturally Now it was clear that he had hair, but that he'd recently shaved his head for some reason. "I never told you," he said. "But it's new business development."

"So does that mean that David Wells is your boss?" I asked.

"No," Stefan replied quickly.

"Oh, I thought he told me that he was the vice president of new business development."

"Well, he is," said Stefan. "So I guess he is, technically, but I have a lot of bosses. You know how it is at these big corporations. It's a huge department, so I don't even work that closely with him. In fact, we hardly ever talk."

This was weird. From the research I'd done, it sounded like Stefan and David worked very closely.

Yet he was so quick to deny it. I framed my next comment carefully. "Nikki Kolista must be his biggest nightmare."

It may have been my imagination, but Stefan seemed to bristle at the mention of Nikki. "Look," he said as he backed away from me, "I don't know why you're asking me about this. I really don't know anything. And, in fact, this is my car. I'd better go. Riley is waiting."

"Riley?" I asked.

"Yes, my golden retriever, Riley," he replied as he quickly opened his car door and then slid into the driver's seat.

"How many dogs do you have, Stefan?" I asked.

"Just one. See you later, Nancy," he replied as he slammed the door shut, and quickly sped off.

As I watched the lights from Stefan's silver sports car disappear into the distance, I knew he was guilty of something. The other day, his dog was named Ollie. And now it was Riley? He couldn't even keep his dog's name straight, which probably meant that there was no dog. Perhaps his whole interest in animals was a front.

I couldn't be sure that Stefan had anything to do with the fire, but I did have a feeling that he was spying for David. If only I could prove it.

I turned around to head back inside and found myself face-to-face with George.

"Hey, George. Things are getting more compli-
cated with the whole fire investigation. I think that
maybe Stefan is involved. Have you noticed anything
strange about him?"

George stared at me with this strange look on
her face, like she had news but dreaded sharing it
with me.

"Did you hear me?" I asked.

"Yeah," she said, kicking at the asphalt with the
toe of her sneaker. "But that's not why I came out
here to find you. The thing is, you would not believe
what Deirdre is doing."

"Deirdre?" She was the last person on my mind.
I couldn't even be bothered. "Who cares about her?
Look, I think that Stefan Kinsley has something to
hide. Maybe he and David are working together to
sabotage the concert. I don't know what's going on
exactly, but we need to get to the bottom of it before
it's too late."

"Okay," said George. "But the thing is . . ."

"Did you tell her?" asked Bess, who was rushing
outside with a worried expression on her face.

"I was about to," said George.

"Tell me what?" I asked.

"Deirdre just invited your boyfriend to some
dance at the country club," said Bess.

"Ned would never go out with Deirdre," I replied.

George and Bess looked at each other without speaking.

"What?" I asked.

"I'm sure he doesn't want to go," said Bess. Her blue eyes were downcast. "But Deirdre is kind of forcing him to."

"She gave him some whole sob story about how her date canceled on her and she's got no one to go with and it's really important to her," said George. "If you ask me, it's a lot of nonsense."

"That, I'd believe," I said. "Anyway, I can't worry about this sort of thing. The more time I waste on thinking about Deirdre, the less time I have for the River Heights Animal Shelter."

"You're right. How's the investigation going?" asked Bess.

"Not well." I shook my head. "I can't find any evidence that this guy Peter Sandover ever existed. I have a feeling that he was actually some random guy who was hired by David Wells to pretend to be a painter so he could get the key. What I don't have is any evidence to prove it. Now I think Stefan is involved too, and I have this icky feeling that things are about to go horribly wrong."

"What if the painter was David Wells himself?" asked George.

"I considered that, but it's impossible," I said.

"David is short with dark hair. The painter was tall and blond. Plus, this Peter guy had green eyes, and David's eyes are brown."

"Someone could dye their hair pretty easily or even wear colored contacts," said Bess. "But I guess height is pretty much a constant."

"Yes," I said. "That's what I was thinking."

"So what's our next move?" wondered George.

"I was just figuring that out," I said, happy that she said 'our' next move, because I definitely needed their help. "I probably need to pay a visit to Rackham Industries after hours, though. Say, at midnight, tonight . . . anyone care to join me?"

Bess and George didn't answer me with words. They didn't need to. From the mischievous grins on their faces, I knew exactly what their answer was.

# 8

# Breaking and Entering

**My adrenaline was pumping** as I slipped out of my house at midnight. I felt like some sort of criminal, which made sense. Not only was I sneaking around like a thief, I was also dressed like one, in dark jeans, gray sneakers, surgical gloves (so I wouldn't leave fingerprints anywhere), and a hooded black sweat-shirt.

I felt bad not telling my dad what I was doing, but I had no choice. He'd never let me leave the house at such a late hour. And breaking into Rackham? Well, there was no way he'd support that.

I had to do it, though. There was too much at stake. I waited on the corner, down the block, for Bess and George to pick me up. Shivering in the cold darkness, I tried not to think about Ned, who would have picked up Deirdre hours ago for the dance. He was probably looking really cute in his navy blue, pin-striped suit. I knew he was only escorting her because he was too polite to say no, so I don't know why I was letting it bother me.

I glanced at my watch, again. It was ten minutes after twelve.

Suddenly I saw blinding white headlights pop up over the hill. Hiding behind a tree, I watched them get closer. It was such a relief when I realized it was Bess and George.

Once they stopped, I climbed into the backseat of the car. Bess and George were also wearing black, although George's shirt was button-down and Bess's had a lace trim.

"Hey, thanks for picking me up. Are you guys ready for this?" I asked.

"I guess," said Bess. Her hair was swept up in a twist and secured with a black velvet bow. Only Bess could turn breaking and entering into an excuse to wear glamorous accessories. And yet, despite her fashionable attire, she seemed nervous.

"Don't worry," I said. "You guys don't even have to go inside. I just need you to drop me off and to be on the lookout."

"What are you searching for, exactly?" asked George.

"That's the problem," I said, fiddling with my flash-light to make sure it still worked. "I'm not entirely sure."

"Whatever it is, I hope you find it," said Bess. "The concert is only a couple of nights away. And if you think David Wells was crazy enough to burn down the shelter, who knows what he might do to stop the benefit."

"No pressure," George added.

As if. I took a deep breath. "The concert will be amazing," I said. "There is nothing David can do to ruin it. Bess, are you still working with Nikki's manager to arrange her flight?"

Bess nodded. "Yup, it's all taken care of. She's arriving at two o'clock on Saturday. I'd pick her up from the airport myself, but that's when we have the first sound check. Mrs. Diver wants me to be there in case any of the equipment is down."

"That's a good idea," I said. Bess would be able to fix any type of mechanical problem. "And I'm happy to pick up Nikki."

"I'll come too," said George. "And, actually, would you mind if Scott joined us? He's been bugging me about Nikki ever since we started organizing this show."

"There's plenty of room for Scott," I said. "Don't worry."

"Thanks," said George. "I know it'll mean a lot to him."

As we approached the Rackham Industries office park, everyone stopped talking. I guess my friends were as nervous as I was.

Bess parked around the corner, off the paved road and in the middle of a clump of trees, so her car wasn't in view. "I really hope this works," she said nervously as she cut the engine.

"You're not the only one," I replied, stepping out of the car.

We walked through the woods, downhill and around the buildings, until we were at the main structure. It was the largest one and in the middle of the group. The buildings had been around for years, and the locks on the doors were the old-fashioned kind, which meant that it was easy to open them with a carefully placed bobby pin. I pulled one from my hair, bent it into place, and put it in the keyhole, fiddling around until I heard a faint click. Then I pulled the door open.

Before walking inside, I turned to Bess and George. "I'll keep my cell phone on. If you see anyone coming, call me."

"Will do," George whispered.

"Good luck," said Bess.

"Thanks," I replied. "I'll need it." I slipped on

through, closing the door behind me.

The office was dark, so I had to turn my flashlight on to look around. The first things I noticed were all of the cubicles spread out across the floor, each with identical desks and computers. There were two rows of printer banks at the front, and offices along either side. I figured a vice president like David Wells would have a corner office. They're usually bigger and go to the employees who are higher up on the corporate food chain. I headed to the corner office closest to me and opened the door. I tiptoed across the room carefully, even though I knew I was alone, and inspected the desk. On top of it was a framed photo of a gray-haired man and what I assumed were his kids and wife. There was a stack of business cards in a cardholder, which told me that this office belonged to someone named Jason Bristol.

Walking out, I moved across the hall to the next corner office and aimed my flashlight at the door. Bingo. The nameplate read DAVID WELLS.

I went inside and surveyed the office. At first glance, there was nothing out of the ordinary. It was meticulously neat, and impersonal. At one end sat a black leather couch. On the other end, a large glass desk. In the center was a coffee table with a stack of magazines—mostly golf- and cigar-related.

Much to my disappointment, there was no closet. I figured that meant there was no place to hide anything, but then I noticed the file cabinet by David's desk. It had three drawers. Crouching next to it, I pulled on the top drawer. It was locked, but that wouldn't be a problem. Using my bobby pin again, I had it open within a matter of seconds.

The first two drawers revealed nothing out of the ordinary—just a bunch of files about the financials of Rackham Industries. It was the same story with the third drawer. I was feeling disappointed when something occurred to me. The files in the bottom drawer sat so much higher than the ones in the other two drawers. That probably meant there was something underneath them.

Lowering my ear to the bottom of the drawer, I knocked. It sounded hollow. I wondered if there was something hidden inside.

I quickly pulled out the files and felt around the bottom of the drawer. It was smooth black metal, with a looped handle in the back. I pulled on the handle and the entire bottom opened up. Beaming my flashlight down, I could hardly believe what I found inside: a bottle of peroxide, some decals with PETER PAINTS printed on them, and a couple of pieces of paper. One was a flyer advertising a new painting business, signed by Peter Sandover.

The other was a letter addressed to the CEO of Rackham Industries. It read:

Dear Mr. Halloran,
Plans for the expansion are moving along smoothly. The city has approved the architect's plans. There's one small stumbling block, but I'm working out how to fix it. Once this is resolved, I expect a promotion.
Sincerely,
David Wells

I read the letter twice more, getting angrier each time. That small stumbling block had to refer to the River Heights Animal Shelter. David was definitely behind the fire, and now I had the evidence to prove it. Not that I took any joy in learning the truth. I couldn't believe anyone could be so heartless. Sure, it looked like he went out of his way to come up with a plan to keep the animals from being burned with the building. But he'd still destroyed their home. He'd still tried to obliterate a nonprofit agency all in the name of corporate greed.

I was so wrapped up in my thoughts that I didn't even notice my cell phone was ringing until it was too late. I missed the call, but saw on my caller ID that it was Bess. I dialed her number right away.

Bess picked up on the first ring. "I'm sorry I didn't call sooner," she said in a breathless tone of voice. "I had to run to a place where they wouldn't hear me. There are cop cars here, two of them. I was hiding in the woods when George tried to distract them. Someone is chasing her right now. And it looks like an officer is approaching the building."

"Yikes!" I said. "Can you tell who it is?"

"Nope," said Bess. "Not from here. Look, I'm going to hang out here for a while. Try to meet me at the car after they leave."

"Will do."

"Good luck, Nancy."

"Thanks," I said.

Hanging up, I could already hear the door to Rackham opening. I hid David's letter, the Peter Paints flyer, and the stickers in my back pocket. I slipped the peroxide bottle into the waistband of my jeans. Then I closed the false bottom, replaced the files, and closed the cabinet.

Next, I ducked down and crawled out of David's office. I could hear someone's footsteps. It sounded like they were opposite the exit, which was about ten feet away. The door was loud and heavy. There's no way I'd be able to leave through it undetected. I had to find another option. It was then that I noticed the window right above my head. If I acted quickly, I'd be able to climb out.

The officer's back was to me, so I quickly popped up, unlocked the window, and opened it. It squeaked loudly, so I dove down behind the bank of printers. Peeking out from behind it, I saw a flashlight beam sweep the area. Luckily, it completely missed me and the open window. When it pointed in the other direction, I hurried back over.

Leaping up, I had my head out the window and could feel the night air and all the freedom it offered. I hoisted one leg up over the windowsill and was almost all the way out when I felt a hand on my ankle.

Turning around, a beam of light flashed in my eyes and someone bellowed, "Well, if it isn't Nancy Drew."

I dropped back down inside, holding up my hands. Whoever it was lowered the beam. I blinked, and my eyes adjusted to the darkness.

Once I recognized the face behind the flashlight, I let out a nervous laugh. "Chief McGinnis," I said. "Funny seeing you here."

# 9

## A Long Ride Home

**B**eaking and entering a private building," said Chief McGinnis, "at one o'clock in the morning."

Chief McGinnis almost never looks happy to see me, but now he seemed downright furious. I felt bad, and not just for getting caught. The way he accused me made me realize something. Breaking and entering was wrong, even if I was only doing it to prevent a bigger wrong. I was in serious trouble. Yes, I had evidence linking David Wells to the fire, but it's not like I could tell the chief that. The timing couldn't have been worse.

"Guilty as charged," I mumbled as I followed Chief McGinnis out to the parking lot, where two squad cars were parked.

"Hi, Nancy," said Joe Rees, another River Heights

police officer who was, fortunately for me, a friend. He was casually leaning against the hood of his car.

"Hi, Joe," I mumbled sheepishly.

"Nancy Drew, is that you?" Sergeant Emily Kim asked as she stepped out of the woods, pulling leaves from her hair.

Feeling my face burn red with embarrassment, all I could do was wave.

"Where's the other one?" asked Chief McGinnis.

Sergeant Kim shook her head. "I couldn't get a positive ID. Whoever it was, was too fast."

Phew, I was happy that George and Bess got away, at least. With hope, they were on their way home, soon to be safe in bed.

The chief turned back to me. "I suppose you're not going to tell us who you were with," he grumbled.

"I'm here alone," I replied. Well, technically, it was true. There was no need to turn in George and Bess. This was my idea, and if anyone had to get into trouble, it should be me and me alone.

"What are you doing out here, anyway?" asked the chief.

I shrugged, which seemed to anger him even more.

"I should really take you downtown for questioning," he said. "But I don't want to put your father through that."

"I've learned my lesson," I said quickly. "This won't happen again, sir. I'm really, truly sorry."

"Hah," said the chief. "I'll believe that when I see it. I'm going to stick around and see if I can't find anyone else. It's the least I can do, after being woken up in the middle of the night over this. Joe, will you take Nancy home?"

"Sure thing, boss," said Joe, opening the front door of his squad car for me.

Before I could get inside, Chief McGinnis said, "Nancy has to ride in back."

Joe looked at me, mouthed a silent apology, and then opened up the back door.

With heavy shoulders and a sinking heart, I climbed inside. The backseat of a police car is one of my least favorite places in the world.

I don't end up there very often, but whenever I do, I feel so suffocated. That's probably because it's nearly impossible to get out of the backseat of a police car alone. They're designed with no door handles so that criminals can't escape. There is also wire mesh and bulletproof glass separating the passenger compartment from the front seat. It's an uneasy feeling, riding in the back. I guess Chief McGinnis wanted to teach me a lesson, and I suppose I deserved it. At least he'd let Joe drive me home.

"So, how did you find me?" I asked Joe as we pulled away from the office park.

He glanced at me in the rearview mirror and said, "Rackham has a silent alarm system now."

I crossed my arms over my chest. This was news to me. "Huh."

"There's a lot of changes over there," Joe went on. "They've got some new hotshot MBA from Harvard, and he's trying to double productivity by the end of the year. Pretty soon, Rackham could take over this entire city."

"David Wells, you mean?" I asked.

Joe nodded. "That's the guy."

"Do you know him?" I asked.

"Not personally, but Chief McGinnis does. So, do I even need to ask what you were doing, sneaking around here at this hour?" asked Joe.

The evidence burned a hole in my pocket. I was afraid to turn it over, though. I needed to think of a foolproof way to catch David Wells.

"I think I'll take the fifth," I said.

"Suit yourself," said Joe, with a shrug. "I'm sure it'll come to light soon."

"It will," I assured him.

"But don't forget, any evidence you may have found at Rackham can't be used in court."

"Huh?" I said.

"Well, you're not the police, and you didn't have a search warrant. If you try to use what you found, you could end up in jail yourself."

"What for?" I asked.

"Breaking and entering, trespassing, theft," said Joe. "And those are just the obvious three. I'm sure Rackham's lawyers would come up with all sorts of stuff."

Just then, something occurred to me. "What makes you think I found anything?" I asked.

I saw, through the rearview mirror, that Joe was grinning. "There's a slight bulge in the back of your shirt," he said. "But you didn't hear it from me. In fact, let's just say that I, like Chief McGinnis, never even noticed it."

I couldn't help but smile. "Notice what?" I asked.

"Exactly," Joe replied.

Moments later we drove past the gates to Mission Hill, and then past Deirdre's country club. I saw Ned's car, and then something even worse: Ned himself. He was opening the door for Deirdre. It's not like they were holding hands or anything, but they were laughing.

I sank down farther in my seat. The last thing I needed was for them to see me in the back of a squad car. Now I was fuming. I just couldn't believe they were out so late together. Ned told me he was going because he was obligated, but he seemed to be having a good time. What did that mean?

If Officer Rees noticed that my boyfriend was out with Deirdre, he didn't say so, and I was grateful for that. We sat in silence for the rest of the trip. After pulling up in front of my house, he got out of the car and opened the backseat door for me. "Have a good night, Nancy. Good luck with everything."

"Thank you," I replied, before disappearing into the house.

After hiding the evidence in my bottom drawer, I changed out of my clothes and slipped into bed. I couldn't sleep, though. There was too much on my mind. Joe had raised a good point. Yes, I now had enough evidence linking David Wells to the crime, but I'd have to prove it some other way.

The case kept me up most of the night. I must have fallen asleep at some point, though, because the next thing I knew, the sun was streaming in through my blinds, making stripes on my plain blue bedspread.

Almost as soon as I opened my eyes, it came to me. Stefan Kinsley worked with David. He was tall and pale, and he had green eyes. His hair was short and dark, but who knows what it looked like before he shaved it?

What if he shaved his head because he had to hide

the fact that he'd dyed it blond? David Wells must have made him pretend to be Peter Sandover to get the keys to the shelter. And if Justine could identify him, we'd be that much closer to proving that David Wells was guilty.

Throwing the covers back, I reached for my phone and dialed Justine's number.

"Hello?" she said in a sleepy voice.

Jumping out of bed, I paced back and forth across my bedroom floor. "I'm sorry to wake you, but this is an emergency. I need your help with something."

"What is it, Nancy?" asked Justine.

"Can you come to the benefit concert meeting tonight? I think I found Peter Sandover."

"Um," said Justine, "I think I can rearrange my study group. What time is the meeting?"

"Six o'clock," I said.

"Okay," said Justine. "I'll be there."

"Perfect."

As soon as we hung up, I called George. "Are you okay?" she asked. "I left you a million messages on your cell phone."

"I know, I'm sorry. I was too depressed to call back. Chief McGinnis caught me, but it all worked out okay. You'll never guess what I found in David Wells's office. . . ."

After explaining my theory to George, I called Bess. They both thought it all sounded just crazy enough to be true.

That night, I waited for Justine outside, feeling really anxious. Before she even showed up, though, Deirdre walked over to me.

"Ned and I had the best time last night," she said.

"Glad to hear it," I replied coolly. No way was I going to let her know how much it bothered me. "Ned's sweet that way. He's always willing to help out a friend in need. Even people who aren't friends. He's the kind of guy who just can't say no."

If Deirdre saw where I was going with my conversation, she ignored it. Flipping her hair over her shoulder, she smiled and said, "I'd no idea your boyfriend was such a good dancer."

I shrugged. I mean, really, what could I say to that? "How's the party planning coming along?" I asked, trying to change the subject.

"It's so great," said Deirdre. "I managed to secure the garden room at the country club. It's small, so there'll only be room for about fifty people, but that's okay. Sometimes more intimate is much nicer, don't you agree?"

"Sure," I said. "And we have about twenty-five

volunteers, so as long as there's room for them."

"Um, actually, I'm not going to be able to invite all the volunteers," said Deirdre.

"You're kidding, right?" I asked.

Deirdre shook her head. "This is a VIP party, Nancy. And there are so many important people in River Heights. Don't you think it would be better for Nikki to spend time with them? I'm sure she's not going to want to hang out with the regular people."

"*Regular* people?" I said, completely incredulous. Just when I think Deirdre has strayed as far from the realm of decent behavior as she can, she takes another step. "It's regular people who have worked so hard to make this concert happen," I said.

"Sure, whatever," she said, handing me a note. "That's not what I wanted to talk to you about, anyway. I need to show you this."

We've met many times and you always play it cool,
But believe me, Deirdre, I'm no fool.
There's no need to hide how we really do feel.
It's time to find out if this could be the real deal.
After the concert, it won't be too late
For us to go on a really fun date.
Sincerely, N

Okay, this was getting ridiculous. I handed the note back to her. "I'm telling you, Deirdre, this isn't from Ned. I just know it. For one thing, that poetry is lousy. He'd do much better."

"Maybe he was in a hurry," said Deidre, happily as she placed the note back in her purse. "We'll find out soon enough, won't we?"

I was so glad I spotted Justine just then at the other end of the parking lot. "Sure thing, Deirdre. Gotta run."

Hurrying over to Justine, I said, "Thanks so much for coming."

"You're welcome, Nancy. I just wish I could stay longer, but I have an exam first thing in the morning."

"This won't take long," I said, leading her into the conference room, where all of the subcommittees were grouped.

Scanning the crowd in search of Stefan/Peter's face, I was disappointed to see that he wasn't even there.

I was about to apologize to Justine when I noticed she was staring at someone else. Pointing across the room, she said, "I think that's him."

Thinking I must have missed him, I followed her gaze.

Then I gasped. Justine was pointing to a tall, pale guy with green eyes and blond hair, but he wasn't Stefan Kinsley.

"Are you sure about this?" I asked.

Justine squinted. "I'm not positive, but it certainly could be him."

I really wished that Stefan had showed. That way, Justine would have someone to compare him to. The guy she was pointing to now was none other than my dentist, Dr. Wolfson.

Did he have some sort of secret connection to David Wells? What could have motivated him to pose as a painter? Clearly there was more work to be done.

The problem was, we were running out of time.

# 10

# Star Struck

**J**ust remember, don't ask for her autograph right away," George warned her brother Scott, who sat in the backseat of my car, wearing a Flying Monkeys T-shirt and carrying his collection of Nikki's CDs in his lap.

"I won't," Scott promised.

"She's had a busy morning of travel, and she's doing us a huge favor," George went on. "So just act friendly, welcoming, and relaxed."

I couldn't believe it was already Saturday afternoon, just hours before the concert, and that I was on my way to the airport to pick up Nikki Kolista. Throwing together the benefit concert so quickly had been thrilling, but also exhausting. I got so busy with last-minute details that I hadn't even had time to get additional proof that David Wells was responsible for the fire. I guess I'd have to worry about that after the show.

"A lot of celebrities just want to be treated like normal people," George said, looking over her shoulder at Scott. "Nikki, especially. I've read a lot about her."

"I said I won't ask her for an autograph. I promise to act totally normal," said Scott, rolling his eyes. "Will you please just chill, Georgia?"

"And don't call me Georgia," said George.

"Why not? It's your name," Scott said, kicking the back of George's seat lightly.

He had a point, but I wasn't about to say so.

Nor did I voice my own concern about Nikki. Since she was Deirdre's first cousin and a world-famous rock star, I had this fear that she would be a snob—as if perhaps Deirdre's snobby attitude were genetic. I was so nervous about meeting her that I'd asked Deirdre if she wanted to pick up Nikki instead. Deirdre claimed to be too busy organizing the party at the country club. "I'm not a chauffeur" I believe were her exact words, which she delivered with a disdainful sneer.

I parked my car in the airport lot, and by the time I got out and locked the doors, George and Scott were already halfway across the parking lot. I had to run to catch up with them.

Nikki's flight had landed early, so there were lots

of passengers from Seattle milling around the baggage claim. Even though the airport was crowded, it wasn't hard to find her. For one thing, the River Heights Municipal Airport is pretty small. But more significantly, Nikki looked just like she did on TV: petite and muscular, with pale skin and long, curly, black and bright pink hair.

Today Nikki was dressed pretty casually, in dark blue jeans and a faded purple T-shirt. She wore a green baseball cap pulled down low.

"Hi, Nikki," I said as I approached. "I'm Nancy Drew. I'll be driving you to the concert hall downtown."

Nikki smiled warmly. "It's so nice to meet you," she said as she offered her hand.

"It's a pleasure meeting you, too," I replied, relieved. Already she seemed much nicer than Deirdre. "Thanks so much for coming to River Heights. It means so much to us all. Please meet my friends George and Scott Fayne."

Nikki gave a small wave to the two, and said to Scott, "Nice T-shirt."

"Thanks," said Scott. "I'm a huge fan of your music."

"That's so great to hear," Nikki replied.

I took Nikki's duffel bag from her hand. Scott reached for her guitar, but she pulled it away. "Um, actually, I always carry this myself," she said with a sheepish grin. "Call me superstitious, but I always need to be within a few feet of my guitar. I even sleep with it under my bed because whenever it's out of reach, I get really nervous."

"That's cool," said Scott. "The car is this way. Come on, I'll show you."

As we followed Scott back to the parking lot, I noticed that George still hadn't said a word.

"Are you okay?" I asked in a whisper.

But George didn't hear me. She was too busy rushing ahead and opening the car door for Nikki.

"Thanks, George," said Nikki.

"Can I have your autograph?" George blurted out. Then, as her eyes widened in surprise and embarrassment, she covered her mouth with both hands. "I'm *so* sorry," she said. "I can't believe I said that!"

"Neither can I," mumbled Scott.

"It's no big deal," said Nikki, pulling a pen out of her back pocket. "What should I sign?"

George felt the pockets of her jeans. "Um, I don't have anything, actually. Wow, this is so embarrassing."

Shaking his head, Scott handed his sister a CD, which she passed along to Nikki.

Once that was out of the way, we all got in the car and drove back into town, with Nikki in the front seat and George slumped in back, looking completely mortified. Scott was next to her and he wore a mischievous grin. Poor George. I just knew her little brother would be teasing her about this moment for a long time.

"So, when was the last time you were in River Heights?" I asked.

Nikki shook her head. "It's been a long time. I went away for college and then moved to London. I was living in Europe when I met the other Flying Monkeys and we sold our first album. Soon after that, we all moved to Seattle. I've been touring off and on for the past few years. Somehow, I've just never found the time to visit."

"But you still have family here, right?" I asked.

"Not really," Nikki replied. "My parents and my brother moved to Chicago years ago."

"But what about the Shannons?" asked George.

Nikki looked out the window at the tall trees and rolling green hills. "Oh, right," she said. "The Shannons. How could I forget?" Turning back to me, she asked, "So, what's the deal with the shelter? How did the fire happen?"

Feeling my shoulders tense up, I frowned. "That's the problem. We still don't know exactly. It could have been an accident, or there might be more to the story. I have my suspicions, but no proof." I went on to tell her about the Rackham Industry threat to the land, leaving out the parts about David Wells and the mysterious painter. There was no need to worry Nikki. Still, even though I didn't say so directly, Nikki seemed to sense that there was more to the story.

"That's the funny thing about River Heights," she said. "On the surface it seems like such a nice place to live. Yet, when you look more closely, there always seems to be something more going on—something brewing beneath the surface. It's almost like the town is somehow cursed."

"We can't argue with you there," I said. "But, luckily, we've raised so much money, thanks to you, that the animals will probably be saved, regardless of whether the mystery is ever solved."

We were approaching downtown. When I turned onto River Street, I could tell that Nikki was getting more excited. "Wow, the concert hall looks exactly the same. I can't believe I'm going to be performing there."

George laughed. "Nikki, you've performed at the most famous clubs in New York, all over Europe, and even in Tokyo, and you're excited about a show here in little old River Heights?"

"Yeah," said Nikki. "This is different. I can't explain it, really, but there's something about coming back to your hometown. There's so much history and so many memories."

"Do you keep in touch with anyone you knew back then?" asked George.

Nikki took off her hat and ran her fingers through her hair. "Not really," she said.

"Well, Mrs. Diver sure is excited about seeing you," I said.

"Oh, I can't wait to see her," Nikki said. "Does she still teach?"

"She sure does," said Scott. "I used to take drum lessons from her."

As I pulled up in front of the concert hall, I said good-bye to Nikki. "Thank you, again, for being here. This means so much to us. I need to go run some errands, but George and Scott are going to take you to your dressing room and make sure you get settled."

"Okay," said Nikki. "Thanks for the ride. It was really nice meeting you, too, Nancy."

I waved. "I'll see you in a couple of hours."

"Definitely," Nikki replied as she picked up her guitar case by its handle and headed toward the concert hall. Scott and George followed close behind with her luggage.

As I hurried over to Joshua's bakery to pick up a batch of banana bread, I noticed that it was already four o'clock. There was so much to do before the show, which began at eight o'clock. As the supervisor of all of the committees, it fell to me to make sure everything was running smoothly. This meant I had a lot of phone calls to make, and a lot of people to see.

I called Ned to see if he could help pick up some slack, but when I dialed his cell phone, a female voice answered and said, "Hello?"

"Hi," I said. "I'm sorry. I must have dialed the wrong number."

"Who are you trying to reach?" asked the voice, which sounded so familiar.

"Ned Nickerson," I replied.

"No, this is his phone. Is this Nancy?"

Suddenly I realized who'd answered Ned's phone. I seriously felt my heart skip a beat. "Deirdre?" I said, hoping it wouldn't be her.

"Yes, this is she. Ned left his phone at my house last night."

"At your house?" I asked. "Last night?"

"Yes, we were working on the party stuff. And then we watched a movie. It was so much fun, Nancy. You should have been there. Or, well . . . I guess you couldn't have been, since you weren't invited." Deirdre giggled.

I didn't want to hear any more. "Is Ned there?" I asked.

"Um, no, but I'm sure he'll be by soon. Should I tell him you called?"

"Sure," I said. Hanging up, I tried Ned at his house, but his mom told me he was out jogging.

I put my phone away. Not only did I not want to worry, but I didn't have time to—so I shoved the thought of Deirdre and Ned out of my mind.

I found Josh quickly at the bakery, and we loaded up my car with delicious-smelling banana bread. Then, after scooting to the concert hall and dropping it all off with Harold and the rest of the food and beverages committee, I went backstage to check in with Mrs. Diver. Luckily the opening act was ready. Everything seemed to be running smoothly until I checked in with the lighting people.

"How's everything going?" I asked Dr. Wolfson, who was bent over one of the spotlights and looking really worried.

"Not good," he replied. "This is the main light, and it's been shattered. It looks like someone kicked it in."

"Weird." I crouched down so I could get a closer look. There was a hole in the center, and the light-bulb was smashed to pieces.

It was pretty ominous, not that I had time to stop and think about it. Whipping out my cell phone, I called a few local lighting stores until I found one that had a replacement light. "Do you have time to drive to Sixth Street to pick up a new light?" I asked.

Dr. Wolfson shook his head. "My car died this morning, so I had to take the bus here. Sorry, Nancy."

"That's okay," I said. "I'll get it."

By the time I made it back to the concert hall with the replacement light, it was time to start the show.

The jazz quartet from the university went on first.

Once I was sure that everything seemed to be falling into place, I went back down to the entrance, where George was collecting tickets with Scott, Nelson, and Bess.

"How is everything going?" I asked.

"Great," said George. "We've sold seventeen hundred tickets so far. That's including the advance-ticket sales, but don't worry. There are still people lined up outside."

I did some quick and simple math in my head. "At ten dollars a piece, that means we've got seventeen thousand dollars so far. We need to sell three hundred more tickets. Do you think there are that many people outside?"

"I hope so," said George. "At the very least, we'll get close."

Close wasn't going to save the animals, but I didn't need to remind my friends of that.

Scott checked his watch. "Nikki is upstairs, meditating. She wanted a five-minute warning," he said. "Which is about a minute away."

"I'll go," I said. "I want to wish her good luck." I headed upstairs and backstage. It was amazing how

106

much work was involved in making sure the concert ran smoothly. I was thrilled it was all going so well.

I knocked on the dressing room door. "Nikki?" I called. "The opening act has just finished, and they're changing the sets. We're going to expect you onstage in about seven minutes, okay?"

Nikki didn't answer.

"Nikki?" I knocked a second time.

Just then, the door opened and out walked Dr. Wolfson. "What are you doing in here?" I asked.

"I wanted to talk to Nikki," said Dr. Wolfson. "But she doesn't seem to be here."

"But she's going to be on in five minutes," I said. "Where could she be?"

Dr. Wolfson shrugged. "I really don't know. Your guess is as good as mine." He hurried off around the corner.

I had the strangest feeling in the pit of my stomach. Walking inside the dressing room, I saw that the place was deserted.

Suddenly the door slammed shut behind me. I jumped, then realized that the window was open and it was the breeze that had forced the door closed.

"Nikki," I called, even though I knew I was alone in the room. "Where could she have gone?" I muttered to myself.

It was then that I noticed Nikki's guitar was

propped up in the corner. Now I *knew* there was something wrong. Nikki had said she was never without her guitar. Why would she have left it now, when she was supposed to perform in five minutes?

Searching the room for some sort of clue, I found a scrap of paper on the floor by the couch. The handwriting on it was messy, as if it had been scrawled out in a rush. It said,

> We have Nikki. Cancel the concert or you'll
> never see her again.

My heart leaped into my throat and I felt short of breath. Who was this "we"? And what had they done with Nikki?

Someone pounded at the door and shouted, "Open up."

I couldn't move. It was like there were anvils strapped to my ankles. I'd brought Nikki Kolista to River Heights, and now she was missing. I knew that David Wells was guilty of causing the fire, yet I hadn't told the authorities. He was obviously dangerous, and I hadn't warned Nikki. Now she was gone—and it was all my fault.

The awful sound of splintering wood filled my ears as someone busted open the door. In rushed Chief McGinnis, followed by Deirdre.

"What are you doing in here?" he asked. "We heard Nikki was missing."

I couldn't speak. Chief McGinnis ripped the note out of my hand and read it out loud. "What's the meaning of this, Nancy?" he asked.

"I just found it," I managed to choke out. "I went to get Nikki to tell her it was almost time, and—"

"Wait a second," Deirdre interrupted, grabbing the note from Chief McGinnis. "Nancy, this is your handwriting."

"No, it's not," I said, completely confused.

Deirdre glared at me, her eyes filled with accusation. She waved the note in my face, asking, "You wrote this, didn't you?"

I turned to her, completely mystified. Did she really say what I thought she said? "Huh?" I said.

"It's you! You kidnapped my cousin," said Deirdre, placing her hands on her hips. "I can't believe you would sink this low."

"No," I said, backing away from her. "How could you—" I shook my head in disbelief. "No! That's crazy, Deirdre."

"This is *so* typical," said Deirdre. "You kidnapped Nikki, and you planted this note—all so you could save her and be the hero. That's what you always do, huh? You just have to be the center of attention."

I looked around, frantic, and tried to swallow the

lump that had formed in my throat. "I don't know what you're talking about. Chief McGinnis, you don't believe her, do you?"

"You're so jealous that Nikki is my cousin," said Deirdre. "You wouldn't even let me pick her up at the airport."

As she stepped forward, I backed away. She was trying to back me into a corner, literally and figuratively.

"You said you were too busy to pick up Nikki, that you were dealing with some party stuff," I said.

Deirdre was relentless. "And you're jealous of my relationship with Ned. You just can't handle the fact that you two may be breaking up."

"We're not breaking up," I cried.

"See how upset you are?" she countered. "I wonder if you burned down the animal shelter too. You did volunteer there, which meant you had access to the building."

"I never had access," I said. "Check with Justine—there were only four keys. This is crazy."

I wished Justine were here to vouch for me, but she was still cramming for exams. She promised to put in an appearance at the concert, but that wouldn't be for another couple of hours.

Bess and George must have heard the commotion, because now they were in the dressing room too.

110

"What's going on?" asked George. "Where's Nikki? The crowd is chanting for her, and she was scheduled to go on a few minutes ago."

Deirdre turned to Chief McGinnis and said, "I cannot believe that you're not questioning Nancy about this."

All this time, the police chief had remained silent. Now he looked down at the note and scratched his head. "It *is* a little strange that you were here alone when Nikki went missing," he said.

"Why don't you talk to Dr. Wolfson," I blurted out, and then immediately regretted it. "He was in here when I tried to get in. He may have left this note." I never jump to conclusions, but I was feeling panicked. I tried to backtrack. "At least, I think it may have been him. It could have been anyone, really. I just don't know how to prove that he's working with David Wells."

"Here we go again with these false accusations of David Wells," said Chief McGinnis. "Nancy, you've gone too far."

He unclipped his handcuffs from his belt.

"Tell him," I said, turning to George and Bess. "Tell him about that night at Rackham. The evidence we found linking David to the crime."

Bess and George both tried to explain, but Chief McGinnis wasn't interested in what they had to say.

He raised his hand, motioning for them to keep quiet. "You claimed you didn't find anything," he said to me pointedly. "And you also said you were alone."

"But I'm telling the truth now," I said. "I promise."

"The thing is, your promises don't mean that much to me anymore," said the chief as he placed my hands behind my back and slapped a pair of handcuffs on my wrists.

"Bess, George, please look into Dr. Wolfson. He really was here," I cried. "And he's the one who told me the spotlight was shattered. I had to run out and buy a new one. Maybe he broke it himself to get me away from Nikki so he could kidnap her."

"There you go again," said Deirdre. "Acting like you're the only one who can get anything done around here. It's highly suspicious."

George shot Deirdre a dirty look. "We believe you, Nancy," she said.

"And call my dad," I said.

"Of course," said Bess. "And I'll just tell everyone that the concert is a bit delayed. We'll find Nikki. This concert will go on. Don't worry at all."

Easy for her to say. As Chief McGinnis led me away in handcuffs, I felt hot tears streaming down my face. I then realized how close to my nightmare of a few nights ago this all was—but it was way worse. This time, it was actually happening, for real.

# 11

# In Trouble—Again

**C**an you at least take the handcuffs off?" I asked Chief McGinnis as he walked me into his office and sat me down in the chair opposite his desk. "Please?"

Police headquarters were only a mile or so from the concert hall. We'd just arrived, but I was already itching to get back.

As upset as I was about being down at the station (and at having to ride in the back of a squad car for the second time in one week), I was even more upset about not being free to find Nikki. She could be in a lot of danger. I tried explaining this to Chief McGinnis, but he didn't want to hear it from me.

"I have all my officers searching the city, Nancy. It's under control."

I tried to argue. "But—"

113

"No buts," he replied sternly.

At least he reached for his keys and undid my handcuffs. As soon as they came off, I started rubbing my wrists. They were aching like crazy. Plus, my skin was itchy and inflamed. "Ouch," I said.

"Hurts to break the law, doesn't it?" asked the chief.

"I don't know about that," I replied, "but it sure hurts to be in handcuffs." I looked him in the eye. "You don't really think I kidnapped Nikki Kolista, do you, Chief McGinnis?"

"Of course not," he replied. "But that doesn't mean you don't deserve to be hauled in. You're not here just because I wanted to get Deirdre Shannon off my back. You are here, Nancy, because you've gone too far. You've been warned many times not to interfere with my department's investigation, and you continue to ignore those warnings. Plus, you broke into a building the other night without a warrant. Obviously, you need to be taught a lesson."

"I'm really sorry for breaking into Rackham," I said, hanging my head low. "It'll never happen again."

"Yeah, tell it to the judge," the chief replied.

"The judge?" I said. Now I really was worried. "Are you going to press charges?"

"No," said the chief, "but I am going to call your father."

In a way, this was worse—especially after Dad's talk earlier in the week. I just hoped that George and Bess were able to speak to him before Chief McGinnis could. Obviously the news would sound much better coming from my friends, who could explain the real story.

Chief McGinnis locked me in his office, and fifteen minutes later my dad showed up. He didn't look happy, but at least he agreed to spring me. As we walked to the car, I tried to apologize

"Dad, I know I wasn't supposed to get involved, but I had no choice. And now Nikki is missing and I have to help find her."

Dad was steely eyed and silent. Rather than answer me, he opened the car door for me and then slammed it shut once I was inside, as if I was going to try to make a run for it.

My cell phone rang as I was putting on my seat belt. I turned to my dad apologetically. "I'd better answer that," I said. "It could be news about Nikki."

He nodded, slightly, so I answered the phone.

It was George. "Nancy, you'll never guess what we found out."

"What?"

"Nikki Kolista and Dr. Wolfson both graduated from River Heights High School twenty years ago. And they used to date."

"Each other?" I asked.

"Yes," George replied.

"No!" I said, completely surprised.

"It's true," George said. "The high school put some of their archives online for their last reunion. Frank—that's Dr. Wolfson's first name—and Nikki were voted cutest couple."

I couldn't believe it. Slapping my hand to my forehead, I cried, "I should have been suspicious of Dr. Wolfson from the beginning. He doesn't like animals, and he isn't into music, yet he volunteered to be on the committee. Obviously it was so he could get closer to Nikki."

"But why?" asked Bess.

My mind spun with theories of revenge. Perhaps Nikki did something to him, and he never got over it. Maybe he resents that she's so successful. "Do you know where Frank is now?" I asked.

"Bess and I are looking for him," said George, "but we haven't had any luck yet."

"Does the crowd know that Nikki is missing?" I asked.

"Nope," said George. "We don't want everyone to panic, so I just announced that the show would be delayed due to technical difficulties."

"Good thinking. I'll be right there," I said, hanging up. Biting my bottom lip, I turned to my dad.

"That's about Nikki, I take it," he said.

I nodded. "George and Bess found a clue. Dad, can I please go back to the concert hall? Once we find Nikki, I promise you can ground me for life. I just—I really need to make sure she's okay. I helped bring her here, and now she's missing and I feel responsible. I need to do everything I can to help find her."

Dad sighed. "It's not often that I doubt you, Nancy. You've always made me proud, and I'm sure that today will be no different." Then he made a U-turn at the next light.

"Thank you so much," I said.

Dad sighed. "Just be careful, Nancy."

"I always am," I replied—then caught myself. "Well . . . ninety-nine percent of the time, I am."

Dad smirked and stepped on the gas.

When we arrived at the concert hall, I immediately noticed a few squad cars outside—and Bess and George in front of them.

"We can't find Dr. Wolfson anywhere," George told me as soon as I stepped out of my dad's car. "Or Nikki, for that matter."

"Did you check the lighting booth?" I asked.

"Why would he be there?" Bess wondered.

"Because he's in charge of lighting."

"Oh," said Bess, hitting her forehead, and we raced backstage. "How could I forget?"

"Aha!" yelled George, opening up the door to the lighting booth and charging inside. "We've caught you."

Dr. Wolfson jumped up out of his chair. "Caught me? What do you mean? What's going on here?"

"You kidnapped Nikki," George said. "Now, tell us why. Was this some sort of revenge? Are you so bitter that you don't want her to perform? Or did David put you up to this?"

Dr. Wolfson's face went pale as he backed away from us. "Wait, you've got this all wrong. Nikki was kidnapped? This is the first I've heard of this."

"So you didn't leave that note in her dressing room?" asked Bess.

"Sure, I left her a note."

"So you *are* guilty," said George. "What are you, some kind of stalker?"

"That's not it at all," said Dr. Wolfson. "Please, believe me. If I'm guilty of anything, it's of breaking Nikki's heart ten years ago. That's all I've done, I promise you. I'm no stalker."

"I don't get it," said Bess.

George crossed her arms over her chest and glared at Dr. Wolfson. "You've got a lot of explaining to do," she said.

"Okay," said Dr. Wolfson. "Let's back up. Yes, Nikki and I were a couple, but you've got everything mixed up. You see, I broke up with Nikki, callously, and I've been feeling bad about it ever since. That's why I volunteered for the benefit concert. So I could get close enough to apologize."

This was quite a twist. Unfortunately, it didn't lead us any closer to finding out where Nikki was. "So you have no idea who kidnapped Nikki?" I asked.

"I didn't even know she was missing," said Dr. Wolfson sadly.

I quickly explained what had happened. Seeing the horrified expression on the doctor's face when he found out about the threatening note led me to believe that he was telling the truth.

"That wasn't my note. I left another note," he said, eyes darting around the room. "We need to go back to the dressing room." He immediately left the lighting booth and hurried downstairs.

We all followed him. Once in Nikki's dressing room, Dr. Wolfson pointed out his note. It was in an envelope marked NIKKI, left on her dressing table. I don't know why I didn't notice it before. I guess I was too focused on the fact that her guitar was missing.

"When I was going into the dressing room, I saw something suspicious," Dr. Wolfson explained. "These two men were leaving with a huge, bulky duffel bag. I'll admit, I did think at the time that it was large enough to fit a person—or at least a small person, like Nikki."

"You don't know where they went, do you?" I asked.

Dr. Wolfson shook his head. "Not exactly. They loaded the bag into a white van that was parked out back. I watched the whole thing out the window of the dressing room. I even wrote down the license plate number, just in case it turned out to be something weird." He pulled a scrap of paper from his back pocket. "It's VXB1435."

"We need to call the police," I said.

Dr. Wolfson said, "I feel horrible. I could have stopped them. I just didn't know they were doing anything wrong."

I believed Dr. Wolfson's story. And I now knew that Stefan and David had kidnapped Nikki.

"What's that noise?" asked Bess.

The crowd was chanting Nikki's name over and over again. "The crowd," I said. "They're ready for some music. I'd better go out there and say something." I left the dressing room and headed toward the stage.

Within moments I was looking at what had to be the biggest crowd River Heights's concert hall had ever seen. "Hello, everybody," I announced. "Thank you for coming here to support the River Heights

Animal Shelter. We're thrilled that you're all here."

"We want Nikki!" someone shouted.

"I do too," I said. "We're having some small problems backstage, but don't worry. She'll be out soon."

This wasn't exactly the truth. It was more like wishful thinking.

And, even though I hated fibbing to the entire town of River Heights, the kidnappers had left me with no choice.

# 12

# The Chase

As soon as I got offstage, I called Chief McGinnis, knowing I was the last person he wanted to hear from. Now that we had proof that Nikki's life was in danger, I had no other option.

"Tonya, it's Nancy. Please put me through," I said to Chief McGinnis's receptionist."

"Are you sure, Nancy?" she asked. "The chief is a little upset with you now."

"It's an emergency," I said. "I wouldn't be calling otherwise."

"Hold on," she said as she connected me.

"You've got to be kidding me." Those were the first words out of Chief McGinnis's mouth.

"I'm sorry," I said. "But this is important. Dr. Wolfson saw two guys leave Nikki's dressing room with a huge, bulky duffel bag. They were really struggling with it too."

"And?" said the chief.

"And he tells me it was large enough to fit a person," I said. "We're thinking they took Nikki. They did leave a note, after all, and we both know that I didn't write it."

Bess and George stood across from me, anxiously waiting for news. All I could do was shrug.

"Is this true?" asked the chief.

"Absolutely. Dr. Wolfson saw them load her into a white van, and because he'd thought it a little suspicious, he copied down the vehicle's license plate number. It's VXB1435."

I left out the part about the two guys being David Wells and Stefan Kinsley on purpose, but if my hunch was correct, all would be revealed soon enough.

As I turned off my phone, Bess asked, "He listened to you."

"Sounds like it," I said. "But I'm going to search for the van too. It could be anywhere."

"I'm parked around back," said Bess. "I want to look as well."

"And I'll hold down the fort," said George.

"What about me?" asked Dr. Wolfson. "I want to help."

"You can come with me," Bess replied. "We'll

123

check out the warehouse district. There are lots of places to hide there."

"Good thinking," I called as I ran to my car.

I made my way through town as quickly as possible, careful to obey the speed limit, which at the moment didn't seem fast enough.

Ten minutes went by, but it seemed to take twenty. I passed the rubble left over from the animal shelter building and sped toward the office park. I didn't see anything out of the ordinary, but I parked at the edge of the woods, where Bess hid her car just a couple of nights ago. Getting out of my car, I noticed tire tracks leading off into the woods.

I passed a white van, which was empty. There were footprints and other markings, like someone had dragged a heavy package through the woods—or maybe a heavy body.

Stefan and David had already burned down a building and kidnapped a rock star. Who knows what else they were capable of doing? I just hoped I could make it there in time.

Bracing myself, I followed the tracks for a couple hundred feet. They lead me to a large willow tree. Underneath it was the body of Nikki Kolista. She was wearing her stage outfit: tight black jeans and a silver, sparkly T-shirt.

She wasn't moving. I got closer, crouching down

beside her. I cradled her head in my lap. "Nikki?" I said, stroking her forehead. "Wake up, Nikki."

Her mouth twitched, and then her eyes slowly blinked open. "Nancy," she whispered, and then started to cough. I helped her sit up.

"Are you okay?" I asked. "Who did this to you?"

"Two guys," she said. "I don't know who they were. My eyes were closed because I was meditating, but I heard a noise and then felt something cover my mouth and nose. It smelled funny and left me feeling light-headed. I opened my eyes and saw two men. Then, the next thing I knew, everything was black."

"Did one have a buzz cut and the other, longer dark hair?" I asked.

"Maybe," said Nikki. "All I remember is the one with intense green eyes."

That had to be Stefan. "I'll bet they laced a rag with chloroform to make you pass out," I said. "How are you feeling now?"

"Okay," Nikki said. "A little dizzy, maybe. What time is it?"

I glanced at my watch. "It's eight thirty."

Nikki gasped. "What about the concert?"

"Don't worry about that. We just need to make sure you're okay."

"I'm fine," said Nikki as she struggled to get up. "And I want to perform."

"Are you sure?" I asked.

"Positive," said Nikki. "The people need to get what they paid for, and the shelter needs the money."

"Okay," I said. "Then we'd better go."

Nikki slung her arm over my shoulder, and I helped her stand up. Together, we headed back to my car.

We were just a few steps away from it when I heard a voice behind me call out, "Not so fast."

I turned around. It was Stefan.

"I'm taking Nikki back to the concert hall," I said.

"No, you're not," said someone else.

I turned around and found myself face-to-face with David Wells. He was blocking my path from the other side. Wielding a tire iron, he said, "You two aren't going anywhere."

13

# Danger Intensifies

**I heard the faint** whine of police sirens in the distance. Of course, they did nothing to ease my fears. The problem? They were growing more faint as the seconds passed.

Not good.

David took a few steps closer. He raised the tire iron up over his head. There was so much anger in his eyes, it scared me. My only defense, I realized, was to try to stall him.

"Come on, David. Think about this," I said.

"I have been thinking about this for a long time." His voice was so deep and menacing, it sounded more like a growl. "I have big plans for Rackham Industries, and no one is going to stop me. You've been meddling in my business for too long, and my

127

business is no place for a girl like you."

I started backing up but then stopped and stole a glance over my shoulder. Stefan was still behind me.

It wasn't ideal, but it could have been worse. He looked almost as scared as I was. "I can't believe this is happening," he said. "I didn't sign up for this."

"Stop worrying," said David. "It'll all be over before you know it."

Nikki and I looked at each other solemnly. Clearly we were both thinking the same thing. That didn't sound good at all.

"Don't listen to him, Stefan," I said. "You know this is wrong."

"He never said anything about hurting anyone," cried Stefan.

"Be quiet," David barked. "If you listen to me, it'll all work out for the best."

"For you two, maybe," mumbled Nikki.

"I told you to keep quiet!" yelled David.

Nikki closed her mouth.

Stefan whimpered. He looked like he was about to crack. Too bad David was the one with the weapon.

"I'm so sorry about this," Stefan said to me and Nikki. "All I wanted was a promotion. David said if I pretended to be a painter and got the keys to the shelter, I'd be in good standing. I didn't know *why* he wanted the keys. I asked, but he wouldn't tell me.

He's my boss, so I listened to him. I never imagined he'd take things this far."

"Rackham needs to expand, and no obstacle is great enough to stop us. This is what it takes to get the job done, Stefan." David's voice was so hard, he sounded robotic.

I could hardly believe my life was at stake, and all for the sake of David's career. It wasn't fair. David waved the tire iron over his head and said, "If they try to take off, you'd better stop them, Stefan. I'm not afraid to use this on you, too."

"Are you sure you want to do this?" asked Stefan.

As they talked, Nikki grabbed my elbow. "On the count of three, run," she whispered softly.

I looked at her as if to ask, *Are you sure?*

She nodded and, under her breath, said, "One, two—"

I darted to the left, and David went after me.

Nikki was too fast for him, though. She moved forward with a flying leap and kicked the tire iron out of his hand.

As it went crashing to the ground, she elbowed him in the gut, grabbed his wrist, and twisted it around his back. Within seconds Nikki had David pinned to the ground, with her knee between his shoulder blades.

"Grab the tire iron, Nancy," she yelled.

I hurried back and lunged for it.

Stefan just stood there, with his hands raised. "I'm not going to fight you," he said. "And I'm so sorry. I can't believe this is happening."

"Sit down on the ground and place your hands over your head," I said.

Just then, the police sirens got louder. Seconds later, three raced up to the scene, kicking up dirt as they slammed on the brakes just a few feet from where we were.

Chief McGinnis stepped out of his patrol car and asked, "Nancy, what are you doing? Your dad told me he was taking you right home."

"He was," I said. "But there was a change of plans."

Once the dust settled, Chief McGinnis noticed Nikki, and he wasn't happy. "Young lady, what are you doing to David Wells? Let him go."

"No way," Nikki said. "Not until he's in handcuffs. This guy is a menace. He broke into my dressing room and kidnapped me. This other guy helped him too," she added, gesturing toward Stefan, who was looking even paler than usual. "Nancy saved my life."

Joe and Emily jumped out of their squad cars, hurried over to the crooks, and had them in handcuffs within seconds.

"Well, I'll be," said Chief McGinnis, shaking his

head. "David, I always thought there was so
crooked about you, but burning down the
shelter? That's low."

David shrugged. "Rackham needed the land. How
else would I get ahead at the company?"

"I didn't know he was going to do this," Stefan
insisted as Emily led him to her squad car.

"But you still posed as Peter Sandover so you could
get the keys from Justine?" I asked.

Stefan hung his head in shame. "It's true," he said.
"I'm guilty of that."

Once the two corporate crooks were loaded into
the back of Emily's police car, Chief McGinnis turned
to me. "Good work, Nancy," he said.

"Really?" I said. This was the highest praise I'd
ever gotten from him. To be honest, it was a little jar-
ring. "Thanks."

He tipped his hat at Nikki. "Sorry about the
trouble. I hope you still have a good concert, Ms.
Kolista."

"The concert!" Nikki and I both exclaimed.

In all the excitement, I'd almost forgotten it. Glancing at my watch, I saw that it was nine. "We should
hurry. I mean, if you're up for performing, Nikki. You
certainly don't have to."

Nikki broke out into a wide smile. "Try to stop
me," she said.

We ran to my car and got in. I called George to tell her that everything was okay and that we were on our way.

"What happened?" asked George.

"Long story," I said. "I'll explain later. Oh, can you call Bess to let her know that Nikki is safe, and she can stop her search?"

"Will do," said George.

"Thanks," I said before hanging up.

We got to the concert hall in record time, since I was able to speed through town with a police escort.

By the time we arrived, Bess and George were waiting outside with Nikki's guitar.

"I've never been so happy to see this," she said, jumping out of my car, grabbing the guitar, and hugging it close to her body.

"The crowd is going crazy," said George. "Are you ready to go on?"

"I'm *so* ready," said Nikki as she ran inside.

When she walked onstage, the cheers were deafening.

"Hello, River Heights," Nikki yelled. "I'm sorry I'm late, but thanks for waiting!"

The crowd went wild with applause, drowning out the rest of her speech.

"Now let's rock," she said, before breaking out in a song.

# 14

# Rock On

**I** **watched the show** from backstage, and I must say, Nikki Kolista was truly amazing. She belted out the tunes in such a soulful voice, and breezed through intricate sequences on the guitar. She had a great stage presence, too. Her personality was so dynamic. Everyone loved her.

I was so caught up in the moment, I didn't even notice that Deirdre was tapping me on the shoulder until she yelled in my ear, "Hey, Nancy!"

I turned to her. "Hi, Deirdre. What's up?"

"My cousin is really talented, isn't she?"

"Yeah," I said, just noticing Deirdre's outfit. She was all dressed up, in a short black skirt, black boots, a green tank top, and a fancy diamond pendant around her neck. Her hair was pulled up in a French twist.

If she hadn't been glaring at me nastily, I'd say she actually looked pretty. "Nikki is awesome," I said. "I mean, I always loved listening to her CDs and hearing her on the radio, but this live show? Amazing."

"It must run in the family," said Deirdre.

"I didn't know you were musical," I said.

"I'm not," said Deirdre, tossing her hair over her shoulder. "I was talking about my all-around fabulousness. There's a certain star quality that's in our genes."

"Oh, of course," I replied, turning back to the show.

"So this is a really big moment for me, Nancy. Do you remember why?"

"Not really," I said.

"Remember my love letters from Ned?"

"They weren't from Ned," I said. Deirdre was crazy to think they were.

"I'll be able to prove you wrong in five minutes," said Deirdre. "He's meeting me around the corner. Does my hair look okay?"

"Great," I said.

Remembering their date at the country club dance, I couldn't help but think twice. What if Ned did like Deirdre more than me?

"And my makeup?"

With Nikki still performing, the last thing I wanted

to do was talk to Deirdre, and worry about my boyfriend. "It's fine," I said, turning to the stage again and hoping that this time, Deirdre would take a hint.

She must have left, but I'm not sure when, since I was so wrapped up in the music. As soon as Nikki waltzed off the stage I gave her a big hug. "That was the most amazing performance I've ever seen," I said.

"Thanks," said Nikki as she dabbed the sweat from her face and neck with a bandanna.

I handed her a bottle of water. After she chugged it down, she wiped her mouth with the back of her hand and said, "I'm just going to head back to my dressing room and wash up."

"Okay," I said.

"Not so fast," said Dr. Wolfson, who stepped out from behind some leftover stage props.

"Yeah?" said Nikki.

"It's me," he said, taking off his glasses and blinking at Nikki. "Frank."

"Frank?" said Nikki, flashing him a surprised smile. "Wow, it's good to see you."

"Is it?" asked Dr. Wolfson, shifting uncomfortably and looking down at his feet. "I feel so bad about the way we broke up. I've been wanting to apologize for a long time."

Nikki laughed. "But that was so many years ago!"

"So you're not still mad?" asked Frank.

"Um, no," said Nikki. "I've been a little busy, pursuing my music and stuff, writing, traveling the world. . . . I'd actually forgotten about our breakup until just now. I mean, no offense. At the time, I'm sure it was very upsetting for me."

"Oh," said Dr. Wolfson as his face turned a deeper shade of red. "Um, sorry to disturb you, then. Congratulations on your great career and everything."

"Thanks," said Nikki. "I guess I should go change now. Maybe I'll see you later."

She left Dr. Wolfson standing there, looking perplexed.

I turned the corner, thinking I'd go find George and Bess, who were double-checking the amount of money we'd raised from ticket sales. But before I made it to the staircase, I saw something strange.

Deirdre had her arms around a guy. He was tall with dark hair and he looked so familiar. I blinked and rubbed my eyes. Realizing what I was seeing, my heart lurched. It was Ned.

My boyfriend and Deirdre were in the middle of a romantic embrace. And it looked like they were about to kiss.

# 15

# A Secret Admirer Revealed

**M**y gaze was completely transfixed. It was like I was witnessing a horrible car wreck. I didn't want to watch, but at the same time, I couldn't tear my eyes away from the scene.

Just then, Ned broke away. "What are you doing, Deirdre?" he asked.

"What do you mean?" asked Deirdre. "You said in your letters that—"

"Letters?" asked Ned, blinking in confusion. "What letters?"

"Come on," said Deirdre. "I know those letters were from you."

"I don't know what you're talking about," said Ned.

"You're just saying that because Nancy is here," said Deirdre.

"What?" Ned looked over his shoulder and, seeing me, started to panic. He turned back to Deirdre. "Look, I promise that I've never sent you any letters."

"Stop lying," cried Deirdre.

Ned turned back to me. "Nancy, this is all a misunderstanding. Tell Deirdre I never sent her any letters. You believe me, don't you?"

"If you say so," I said in a croaky voice. I bit my bottom lip to keep it from trembling. I was too upset to say anything else. I had to wonder, did Ned really not send the letters? Or was Deirdre right? Was he just saying that because I was there?

"If you're not my secret admirer, then who is?" asked Deirdre angrily. "Someone wrote those letters."

"I did," said Nelson Fadley as he stepped out of the shadows. Apparently he'd left Iggy at home. His normally floppy dark hair was slicked back with so much hair gel, it looked like plastic. And he was wearing a tie.

"You did *not*," screamed Deirdre, stomping one foot on the ground. She glared at Nelson so coldly, I could almost see the icicles flying from her eyes. I felt bad for the guy.

Ned looked at me, completely baffled. "What's going on here?" he asked.

"Deirdre has had this secret admirer for the past

few days," I explained. "And she was convinced it was you."

I was just explaining what was happening. I didn't mean to embarrass Deirdre, but that was the effect of my words. She looked not just flustered, but completely mortified.

"But you're my girlfriend, Nancy," Ned said. "I'd never do that to you."

"That's what I tried to tell her," I said.

Nelson was nervous, but he stumbled through an explanation. "I know there's a big age difference between us," he said to Deirdre, holding out a bouquet of pink and white carnations. "But I'm very mature for a twelve-year-old. Everyone says so."

"What?!" Deirdre screamed. "You humiliated me!"

"But . . . but . . . ," Nelson stammered.

"This is unacceptable. I'm so angry, I could scream!"

"She's already screaming," I whispered to Ned, then immediately regretted it. Deirdre isn't my favorite person—but I didn't want her to be humiliated.

"Let's just forget about this," I said, stepping between Deirdre and Nelson before Deirdre did any more damage to the poor kid.

"No way. Nelson Fadley, this is . . . this is . . ." Deirdre emitted a strange sound, like a strangled choke.

"Are you okay?" asked Ned.

She breathed heavily, with her hand over her chest. Her eyes were tearing.

I had to blink and look twice before I could accept what I was seeing, because it looked as if Deirdre was actually laughing.

"I can't believe it. You, Nelson. With the iguana! I've never even seen you without your skateboard, and you were writing poetry?" she asked between gasps.

Now it was Nelson's turn to be embarrassed. His face began to flush. "I just love the way you always take control of everything," he said. "You're the strongest girl I've ever known."

Deirdre shook her head. "Nelson, you're a nice kid, but, um—I normally don't date guys who are so much younger than me. How about if we just stay friends?"

"Will you still take the flowers?" he asked, offering them to her again.

"Sure," said Deirdre. As she took them, she ruffled his hair.

Just then, Nikki walked over. She had changed into ripped jeans and a red T-shirt, and her hair was pulled up in a loose ponytail. Her eyes were shining.

"Amazing show," I said.

Everyone agreed.

"Thanks," said Nikki. "I had so much fun. And I can't believe Frank Wolfson showed up. What a crazy blast from the past."

"Speaking of," said Deirdre as she hugged Nikki. "It's so great to see my long-lost cousin after so many years!"

"Huh?" said Nikki, looking totally confused.

"It's me," she said. "Deirdre Shannon. Well, last time I saw you, I went by DeeDee. But that was years ago. I'm *way* over DeeDee."

"Yeah—it's been a while since I've heard your name," said Nikki.

"Come on, we're going to be late," Deirdre said, pulling on Nikki's elbow.

"Late for what?" asked Nikki.

"The after-party, of course," Deirdre said impatiently. "Didn't they tell you? I'll give you a ride. I tried to get you a limo, but Nancy said it wasn't in our budget. My car is nice, though. Don't worry."

"Um," said Nikki. "Okay, I guess." She turned to me and said, "Nancy, why don't you ride with us?"

"Oh," I said, looking down at my feet. "Actually, I can't. I'm not invited to the after-party."

Nikki smiled. "Very funny. Come on, now."

"Seriously," said Deirdre. "The country club gave us one of their smaller rooms, so the volunteers can't come. It'll be very intimate. Strictly VIP."

"The country club?" asked Nikki. "The old one by Mission Hill?"

"Of course," said Deirdre. "Only the best for you, Nikki. The most important people in River Heights are there, waiting."

"Really?" said Nikki, with this strange look on her face.

I didn't know her all that well, so I couldn't say for sure—but it looked to me like she was kind of annoyed. Maybe even angry. "And who might that be?" Nikki wondered.

Deirdre ticked off the names on the fingers of one hand. "Mayor Simmons, Jack Halloran, the CEO of Rackham, all the Shannons. My parents can't wait to see you."

"I can't go to that party," said Nikki. "I could never stand that country club when I was a kid, and I can't stand it now. It's so exclusive."

"But I planned this for you," said Deirdre. "Is that how you treat your family? Leave town and never call or write, then come to visit and refuse to spend time with us?"

"I'm here for the River Heights Animal Shelter," said Nikki. "I thought everyone knew that."

"Well, you had your concert, so you may as well have some fun now," said Deirdre.

"That sounds great, but a fancy party at your country club just isn't my idea of fun," Nikki explained. "I don't want to sound ungrateful, but I'm not into going to a party that excludes all of the people who made this concert happen."

"I don't understand," said Deirdre.

Nikki shook her head. "I wasn't going to bring this up because I'm not one to hold a grudge, but you've given me no choice, Deirdre. Your family has always been horrible to us Kolistas. As far as I'm concerned, the Shannons are a bunch of snobs."

"What do you mean?" asked Deirdre.

"My mother married a poor artist from the wrong side of the tracks, while your mother married a successful lawyer," said Nikki. "And my family was shunned. We were always the poor cousins. The charity cases. Do you know that your parents have been having parties at the country club for years and my family was never invited?"

"No," said Deirdre. "I had no idea."

"Did you know what my summer job was when I was in high school?" asked Nikki.

Deirdre shook her head.

"I waited tables at the country club dining hall. And I have never met such rude and snobby people in my entire life. Your family wouldn't even acknowledge that I was related to them when I was working."

"That's horrible," said Deirdre, looking down at

her feet. "I had no idea. I'm—I'm so sorry."

"Yeah, you're all sorry, now that I'm famous," said Nikki.

"No," said Deirdre. "I mean, I'm sorry that my family treated your family that way. It wasn't right. And I'm not just saying that because you're a rock star. No one should be judged on such a superficial basis. But especially not you. It was so nice of you to come to River Heights for the animal shelter. Everyone has worked so hard to put this concert together. I could have done more, and I should have organized a party for the volunteers."

I was too stunned to speak. Deirdre was actually being kind and sincere. I didn't know she had it in her.

I don't know when George arrived, but she must have heard Deirdre and Nikki's discussion because she stepped forward and said, "Actually, there is another party for the volunteers, and we have plenty of room for anyone who wants to come."

"Really?" said Deirdre.

"Yup." George nodded. "We're having a cookout in the town square, right across the street from here."

"Now, that's what I'm talkin' about!" said Nikki.

Nelson tugged on Deirdre's sleeve. "You know how you were saying no one should be judged superficially? I think that could apply to age, too."

"Be quiet, Nelson," Deirdre snapped.

Ned and I smiled at each other.

I think Deirdre must have realized what she sounded like, because she put her arm around Nelson and said in a kind voice, "I'm sorry, but I just can't see this working. No offense. We can be friends, though— as long as you keep that lizard away from me."

"Okay," said Nelson, nodding seriously.

Just then, Bess ran over. "I have the ticket sales all tallied up."

"We've got nineteen thousand, five hundred dollars," she said.

"That's a lot of money, but we're still five hundred dollars short," I cried. My heart sank. We'd come so far, and we were so close.

"Wait a minute," said George. "You forgot about the banana bread sales." Whipping out her cell phone, she made a quick call to Harold to get the numbers from the food and beverage tables.

Moments later, she was grinning like a madwoman. "They made eight hundred dollars. We have enough," said George, jumping up and down in excitement. "We have more than enough!"

"I'm calling Justine right now," I said. "She'll order the temporary structures, and we can have them up by next week. The animals are saved!"

We all cheered.

"Well, what are we waiting for?" asked George. "Let's party."

Deirdre stepped forward. "I have to make an appearance at my party, you know, to explain why Nikki isn't going to be there—but I'd like to stop by later, if you'll have me."

"Hey, why not?" said George, smiling wide. "The more the merrier."

Ned and I, Nelson, Bess, George, and Nikki all headed to the party in the town square, and were met with loud cheers from a huge crowd. The party was a blast. It was a fabulous night, and the perfect way to celebrate the happy ending of one more adventure that I'll never forget.

# Sleuthin' Supplies

Stationery, Journals, Notepads,
Address Books, and more!

Nancy Drew® is a registered
trademark of Simon & Schuster, Inc

Available at a retail store near you or at
**www.chroniclebooks.com/nancydrew**

CHRONICLE BOOKS

# DON'T MISS NANCY DREW IN ALL-NEW GRAPHIC NOVELS!

## ALL-NEW STORIES! ALL-NEW FULL-COLOR COMICS.
### A new one every 3 months.

**NEW!**
Nancy Drew graphic novel #6
"Mr. Cheeters Is Missing"
Stefan Petrucha, writer
Sho Murase, artist

When the eccentric Blanche Porter reports that her beloved Mr. Cheeters has vanished, it isn't your standard missing persons case. As Nancy Drew soon discovers, Mr. Cheeters is a pet chimp. Or is he? The River Heights police dismiss the case as bogus, but Nancy Drew discovers there's a missing diamond necklace as well! Can Nancy recover the chimp and the necklace, or has Blanche Porter made a monkey out of Nancy Drew?

96pp., 5x7 1/2, full-color;
paperback: $7.95, ISBN 1-59707-030-0
hardcover: $12.95, ISBN 1-59707-031-9

**NEW!**
Nancy Drew Boxed Set Volume 1–4
With free Nancy Drew computer game!
A $20 value!
Total of 384 pages of full-color comics!
Specially priced at $29.95! ISBN 1-59707-038-6

## SEE MORE AT
## WWW.PAPERCUTZ.COM

# PAPERCUTZ™

Distributed by Holtzbrinck Publishers
Order at: 40 Exchange Place, Ste. 1308,
New York, NY 10005, 1-800-886-1223 (M-F 9-6 EST)
MC, VISA, Amex accepted, add $3 P&H for 1st item, $1 each additional.

She's sharp.

She's smart.

She's confident.

She's unstoppable.

And she's on your trail.

**MEET THE NEW NANCY DREW**

Still sleuthing,

still solving crimes,

but she's got some new tricks up her sleeve!

# NANCY DREW

girl detective

# REDISCOVER THE CLASSIC MYSTERIES OF NANCY DREW

$5.99 ($8.99 CAN) each
AVAILABLE AT YOUR LOCAL BOOKSTORE OR LIBRARY

Grosset & Dunlap • A division of Penguin Young Readers Group
A member of Penguin Group (USA), Inc. • A Pearson Company
www.penguin.com/youngreaders

# THE HARDY BOYS

### UNDERCOVER BROTHERS™

They've got motorcycles,
their cases are ripped from the headlines,
and they work for ATAC:
American Teens Against Crime.

## CRIMINALS, BEWARE:
## THE HARDY BOYS ARE
## ON YOUR TRAIL!

Frank and Joe tell all-new stories of crime,
danger, death-defying stunts, mystery, and teamwork.

## Ready? Set? Fire it up!